Imaginative Apologetics

Imaginative Apologetics

Theology, Philosophy and the
Catholic Tradition

Edited by

Andrew Davison

scm press

© The editor and contributors 2011

Published in 2011 by SCM Press
Editorial office
13–17 Long Lane,
London, EC1A 9PN, UK

SCM Press is an imprint of Hymns Ancient and Modern Ltd
(a registered charity)
13A Hellesdon Park Road
Norwich NR6 5DR, UK

www.scm-canterburypress.co.uk

British Library Cataloguing in Publication data

A catalogue record for this book is available
from the British Library

978-0-334-04352-2

Originated by The Manila Typesetting Company
Printed and bound by
CPI Antony Rowe, Chippenham and Eastbourne

Contents

CONTENTS

This book is dedicated to two sets of friends, preachers and theologians who saved my faith as an undergraduate: to those who introduced me to the Christian philosophical tradition of the West, among them Caroline and Hans Pung, Fr Tom Weinandy and David Albert Jones, and to those who reintroduced me to the humane dignity of the Church of England, among them Fr Mark Everitt and the community at Merton College Chapel. If I owe these people a debt that I cannot repay, then I hope that I may at least join in their work.

Contributors

Stephen Bullivant is Lecturer in Theology and Ethics at St Mary's University College, Twickenham. He has written widely on Catholic social teaching and Catholic responses to atheism. He is the co-director of the Non-religion and Secularity Research Network. His forthcoming monograph on Catholicism and atheism is entitled *The Salvation of Atheists and Catholic Dogmatic Theology*.

Richard Conrad is a Dominican friar. He teaches Christian doctrine and sacramental theology at Blackfriars, Oxford, where he is the vice-regent. He is also a part-time lecturer at the Maryvale Institute, Birmingham. He is the author of *The Catholic Faith* (Continuum, 1994) and *The Seven Gifts of the Holy Spirit* (CTS, 2009).

Andrew Davison is the Tutor in Doctrine at Westcott House, Cambridge, and an affiliated lecturer of the Cambridge University Divinity Faculty. He has been Tutor in Christian Doctrine at St Stephen's House, Oxford, a member of the Oxford University Theology Faculty and Junior Chaplain of Merton College, where he had previously studied chemistry and biochemistry.

Craig Hovey is Assistant Professor at Ashland University in Ohio, where he teaches Christian ethics and doctrine. His publications include *To Share in the Body: A Theology of Martyrdom for Today's Church* (Brazos Press, 2008), *Nietzsche and Theology* (T&T Clark, 2008), *Speak Thus* (Cascade, 2008), and the forthcoming *Bearing True Witness: Truthfulness in Christian Practice* (Eerdmans).

John Hughes is the Chaplain of Jesus College, Cambridge. His interests and publications span theology, philosophy and ethics. His book on the theology of work, *The End of Work*, was published by Blackwell in 2007.

Donna J. Lazenby is training for ordained ministry at Westcott House, Cambridge. She gained her PhD in theology from Cambridge University in 2009, writing on points of contact between Christian mysticism and the literary aesthetics of Virginia Woolf. She is author of a forthcoming book on Christian apologetics and the occult in contemporary literature (Cascade – Wipf & Stock).

Alister E. McGrath is Professor of Theology, Ministry, and Education, and Head of the Centre for Theology, Religion and Culture at King's College London. He has written extensively on the relation of Christian theology and the natural sciences, and has a special interest in the area of Christian apologetics. He also serves as President of the Oxford Centre for Christian Apologetics.

Alison Milbank is Associate Professor of Literature and Theology at the University of Nottingham and Priest Vicar of Southwell Minster in Nottinghamshire. Her books include *Dante and the Victorians* (Manchester University Press, 2009), *Chesterton and Tolkien as Theologians* (Continuum, 2007) and (with Andrew Davison) *For the Parish: A Critique of Fresh Expressions* (SCM Press, 2010).

John Milbank is Professor in Religion, Politics and Ethics at the University of Nottingham. His books stand as some of the most significant contributions to recent philosophical theology and Christian political theory. They include *The Future of Love* (SCM Press, 2009), *Being Reconciled* (Routledge, 2003) and *Theology and Social Theory* (1990, second edition 2005). With Graham Ward and Catherine Pickstock he was editor of *Radical Orthodoxy* (Routledge, 1998).

Graham Ward is Head of the School of Arts, Histories and Cultures and Professor in Contextual Theology and Ethics at the University of Manchester. Recognized as a foremost theological commentator on culture, his many publications include *The Politics of Discipleship* (SCM Press, 2009), *Christ and Culture* (Wiley-Blackwell, 2005), *Cultural Transformation and Religious Practice* (Cambridge University Press, 2004), *Cities of God* (Routledge, 2000) and *Theology and Contemporary Culture* (MacMillan, 1996). With John Milbank and Catherine Pickstock he was editor of *Radical Orthodoxy* (Routledge, 1998).

Michael Ward is the Chaplain of St Peter's College, Oxford. He was previously the Chaplain of Peterhouse, Cambridge. Acknowledged as 'the foremost living Lewis scholar' (Tom Wright in *The Times*), he is the author of *Planet Narnia* (Oxford University Press, 2008) and *The Narnia Code* (Authentic Media, 2010), and an editor of *The Cambridge Companion to C. S. Lewis* (Cambridge University Press, 2010).

Foreword

An Apologia for Apologetics

JOHN MILBANK

'Apologetics' now has unfortunate connotations. Demotically it suggests at worse saying sorry, at best a defence of a doubtful or compromised position. Technically it has come to mean a theologically secondary exercise: not the exposition of the faith, but the defence of the faith on grounds other than faith – on one's opponent's territory, where one risks remaining in a weak or even a false position. The best that such a posture can hope to achieve would be the occasional demonstration that one's adversary has somehow missed the authentic wider ground of her own standing. But calling this very standing into doubt would appear to be beyond the apologetic remit.

For these reasons apologetics often fell into disfavour within twentieth-century theology. Instead, what was recommended was an authentic exposition of faith, capable of persuading the non-believer to start to inhabit the alternative world which that exposition can invoke. In this light apologetics appeared to be a compromised exercise, unlikely in any case to succeed. And yet, the latter assumption was belied by the wide popular reach of some apologetic writing, most notably that of C. S. Lewis – the sign of the success of his *Screwtape Letters* being that they were often much admired even by those whom they did not convince. Meanwhile, the recent rise of the 'new atheism' has left many ordinary Christians feeling that they need the assistance of an upgraded apologetic weaponry in the face of newly aggressive scientistic assaults.

For both these reasons the time seems ripe to reconsider the apologetic role. And perhaps the first question to ask here is whether this role is really a secondary and subsidiary one after all. Perhaps the exposition of faith always includes an apologetic dimension? This might suggest that any successful exercise of apologetics, like indeed that of Lewis, must contain a strong confessional element which convinces precisely because it persuades through the force of an imaginative presentation of belief. Conversely, however, this possibility would equally suggest that confession has to include a reasoned claim, just as 'argument' denotes both the plot of a narrative and the sequential unfolding of a logical case.

A brief glance at the history of the relationship between Christianity and apologetics supplies immediately a positive answer to this question. *Apolegein* in Greek means 'to tell fully' and therefore simply *to narrate*, with a fullness that is acquired from a slightly detached perspective, as indicated by the prefix *'apo'* meaning 'away from', 'off', or 'standing apart'. Therefore the very word would suggest that an *apologia* is the primary narrative testament of faith, yet with the interesting proviso that even an initial, committed, heartfelt, interior-derived confession must already stand somewhat apart from itself, rendering a reflexively felt judgement upon the spontaneously felt commitment to the Triune God and the incarnate *Logos*. From the very outset, therefore, the *'apo'* in 'apologetics' calls to mind the *'apo'* in 'apophatic' – etymologically the 'away-disclosure' of negative theology, or that caution in the face of mystery which alone allows a genuine adherence to mystery's manifestation.

More specifically, *apologia* in ancient Greece referred primarily to the defence speech spoken at a trial, in contrast to the *kategoria* proffered by the prosecution. This pairing shows that the echo of 'apophatic' we have just noticed is matched by the echoing of the term for the prosecuting case by the term for positive theology: *kataphasis* or 'down-disclosure'. In either case one has the sense of something being 'pinned-down', at least provisionally 'located'. One can think here of our word 'category', but also of our word 'catalogue' since this derives from the more etymologically precise, if not legally opposite number to *apolegein*, namely *katalegein*, meaning to pick out, enlist, enrol, include, enumerate. So a 'catalogue' of one's life or views on life might be a list of isolated events, achievements and propositions – unlike an *apologia* it would *neither* be a sequential story, nor a provisional attempt objectively to assess oneself and one's commitments.

Perhaps surprisingly then, if an *apologia* is indeed an argument, it is also a narrative, and if it attempts to be detached, this is only because it springs from the most authentic heart of interior commitment.

And this turns out to be true of the three most famous legal defences in Western history, which are the three original sources for the true sense of Christian apologetics. First there is the *apologia* of Socrates as written by Plato. This was a defence before the city not only of the quest for a truth that is prior to the city's foundation, but also of a certain unknowing as the condition for that quest which is not abolished by the quest's partial achievement.

Secondly, there is the defence of Jesus before Pilate. Here we have a denial by Jesus that he is a worldly rebel against the city, but, as with Socrates, the affirmation (at least in John's gospel) that he is witness to a truth beyond the city and beyond this world. But in excess of Socrates Jesus claims to be in some sense the King of an unworldly kingdom. Whether or not he is thereby the 'King of the Jews' he mysteriously leaves in the hands of human acclamation (Mathew 27.11; Mark 15.2; Luke 23.3; John 18.34). Beyond these points his defence is his silence and he does not elucidate Pilate's query as to the nature of truth (John 18.28–38).

In the case of both Socrates and Christ, therefore, their teaching is accentuated and has to 're-commence' as a *defence* before it can be an affirmation, precisely because it concerns a truth beyond all known legal and cosmic bounds, and therefore a truth that is threatened with legal and scientific exclusion. In speaking for the truth Socrates is consequently threatened by the city with death. In identifying himself as the truth and as the real ruler with a kind of casual indifference to the city's norms, Christ is likewise threatened with legal execution.

The third defence is that conducted by Paul before Festus and Agrippa in the book of *Acts* (Acts 25–26). This is explicitly described as an *apologia.* (Acts 26.2). Paul's speech is at once a narration of his life, a justification of his learning and status, a 'saying sorry' for what he has done in persecuting Christians, including a certain 'excuse' in terms of his rigid Pharisaic commitment, and a confession of his faith in Christ. The 'full narration' of the latter includes most spectacularly Paul's account of his vision of the resurrected Christ and hearing of his words. So at this point his 'apologetics' contains a highly 'cataphatic' moment in which a vision 'comes down' to him in the middle of his journey. One could say that the inclusion of this moment indicates how an apologetic discourse which is primarily a narrative and a detached assessment can suddenly reach for the positive hymnic testament of the disclosing imagination and reception of apostrophising address. It is, one might suggest, the interweaving of all these things in Paul's speech which is convincing.

In all three cases then, 'apology' turns out to be *theologico-political* in some fundamental and constitutive sense. And yet this sense is thoroughly ambivalent: it involves a certain appeal beyond the city which is, and yet is not, against the city, which is indeed in some measure in its support, but which also leaves the city behind in its own vanity. What we have here is an apology *for the ultimate* and for the primacy of the ultimate over the quotidian. And yet there is a certain caution in this apology, even a hesitating shyness. For no claim can be made fully to present the ultimate here and now, even in the case of Christ wherein God is fully shown and yet still secreted for now, since he is manifest in a human being. Hence the everyday and the customs and laws of the everyday remain respected even where they are condemned with the most ironical extremity.

Of the three defendants, Paul is of course the most forthright. And yet an aspect of reserved submission is shown in his request to be taken before Caesar, although it is clear that he would have been discharged by Agrippa and Festus. Rather than this being merely to do with the superficialities of pride in Roman citizenship, it is as if Paul is saying at this point that this contestation must now be between Christ and Caesar, between the Kingdom of heaven and the Roman imperial legacy. And yet this contestation ends in Acts with the banal anticlimax of Paul's long house-arrest in Rome – as though to say, this contestation is only just begun and will define the age between now and the final apocalypse.

In this respect, should we see it as merely accidental (symbolically and theologically) that the Caesar Augustus to whom St Paul submitted, the Emperor Nero, was the fourth successor to that first Augustus Caesar in the Julio-Claudian dynasty who, uniquely amongst emperors, left an *apologia* inscribed upon pillars of bronze outside his tomb: the *Res Gestae Divi Augustus*? – as if the historical irruption of defence against the city in the name of the eternal, beginning with the Incarnation during the first Augustus's reign, had already incited in *riposte* a new sense of the need to apologise for political coercion – whether by the internal judiciary or the external expropriations and military police actions of warfare? The Christian event would at once require such a counter-apologetics, though bring it under extreme suspicion, and yet again – given the reserve before quotidian law of the three defendants – not be necessarily always able to deny its cogency.

Apology as narrative, argument, confession and imaginative witness *by the human person* in the name of divine personality against the hitherto impersonality of the city – that is the very heart of Christian theology. This is why theology *began,* with Paul, Justin Martyr and Irenaeus as 'apologetics' – not just against pagan accusations and misconceptions, but also in continued expansion of Paul's defence of the God-Man, the infinite personality made flesh, before a human jurisdiction. A defence that continues, after Paul, to be a witness to the real eternal life of Christ's spirit, soul and body as untouchable by either time or finite verdict. But a defence that must therefore begin to elaborate an entire metaphysical vision that seeks to imagine a reality in which all is divine gift; in which all creatures belong to an eternal kingdom that will overcome every kingdoms of this world.

The point then is that Christianity is a refusal to allow that the three trials are over, because they *always were secretly cosmic trials*. And because they are, still, cosmic trials, the act of political defence must here take the form of a new elaboration of metaphysics, as commenced by Plato, but now in terms of the disclosure of God as personal because interpersonal, and as assuming into himself his creation through his entire inclusion of one human being into the personhood of the divine Son. Thus in the course of his *Apologeticus* Tertullian first defined Christianity as *vera religione*, in a new linking of cult with philosophy that Augustine will later much further elaborate. Eventually it will have to be shown how this metaphysics – Christian *sacra doctrina* – better saves the appearances of everyday reality than does any other doctrine.

For it is at this point that the apophatic Christian *apologia*, out of its own internal structure, always *makes room for* the counter-apologetics for the quotidian. Jesus allows Pilate's questioning of truth to have the last word, precisely because he has not, as yet, fully answered this question; because the questioning still goes on and is even most radically instigated by the enigmatic presence of the truth in very person. For, since Christianity is not Gnosticism or Marcionism, its qualified world refusal will, even at the *eschaton,* allow the world a place, including a place for political law, in the sense of positive just distribution which the fulfilment of love itself requires. As W. H. Auden wrote, quoting Franz Kafka, 'God will cheat no one, not even the world of its triumph'.[1] At the end, indeed, the need for law as negative coercion and appeal to people's lesser or even base instincts will vanish; yet for now even this must be accorded some respect, else the innocent will not be able to live in freedom and true *apologias* will not be granted the civilised space in which they can be made.

What we are beginning to see then is that there are two seemingly contradictory things that must be said about the apologetic process. In the first place it is not that weazly, insidiously weak thing that so many imagine: rather it is bold proclamation and confession in the face of extreme danger. It lies at the very heart of faith and of theology. And yet, after all, in the second place, it introduces into that heart something complexly cautious and even ambivalent. It is indeed imaginative vision, but it is also apophatic reserve. As the former it instigates a new self-distancing of the world from the world's self – a felt need to render a counter-apology.

---

1 W. H. Auden, 'For the Time Being: a Christmas Oratorio', in *Collected Poems* (New York: Vintage, 1991), p. 400.

And yet as the latter it allows the world and the city of this world also to make a continued self-affirmation – albeit provisionally and only up to a point. This affirmation lies 'outside' theology – it is that with which theology is in apologetic dialogue – and yet, more fundamentally, it is not outside theology at all. For the distancing of the world and the city from itself is the difference made to it by theology, and in this very difference theology is able to sketch certain further more positive imaginings of the divine. The initial world-refusing here turns out to be a compassionate world-understanding that is yet more ultimately a world-transfiguring.

In the history of the English language, 'apology' initially meant defence; then it came to mean 'excuse'; later still 'acknowledgment of offence' and finally, also, 'a poor substitute'. And yet this entire development, one could claim, was always latent in the Greek sense of the word and its application in the course of the three trials. It has already the sense of 'excuse' for Paul in *Romans* (Romans 1.20 – the pagans are without any), while admission of the *appearance* of public offence is assumed by the legal settings. Finally, Jesus died because the crowd saw him as but a 'poor substitute' for Barabbas – 'a mere apology of a law-breaker', if you like – even though he was in reality the richest possible substitute for all of humankind.

All this negativity of connotation is indeed only breached and rendered convincing by our witness to this substitute for ourselves: the very instance of our positive imaginative envisionings of Christ. The procurator of Judea, Porcius Festus, already recognised the bizarre coincidence of cautious reflection and exorbitant claim involved in Christian *apologia* when he expostulated to Paul, 'thou art beside thyself; much learning doth make thee mad'. To which Paul, who has just recounted the extraordinary events on the road to Damascus, implausibly replies, 'I am not mad, most noble Festus, but speak forth the words of truth and soberness' (Acts 26.24–25, Authorised Version).

Indeed we have seen how Paul nomadically located himself between the *élan* of personal vision and the allowance for the role of Roman judgement, just as in Acts he also allows for the role of Greek philosophical testament to the participated and parental God 'in whom we live and move and have our being' and of whom we are natural 'offspring' (Acts 17.28). And I have tried to argue how this shifting location between the defence *against* the world on the one hand, and defence *of* worldly *nomos* and worldly *logos* on the other, is not really a tension between Christianity and something else, but rather a tension constitutive of Christianity itself as refusing the Gnostic or the Marcionite path.

Perhaps no-one grasped this with more unsettling subtlety than the Victorian poet Robert Browning. Nearly all his characteristic dramatic monologues take the form (in some measure) of apologias, which are never without extreme ambiguity. In his first long poem, *Paracelsus,* the message would seem to be that the speaking protagonist has tried to perfect the human race through power under the inspiration of romantic love, while wrongly despising the little that can be made of faint loves or even hates that conceal an unadmitted love at their hearts. And yet he is brought to the realisation that he is 'from the over-radiant star too mad / to drink the light-springs' by one 'Festus', whose very name surely invites caution in the reader who recalls Acts and another eponymous diagnostician of supposed insanity. This surely further invites her to read Paracelsus' final hope for a day when human advance through a mere refusal of the worst will be surpassed, and his own offer of full 'splendour' can be admitted on earth, as truly belonging to Christian eschatology parsed in terms of a magical or technological release of all natural powers.[2]

But in other poems by Browning this order of apologetic and of suspicious counter-apologetic is exactly reversed. Thus in *Fra Lippo Lippi* the painter protagonist offers us a counter-apology for his sensual inability to paint soul and spiritual symbol by persuasively suggesting that our only human way to these things must be through physical beauty, and that we need to be constantly reminded of this by a humbly mimetic art.[3] More complexly, in *Bishop Bloughram's Apology,* Browning's supposed satire on Cardinal Wiseman, we are drawn into a smug contempt for the Bishop's defence of a half-belief ensuring his own worldly comfort far more readily than any other *metier*, only to be drawn up short by the circumstance that this very crassness has given him an insight into the 'dangerous edge of things / The honest thief, the tender murderer, / The superstitious atheist, demirep / That loves and saves her soul in new French books.'[4] Similarly, we are easily led to despise Bloughram's offering to people of semi-mythological consolation, only to be once again surprised by his profundity in the face of the implications of the modern scientific outlook when he suggests that if we lose the idea of Pan's face appearing in the clouds, we will soon lose also our belief in the reality of the clouds themselves.[5]

Bloughram proves himself to be, despite everything, in this Protestant satire, the Catholic spokesperson for the half-hints of the sacramental

---

2 Robert Browning, 'Paracelsus', Book V, in *Poems of Robert Browning* (London: OUP, 1912), p.498.
3 Browning, 'Fra Filippo Lippi' in *Browning: a Selection,* ed. W.E. Williams (Harmondsworth: Penguin, 1974), pp 194–206.
4 Browning, 'Bishop Bloughram's Apology' in *Browning: a Selection,* pp 220–51; this quotation p. 232.
5 'Bishop Bloughram's Apology', p. 247.

and the halting virtue of the ceaseless resort to the confessional, which is perhaps why Wiseman famously did not take offence and later a Catholic novelist, Graham Greene could make Brougham's 'interest' on the 'dangerous edge' his very own. And yet of course this *apologia* for the unsatisfactory remains, in the end, precisely unsatisfactory, and has to be tempered by Paracelsus's reformed and alchemical apologia for the marvellous, the ideal and the utopianly transformative, despite his eventual admittance of Festus's tempering of this vision in terms of the prerogatives of the gradual and the partial.

This authentic Christian fusion and balancing of the apologetic and the counter-apologetic insofar as *both* are elements of apologetic itself (this being another version of the oscillation of the apophatic and the cataphatic) stands in stark contrast to the pathos of false apologetic as satirised by Browning in his *Caliban upon Setebos,* where the blind monster provides a 'natural theology' of his god, based merely upon projections from his own sensory experience and self-centred cravings.[6] All he can do on this basis is reason to a god who has created out of boredom and a need to exercise a playful cruelty. Imagination does *not* enter into this, except at the point where Caliban postulates a 'Quiet' beyond Setebos, whose goodness amounts at most to an indifference, at worse a favouring of Setebos alone – though Caliban recalls a rumour that Setebos may be demiurgically 'vexing' the Quiet. All merely natural theology, Browning implies, which falsely and idolatrously poses as a necessary adjunct to natural science (as if divine and material causality lay on the same univocal plane) is idolatrously like this, risking a reactive inversion to a Gnostic demonisation of the material cosmos. By contrast Bloughram is cynically nearer a genuinely pious consideration when he suggests that the creation exists in order to conceal God and prevent us from a premature confrontation that would be too overwhelming to survive.[7]

Instead of such a falsely 'neutral' approach (and one can think here of the folly of much 'science and religion' debate in our own day) which accepts without question the terms and terminology of this world, we need a mode of apologetics prepared to question the world's assumptions down to their very roots and to expose how they lie within paganism, heterodoxy or else an atheism with no ground in reason and a tendency to deny the ontological reality of reason altogether.

---

6 Robert Browning, 'Caliban upon Setebos; Or, Natural Theology in the Island', in *Poems of Robert Browning,* pp. 650–5.
7 'Bishop Bloughram's Apology', pp. 240–1.

But such a mode of apologetics does not pretend that we have any access to what lies beyond the world save through the world and its analogical participation in that beyond. For this reason its mode is bound to be, like Browning's idiom, fragmentary and 'spasmodic' (to use the term applied to the now forgotten literary school which he largely despised and yet to which he himself undoubtedly helped to give rise). And yet, through and beyond out human spasms, this participation is consummated in the Incarnation where God and the world become one through a specific point and event of identification. And it is here that God himself in human guise offers an *apologia* for himself in both word and deed.

Christian apologetics must therefore always remain Christological. And this means true to an uncompromising offer of splendour which has once (unlike Paracelsus's pretentions) had the full divine power on earth, mediated from the outset by a sublime patience (which Paracelsus had to learn), of magical transformation of all things through mere verbal utterance – a power that is still faintly transmitted to us through the ecclesial offices. And yet true also to the memory of the refusal of this power by the world and its law and wisdom, and true once more to Christ's refusal violently to respond to this refusal – in the interests of a complete persuasive and demonstrative overcoming of this refusal in the end.

Since then, the Church has been adjured to remain faithful both to Christ's offer and to his refusal of violence in the face of rejection by the world, whose sphere of legitimacy he also recognised. But after the inevitability of the Constantinian moment, the Church has had fully to realise that the counter-apologetic belongs also to the apologetic and that the frailties of the human physical vessel, unlike the auto-rising body of the God-Man (since the power of the Trinity is undivided) means that the true interests of the human spirit cannot be entirely disentangled from the need to defend and keep the space of civil peace and order – think, for instance of the case of systematic attacks upon sacred buildings, whether by terrorists or regular forces.[8] The Church has tried to avoid and minimise coercive defence of its own polity, and must hold to the ultimate witness of preparedness to die for the eternal truth which needs not worldly de-

---

8 No clear distinction between a 'just' and a 'holy' conflict was ever made before the early modern era, when the distinction then coincides with a dubious downgrading of international justice to merely procedural and not substantive criteria, even though Christianity did not, like Islam, usually or authentically (in Christian theological terms) endorse holy wars for purposes of religious expansion – the Crusades being – understandably, given the initial circumstances – viewed as a defensive enterprise. See Jonathan Riley-Smith, *The Crusades, Christianity and Islam* (New York: Columbia University Press, 2008) and James Turner Johnson, *Just War Tradition and the Restraint of War: a Moral and Historical Inquiry* (Princeton, NJ: Princeton University Press, 1981).

fence, yet in the penultimate secular finality of crisis, the fate of State and Church, of physical survival and the very possibility of offering salvation here on earth have proven to be ineluctably and by no means altogether improperly bound up together.

In like mode, while the truths of the Creation, the Incarnation, the Trinity and of Grace, are replete of themselves, they complete and safeguard rather than destroy our sense of natural order and human dignity. This means that they themselves presume such a defence, and therefore that belief in these supernatural truths cannot survive the threatened collapse of the ordinary and perennial human belief in soul, mind and will, and its intuition of a teleological purposiveness in all existing things.

For this reason today apologetics, which is to say Christian theology as such, faces the integral task of at once defending the faith and also of defending a true politics of civic virtue (rooted in Platonic and Aristotelian assumptions), besides a renewed metaphysics of cosmic hierarchy and participatory order.

Yet today also we have a more specific sense that such a metaphysics was lost through an assumption that the only 'reason' which discloses truth is a cold, detached reason that is isolated from both feeling and imagination, as likewise from both narrative and ethical evaluation. Christian apologetics now needs rather to embrace the opposite assumption that our most visionary and ideal insights can most disclose the real, provided that this is accompanied by a widening in democratic scope of our sympathies for the ordinary, and the capacities and vast implications of the quotidian – like the road running outside our house which beckons to endless unknown vistas.

It is of course just this combination (and indeed this very image of the open road) which was recommended by the Romantic poet William Wordsworth who provided (like Browning later) such an inspiration for nineteenth century Anglicanism and for the new *apologia* for the ancient faith by the Oxford Movement in the face of English civil distortions. As Simon Jarvis has pointed out, Wordsworth's own poetic apology, *The Prelude,* reaches a point of consummation when he remembers himself, standing above the mists of the mountaintops in Snowdonia, as coming to the realisation that the power of the imagination, which is the whole force of the mind, is something that belongs objectively within nature itself as its very core and key to its underlying enigma:

> The universal spectacle throughout
> Was shaped for admiration and delight,
> Grand in itself alone, but in that breach

Through which the homeless voice of waters rose,
That deep, dark thoroughfare, had nature lodged
The soul, the imagination of the whole. [9]

What Wordsworth here glimpses is an image of the imagination itself: within nature we often see a 'domination' revealed, or else one over-whelmingly impressive object, both of which call attention to the usually concealed primacy of *natura naturans* over *natura naturata* ('nature na-turing' over 'nature natured'). It is this very shaping power which is most acutely shown in the natural object 'humanity', within whom, as 'the imagination', it similarly stands out in dominance over all other intel-lectual capacities. It is the imagination which intuits 'the underpresence' of God and can 'build up greatest things / From least suggestions', be-ing 'quickened' but not 'enthralled' by 'sensible impressions' and 'made thereby more fit / To hold communion with the invisible world'. It is this power which gives rise to religion and faith which concerns an atuned 'Emotion which best foresight need not fear / Most worthy then of trust when most intense'. [10]

As with Paul then, it is the true exercise of the imagination which in-duces a paradoxically sober *furor* and guides and cautions our discursive judgement. But the vision of human imagination in the mountain cleft most truly attains Wordsworth's desired collapse of the subjective into the objective and vice-versa, when it is the vision of Christ, the God-Man who exercised for our redemption the supreme imaginative act of recre-ation here on earth. [11]

A true apologetics negatively defends this imaginative action against assault by positively perpetuating its performance. It is this task which the authors of the present volume seek to renew in our time.

---

9 William Wordsworth, *The Prelude: the Four Texts* [1798, 1799, 8105, 1850] (London: Penguin, 1995), [1805 version], Book XIII, 60–5, p. 512; Simon Jarvis, *Wordsworth's Phil-osophic Song* (Cambridge: Cambridge University Press, 2007), pp. 214–23.
10 Wordsworth, *The Prelude* [1805], Book XIII, 66–122, pp. 514–16.
11 See Stephen Medcalf, 'The Coincidence of Myth and Fact', in *The Spirit of England: Selected Essays of Stephen Medcalf*, ed. Brian Cummings and Gabriel Josipovici (London: Legenda, 2010), pp. 20–40.

Introduction

ANDREW DAVISON

The approach to apologetics offered in this book is imaginative twice over. There is an interest in the imagination in the more expected sense of 'works of the imagination': several of the authors consider the role that literature and the visual arts can play in apologetics. These might be works that illustrate the Christian faith, or argue for it, or they might be works further from the Christian fold, and here especially novels, that disclose something important about the cultural context within which we present the gospel.

Apologetics concerns faith's appeal to reason. It is useful here to take a step back and consider the nature of reason. Our apologetics will be the better for it. Properly Christian apologetics requires a Christian understanding of reason. More than that, a theological account of reason is part of what we offer with the gospel. The Christian faith does not simply, or even mainly, propose a few additional facts about the world. Rather, belief in the Christian God invites a new way to understand everything.

There is therefore a second and more fundamental interest in the imagination among the authors of these chapters. Going beyond the imaginative work of the creative few, they insist that all *human reason is imaginative*. Throughout this collection there is an enquiry into the nature of reason and the role, within it, of the imagination: is reason wide or narrow, warm or cold, only a matter of logic, or of imagination also? The contributors remind us that reason both knows *and desires*, and that these two aspects lie very close together. As Thomas Aquinas put it, 'truth is something good, otherwise it would not be desirable; and good is something true, otherwise it would not be intelligible'.[1] God satisfies both the intellect and the desire – he is both true and good – which is why apologetics should embrace both.

---

1 *Summa Theologiae* I.79.11 ad 2. References are from the 1920 translation by the Fathers of the English Dominican Province, 22 vols (London: Burns, Oates and Washbourne).

A Christian vision of reason will let go of neither intellect nor will. Intellect is important; although the 'New Atheists' portray Christian commitment as an absurdist leap in the dark, it cannot be that. Christianity is, after all, the religion of the Word, the *Logos*. We therefore rebuff the New Atheists not for being too rational but rather for *not being rational enough*. Their reductive account of reason suppresses the impulse to ask *why*; it ignores too many important features of the world. As Denys Turner has said, the best way to be an atheist is to avoid asking certain questions.[2] Sure enough, New Atheist polemic curtails reason, turning to a caricature of the (supposedly singular) method of the physical and natural sciences. It praises the inquisitiveness of scientists but discounts inquisitiveness in theology, ethics or metaphysics. The result is an unimaginative reason that is therefore incompletely reasonable.

In this book we celebrate reason, but not so as to make apologetics rational in some cold or arid fashion. Apologetics should be a matter of wonder and desire, not least because reason at its most reasonable is itself a matter of wonder and desire. It is the work of the apologist to suggest that only in God does our wonder reach its zenith, and only in God do our deepest desires find their fulfilment. The apologist may labour to show that the Christian theological vision is true, but that will fall flat unless he or she has an equal confidence that it is supremely attractive and engaging.

These chapters go under the subtitle 'theology, philosophy and the catholic tradition'. The authors put a high premium on theology. This goes hand-in-hand with our shared sense that apologetics cannot be a matter of *technique*. Apologetics is not an instrument to be deployed upon the person with whom we are speaking, not least because that fails to take each person's particular personhood sufficiently seriously. Rather, authentic Christian apologetics should resemble authentic Christian morality as portrayed within the 'virtue' tradition of ethics: the best Christian apologetics is the product of a thorough immersion in the Christian tradition combined with careful attention to the person with whom we are speaking and the context in which we find ourselves. As a consequence, training in apologetics is inseparable from the business of learning the faith (what we might call 'catechesis'). To make this apologetics–catechesis link is not simply to say that apologetics should be part of any comprehensive programme to teach the faith in our churches

---

2 'How to be an Atheist: An Inaugural Lecture Given in the University of Cambridge 12 October 2001' (Cambridge: Cambridge University Press, 2002). Reprinted in Denys Turner, *Faith Seeking* (London: SCM Press, 2002), pp. 3–22.

(although it should be). More fundamental still, it is to say that the best way to be prepared to explain and defend the faith is to have learned it thoroughly, to have thought it through seriously, and to have made proof of it by living according to its vision of the world.

That is to say something about how and why these chapters are 'theological'. Many are also gently but decidedly philosophical. This arises from the conviction that everyone is a philosopher at heart, and from its corollary, that the best philosophy relates to the topics closest to the heart of every human life: love and loss, birth and death, good and evil, transgression and redemption. The philosophy most worthy of its name – the 'love of wisdom' – never wanders far from such theological questions. To be an apologist is to accompany our fellow searchers as we consider whether the Christian faith, or atheism, or any other worldview, does or does not make sense of these matters.

Where these chapters are philosophical it is because knowledge of philosophy is quite simply *useful* for the apologetic task. We can turn again to Thomas Aquinas, who suggests two reasons why it is worth thinking about philosophy for the purposes of apologetics: philosophy both helps Christians to understand their own faith and helps them to understand the positions of others.[3] When philosophy is ruled by theology, and not the other way round, it helps us both to think about Christianity clearly and to think our way into non-Christian understandings of reality. Both of these approaches are to be found in these chapters. Most of all, the authors are enthusiastic about philosophy because they believe that the Christian faith offers the best of all philosophies – the best way to understand the world and what it means to be human at its fullest breadth.

These chapters are *theological* and often *philosophical*. The third part of the subtitle refers to 'the Catholic tradition'. Christian theology today is an ecumenical endeavour, which is an enduring benefit of ecumenism in the twentieth century. Most of the contributors to this volume are either catholic-minded members of the Church of England or Roman Catholics; all of the authors would admit their debt to classical catholic thought. We have found in that tradition treasures theological,

---

3 Both points are made in *Summa Theologiae* I.1. Sacred teaching 'can in a sense depend upon the philosophical sciences, not as though it stood in need of them, but only in order to make its teaching clearer' (5 ad 2). Aquinas later notes that appeals to Scripture are ineffectual if the person with whom we are speaking does not accept its authority: 'there is no longer any means of proving the articles of faith by reasoning, but only of answering his objections — if he has any — against faith' (8 resp). In order to answer these objections it is useful to understand his or her philosophical worldview. This is also helpful when it comes to pointing out internal inconsistencies.

philosophical and imaginative. We hope these chapters will bring some of what we have found to the attention of readers of all traditions. Nor, given our emphasis on the imagination, do we wish to forget the original sense of the word *catholic*, as meaning 'whole'. We argue for a version of Christian apologetics – theological, philosophical and 'catholic' – that embraces the whole of human reason and takes an expansive view of what it means to be a human being.

Faith and Reason Reconsidered

I

Proofs and Arguments

JOHN HUGHES

John Hughes argues that 'modern' apologetics often seems at once both too modest and too arrogant. It is too modest in thinking that the question of Christian faith is just another question, about some more 'facts' within an otherwise self-evident world, rather than something that changes the way we think about everything. And it is too arrogant in thinking that we can attain 'proof' of these ultimate matters, as if we could step outside the limitations of our human reason. For Hughes, this modern approach to apologetics is complicit with an ahistorical, uncritical and anti-Christian account of reason. To illustrate this, and help us find a way out of this cul-de-sac, he recounts the history of how we got here, arguing that such narratives and genealogies of thought are an important part of the apologetic task. For Hughes, beyond both modernist foundationalism and postmodern relativism, faith may be incapable of proof in the narrow sense, but it is no less rational for that. **A.D.**

If apologetics is partly about arguing or persuading people to believe the Christian faith, then it is worth stopping first of all to think about what we mean by 'argument', 'proof' and 'persuasion'. This touches on some of the big questions of what is sometimes called 'fundamental theology' or philosophical theology, questions such as: the limits of reason, the nature of faith, arguments for and against the existence of God. For reasons that will become clear in a moment, I would like to explore these questions by way of a little historical story, before leading into some more general contemporary conclusions.

This story begins not so long ago, perhaps 20 or 30 years past. In those days, perhaps especially in the English-speaking world, everyone seemed to have enormous confidence in reason and common sense. Whether they were believers or atheists, they shared a common set of basic assumptions about what was reasonable and so were able meet each other on this safe, common playground. This made philosophy of religion very easy: you could simply line up arguments for and against questions like the existence of God, the problem of evil and all the rest, and simply make up your own mind on the balance. Down at the street level, this overflowed into the more confessional business of popular apologetics. There was quite an industry of popular books of apologetics that aimed to prove the things of faith to ordinary people on the basis of simple rational arguments. If you were Roman Catholic, these things would normally begin from 'natural theology', and the so-called 'proofs' for the existence of God, usually based upon the *quinquae viae*: the five ways of Saint Thomas Aquinas. Any sensible person could observe motion, causation, contingency, teleology and hierarchies of excellence in creation, and so they could deduce from this their Origin and Goal, *quod omnes dicunt Deus,* 'which everyone calls God'.[1] If you were Protestant on the other hand, your apologetics would usually begin by demonstrating the rationality of revelation, whether this was proving the Bible's authority from prophecies that have been fulfilled, or its authenticity from biblical archaeology, or the evidence for the resurrection of Christ, often considered in the manner of a legal trial. Both these traditions can be seen merged in the figure of the former Nolloth Professor of Philosophy of Religion at Oxford University, whose influence continues to be disturbingly widespread. Richard Swinburne famously claims to calculate the statistical probability of the existence of God and the resurrection of Christ.[2] It is worth pausing to consider this for a moment. This is problematic, to put it mildly, not only in that these calculations clearly fail to resolve the matter (or else why would there still be atheists), but also absurd in suggesting that the existence of God and the resurrection of Christ are things whose probability can be measured like any other ordinary 'thing' in the world, in the same way one might wonder about the existence of an ancient Greek battle or another planet in our solar system, rather than something *much* more fundamental which alters one's entire view of *everything*. Swinburne's efforts, and many similar attempts were of course honourable in intent, building on a long tradition, and various people continue them today (Alvin Plantinga among Protestants, and Scott Hahn among Roman Catholics), but they reached some quite curious and problematic conclusions as we have suggested.

We can trace the origins of this project of proofs back through history to understand where it came from, before we go on to see how it may have run aground. This project of proving the foundations of

1 *Summa Theologiae*, Ia q.2, a.3, rep.
2 Richard Swinburne, *The Existence of God* (Oxford: Clarendon Press, 2004); and *The Resurrection of God Incarnate* (Oxford: Clarendon Press, 2003).

faith by reason goes back into the nineteenth century, where we find the First Vatican Council affirming on the basis of Neo-Scholastic philosophy that the existence of God is a truth that can be known by reason unaided by grace or faith. In Anglican circles a similarly confident rationalist natural theology was represented by William Paley's famous analogy of the watch found on the beach, from which one can deduce the existence of a watchmaker, which remained a staple of Anglican textbooks well into the twentieth century. But the project goes back before Pius IX and Paley, enjoying its heyday in the eighteenth century, with such supremely confident rationalists as Leibniz and Wolff, and arguably taking off even earlier, in the seventeenth century with the so-called 'founder of modern philosophy', René Descartes. Descartes famously sat alone in his boiler room, stripping away all potentially doubtable beliefs founded upon traditional authorities such as Scripture or the Church, in order to find a common, neutral, indisputable rational foundation upon which everyone could agree. This 'Cartesian method', of using doubt to find certainty, supposedly born in reaction to the European Wars of Religion, was to become classically modern. This is what people sometimes call 'foundationalism', the quest to find a rational foundation 'behind' all the different views people have, upon which they must all agree.[3]

The point to be made here is that the project of trying to 'prove' God's existence and the truth of the Christian faith, according to supposedly 'pure' reason, while it might have precursors, is not so ancient as we might think, but actually belongs to this particular philosophical project, which we call modernity and the European Enlightenment, and more specifically to rationalist foundationalism. If this is so, then we might well have good reasons for being more than a little suspicious of its hidden agendas and unseen consequences.

The first thing to note is that it simply does not seem to work. Hume and Kant in the eighteenth century famously spelt out the problems with the cosmological and teleological 'proofs' of God's existence: Why could there not just be an infinite regress? Why does someone have to start causation and motion off? Is it legitimate to argue from patterns within a series to explanations for the entire series itself? The order in the universe is at least as susceptible to being read in terms of organic generation or chance as it is in terms of design. And so on. This debate was summed up by the famous encounter between Bertrand Russell and Fr Copleston,

---

3 See Stephen Toulmin, *Cosmopolis* (Chicago: University of Chicago Press, 1992); and Thomas Nagel, *The View from Nowhere* (Oxford: Oxford University Press, 1986).

when Russell insisted that the universe needed no explanation beyond itself but 'just is'. There is nothing to prevent the atheist sidestepping the argument's premises in this way. If these are 'proofs', then they seem to have failed.

The second thing to notice seems to me to be more important for apologetics today, but less frequently commented upon. This is the pernicious consequences of this rationalist foundationalism for faith. It was some of the Romantics in the late eighteenth and early nineteenth century who first noticed that if you made the Christian faith into something that could be proved by reason, one effectively placed reason above faith, belittling faith in the process. In the twentieth century, Karl Barth made a similar point in his attack on natural theology, which, he argued, required God's revelation to be squeezed into the meagre categories of our human reason. For this rationalist foundationalism, faith now seems to be characterized as dealing with the most *uncertain* things, rather than the most important. Belief in God is presumed to be self-evident, so no longer requires the will to be combined with the intellect as in ancient accounts of faith, so it is no longer really a free response. Other beliefs, which are still based on faith, such as those deriving purely from revelation, now look rather vulnerable by comparison. Most crucially God himself is reduced to just another, very big 'being' among others, on the same plane as everything else, and subject to the same laws, such as probability. The mysterious timeless, simple, unchanging God of the Fathers and medievals has become the 'Supreme Being' or the 'Ultimate architect' of the eighteenth-century rationalists. This rationalist, foundationalist project of proving God's existence has unwittingly smuggled the Christian God out of the back door and replaced him with the cheap imitation god of the deists. Such a *deus ex machina*, a god of the gaps, is largely useless and readily dispensable, so from here it is but a short further step to atheism, to Laplace's famous remark to Napoleon, 'I no longer have need of that hypothesis.' Michael Buckley has brilliantly traced these developments from natural theology through deism to atheism in his book *At the Origins of Modern Atheism*.[4] Much more could be said about this sub-Christian view of God, particularly in relation to the voluntarism that made him seem like a capricious tyrant. It is arguably *this* god, not the Christian God, whom John Robinson wanted to leave behind in his *Honest to God*, and whom Heidegger rejected under the term 'ontotheology'. Some have traced him back before Descartes

---

4 Michael J. Buckley, *At the Origins of Modern Atheism* (New Haven, CT: Yale University Press, 1990).

to Duns Scotus and his doctrine of the univocity of being. But that is another story.[5]

The point that should be grasped is just that the rationalist project of proofs has sold out the Christian faith to deism and turned the God of Jesus Christ into an idol of human reason. There is a crucial issue here about our fundamental views of the world, which applies just as much to secular worldviews as religious ones: the foundation of one's belief cannot, by its very nature, be based on some other foundation without that becoming the more ultimate instead. So if one proves God on the basis of reason then secretly one establishes reason as the more ultimate foundation and thus the real object of worship. The other consequence of this is that worldviews are essentially incapable of proof, because the only possible premises come from within the system itself. The views themselves determine what would even count as evidence; one's ultimate stance affects the significance of every possible 'fact'. *All* ultimate questions, our positions or existential stances upon them, are therefore supra-rational, incapable of proof. They are more than empirical; they are properly hermeneutical, questions of interpretation. How important it is to remind secularists of this, again and again!

But to return to our historical story, foundationalism has not only been rejected in terms of religion, it has now come under considerable attack in all areas of knowledge. Beginning with Nietzsche's attack on the notion of one absolute truth in the nineteenth century, this critique of rationalism has gained strength throughout the twentieth century, first in Continental philosophers such as Heidegger and Derrida, to become mainstream in the last 30 years in what people loosely call 'postmodernism'.[6] It is easy to get caught up in debates over definitions here, but if we can see modernism as characterized by the assertion of human freedom and scientific reason against tradition and authority, an era which climaxed with the enthroning of the pagan cult of Reason in Notre Dame during the French Revolution, then much of this era seems to have come to an end. Now, it seems, the rationalist attempt to establish consensus through an appeal to universal reason has been deconstructed and unmasked as in fact just one particular way of looking at the world (Western, scientific, male, dominating and so on). Science is no longer the paradigm of all knowledge, and indeed many philosophers of science point

---

5 See Catherine Pickstock, 'Duns Scotus: His historical and contemporary significance', *Modern Theology* 21 (2005), pp. 543–74.

6 See Graham Ward (ed.), *The Postmodern God: A Theological Reader* (Oxford: Blackwell, 1997).

out that even science does not have the universal ahistorical certainty that some have pretended for it. All knowledge is embedded in time and space. Our knowledge always begins not with some universal foundation but 'in the middle of things'. So now, the tools of deconstruction, questions such as 'where did these ideas come from?', 'whose interests do they serve?', 'what voices are being silenced here?' are no longer simply used against theology, but are turned back upon the secular rationalism that had attacked it. Theology may be in a strong position here, as the first area of human knowledge to face up to these challenges, the limitations of its own certainty. The ball has now returned to the rationalists' court. We may no longer be able to prove God, but perhaps proof and the particular sort of rationalism that went with it has had its day more generally. We are no longer quite so sure about the infinite progress of the march of reason, sweeping away all other traditions and authorities before its advance.

Does this mean that we are all postmoderns now? Has reason had its day? It sounds like all we are left with is fideism, the arbitrary decision, the leap of faith. Some existentialist Christians and Barthian Protestants, and non-realist postmodern theologians such as Don Cupitt, have found they could make themselves at home in the postmodern world in this way, but at what cost? Disturbingly, it sounds as if there can be little point in apologetics, in any discussion and conversation with other people, on this account, because after all everybody has their own particular view and nothing could persuade them to change it. If we cease to believe in rationalism, do we throw out all belief in reason and truth? If so, we are left with nothing but the bleak self-assertion of millions of different perspectives, Nietzsche's will to power. This is the anarchy of complete moral, theological, political and philosophical relativism.

This sort of postmodernism seems after all to be not so different from modernism, just an extension of its basic premise of individualistic freedom to fit with the more extreme forms of consumer capitalism that have developed in the last 50 years or so, as Terry Eagleton and others have argued.[7] It is not surprising then that we treat our worldviews just as we treat everything else, like commodities to be purchased from our global pick 'n' mix and consumed until we grow bored with them. This sort of postmodernism is not only politically sinister, it is also contrary to basic Christian beliefs such as the idea that God is Truth and that the Christian faith is not just a private language, but can and should be shared with everyone. More fundamentally, we can argue that this sort of

---

7 Terry Eagleton, *The Illusions of Postmodernism* (Oxford: Blackwell, 1996).

postmodernism is internally incoherent. Inasmuch as it claims that there are no truths, only perspectives, it reveals the hidden truth that it does actually have its own fundamental belief which positions all the others; and insofar as it still bothers even to engage other positions in dialogue, it shows a commitment to the very possibility of communication and changing one's mind, which can only be understood as a hangover from the belief in something like Truth. We would be foolish to sell out to postmodernism after all.

It is not simply that we can use deconstruction against modernist rationalism, we can also deconstruct the irrationalism of the postmodernists. This was the strategy of Alasdair MacIntyre in his books *After Virtue* and *Three Rival Versions of Moral Enquiry*.[8] MacIntyre proposes that we take on board the postmodern critique of rationalist foundationalism, but that we should not abandon reason altogether. He points to the practices of the medieval university as embodying a commitment to ultimate truth, mediated through specific socio-historical traditions and authorities, yet precisely because of this belief, open to dialogue with all seekers after truth. In this situation there may no longer be room for proofs, because there are no longer common foundations upon which everyone agrees; the starting points may be many and various. But there is still the possibility of real debates and discussions, more modest and pragmatic arguments, based on the partial and provisional acceptance of certain non-ultimate premises. MacIntyre demonstrates this method in the way he plays the rationalism of the Enlightenment off against the irrationalism of the postmodernists. He has no knock-down proofs against them, but he can employ a complex series of attacks: situating them genealogically, unmasking their agendas and inconsistencies, allowing them to deconstruct themselves and one another. And because we are creatures of flesh and blood rather than pure intelligences, these arguments will persuade us not by some irrefutable logic, but also by all the powers of persuasion, by their goodness and even their beauty. They will be arguments which must be enacted in our lives as well as in our words. But if they are authentic then their rhetoric will persuade by virtue of their *inherent* beauty and goodness, rather than because of some added spin or window-dressing. Form is not accidentally related to content: the medium must fit the message. It may well be that these are the sorts of arguments that will be appropriate for a twenty-first century apologetics: not proofs, but critiques, genealogies and

---

8 Alasdair MacIntyre, *After Virtue* (London: Duckworth, 2003); and *Three Rival Versions of Moral Enquiry* (Notre Dame, IN: University of Notre Dame Press, 1990).

explorations, persuasive and attractive narratives that help us to make sense of our intellectual and cultural situation and inspire us to participate in them. For those today who would be teachers and preachers of faith, we must learn again the importance of rhetoric, and not as mere wordmongering, but as the art of faithfully performing our proclamation of the faith.

Many of the more ancient arguments for the existence of God, whether Anselm's or Aquinas', can be rehabilitated within this more modest rationalism: not as unquestionable proofs, but as arguments that draw out the logic of a certain position or line of thought, that lead people from particular phenomena, such as contingency or degrees of excellence, towards the idea of God. Many have taken Anselm's famous phrase to describe this more modest project of apologetics: *fides quaerens intellectum*, 'faith seeking understanding'. Faith is not completely irrational after all: reason and faith can collaborate together. Faith can deploy a more modest reason in its service, and this more modest reason may well even lead people to faith, without being able to 'establish' it. Indeed, one of the most powerful arguments that might be made in favour of faith is that the common-sense notions of reason that we take for granted are historically derived from and only really make sense in relation to faith in a God who has rationally ordered creation. Nietzsche here can help us see that if people are going to be consistent in abandoning God then perhaps they should abandon belief in truth and goodness as we have known them as well.

Perhaps particularly in the last ten years or so, we have seen a revival of Christian philosophy, of a certain modest Christian rationalism beyond secular rationalism and postmodern irrationalism. The encyclical *Fides et Ratio* can be read in this way, as can the more general revival of interest in metaphysics.[9] Some have even argued that faith and reason belong so closely together that they are more or less indistinguishable: reason is always a certain leap of faith, while faith is always a certain sort of rationality.[10] If this is so, then the old boundaries between apologetics and dogmatics begin to fall down. Whereas 30 years ago, we might have been convinced by the postmodern relativists that we had heard the last of apologetics, it now seems that *everything* is apologetics! Christian faith can articulate itself only through an engagement with culture. *All*

---

9 See John Paul II, *Fides et Ratio* (London: Catholic Truth Society, 1998), Peter M. Candler Jr and Conor Cunningham (eds), *Belief and Metaphysics* (London: SCM Press, 2007); and D. Stephen Long, *Speaking of God: Theology, Language, and Truth* (Cambridge: Eerdmans, 2009).

10 See John Milbank, *The Suspended Middle* (London: SCM Press, 2005).

God-talk, from formal theology, to the liturgical proclamation of the word, to the conversations in pubs and cafes, should be apologetic; not in the sense of establishing common neutral foundations for faith, but in setting forth the Christian faith in a way that engages with, criticizes and responds to the other views that are current in our world, and that is attractive and persuasive in itself.

2

Christian Reason and Christian Community

ANDREW DAVISON

The Christian faith, in the words of Saint Paul, calls for 'the renewing of your mind'. In this chapter I argue that a distinctive understanding of reason is part of what Christianity offers in the gospel. The further patterns of Western reason depart from their Christian roots the more important this becomes, and all the more part of the Good News. What we take reason to be has consequences for the kind of apologetics we use. Many classical approaches to apologetics attempt to work with a 'neutral' account of reason, which is supposed to be shared by all. I argue that this fails to recognize the plural, fragmented varieties of reason with which we are now faced. It also fails to make the most of Christian reason as something distinctive and attractive, as something we have to offer. The chapter concludes by relating reason to community. If, as Wittgenstein said, 'Words have meaning only in the stream of life', then we have one more reason why any invitation to Christian belief must be an invitation to membership of the Christian community, and why any exploration of ideas must also be an invitation to the life of the Church. **A.D.**

Christian Apologetics and Christian Reason

To acknowledge that there is a God, and that God created all things, is more than to add an additional item of information to the list of propositions we understand to be true. Coming to believe in God involves more than changing your mind as to whether there is a deity. It changes the way in which you understand everything. The Christian faith is therefore not so many intellectual propositions; it is a different way to think.

In the words of Saint Paul in Romans, turning to Christ involves a 'renewing of your minds'.[1] The further our culture shifts from its Christian roots, the more important this renewal becomes for apologetics. Christian patterns of thought may live on elsewhere as remnants, but increasingly they are eclipsed, displaced by ideas and conceptualities alien to the Christian understanding of reality. More and more then, the mission of the Church in its intellectual mode offers with the gospel a revolution in reason.[2]

In the first half of this chapter I will approach this idea from three different angles. The first argues that Christianity offers not only new conclusions but also new starting points for thought. The faith challenges our axioms, what we hold to be most fundamentally true. From a second angle, the apologist is concerned with what people take to be *real*. Christianity and secularity, along with various other contemporary religions and quasi-religions, offer incompatible answers to this question. Finally, we have in view nothing less than the scope of reason and the manner of its operation.

The phrase 'common sense' is so familiar to us that we are unlikely to enquire after its origins. Its roots are in the Christian theology of the Middle Ages. The scholastics noticed that the five senses bombard us with a constant stream of information. For all that, we quite easily make something of this maelstrom. In the mind, diverse and potentially overwhelming torrents of sensation are woven together into a unified and rounded perception of the world. The schoolmen called the human faculty that allows us to do this our *sensus communis*, or common sense.

A similar dynamic applies in the realm of thought more generally. Human beings are animals who discern meaning. This is quite some task. We must integrate memory, perception and reason, desires, hopes and fears. We interpret all these and relate them one to another. With so

---

1 Romans 12.1. Scripture quotations are from the New Revised Standard Version of the Bible, copyright © 1989 by the Division of Christian Education of the National Council of the Churches of Christ in the USA.

2 For the sake of simplicity, in this chapter I argue for the significance to apologetics of '*the* Christian account of rationality' or '*the* Christian worldview'. This is necessarily to pass over divergence between churches and between Christians within any particular church. It is worth making two points in response. The first is that against the backdrop of a rationality or worldview that is decidedly not Christian it is often the broader outlines of the Christian faith that make the most difference. These broader outlines are what Christians share rather than that on which they differ. The second point is that apologetics is not at its best when it is apologetic in the usual contemporary sense of the word. We can only really be apologists for something that convinces us. A certain vision of Christian theology has persuaded me, and it is for this that I argue here.

much rushing around in our minds, and so much information flooding in upon us, we need some stable landmarks. For the sake of this chapter, I will call these our axioms.

Axioms are our touchstones of thought. They are the lamps by whose light we see other things. They are the sticks we hold up to the world to find out what is straight and what is curved. They are what we can take for granted, providing enough stability for us to make sense of what comes our way.

Any set of convictions that are this basic will be 'theological'. Whatever our axioms, they take a position one way or another on a whole host of philosophical questions that are very directly 'religious'. To give just a few examples, there are assumptions about time (whether the past is lost; whether the future is already fixed), communality (my fundamental outlook can be individualist or communitarian; I can see my good as in competition with my neighbour's good, or to be found in it) and ethics (whether there are such things as good and evil, and if so how they are related; whether things have a purpose or not). We could call the sum of the positions we take over such questions as our worldview. We could also call it our faith.

'Faith' is a good word for these basic convictions for a number of reasons. For one thing, they are so basic that we cannot argue our way to them from something more fundamental. This does not mean that faith is irrational, just that it is where reason begins rather than where it ends. Our faith or worldview is not beyond scrutiny. It can and does change. We scrutinize it by asking whether it does a good job of making sense of things. If not, we adapt it; we come to new conclusions about that on which every other conclusion must rest. All the same, changing one's worldview or faith can be a traumatic affair. We tend to avoid making adjustments unless we need to. It often takes a crisis to force us to think again – the sort of crisis that shows us that our previous mechanisms for interpreting the world were just not up to the task.[3]

It follows from this conception of faith that it is something 'non-religious' people have just as much as 'religious' people. Everybody has a working hypothesis about reality, in the light of which they act and understand. We all have axioms to start from. This is our 'faith'. As with faith more traditionally conceived, this worldview–faith is a communal affair. It is part of what we pick up from our parents and the community in which we grow up. It can change, but we have to start somewhere. Diligent

---

3 This is similar to the sort of reasoning that the American philosopher Charles Sanders Peirce called *abduction*.

parents might think that providing good axioms is among the most important responsibilities in bringing up a child. It is part of equipping a child
with a rounded and healthy understanding of the world. The communal
aspect of faith will be important in the second part of this chapter.

To present the Christian faith is to present a new way to understand
life and the world in which we live. Put another way, Christian faith is
a new way to understand what is *real*. Clashes of worldview crystallize
around this question. What each of us counts as real or unreal sets a very
strong filter on how we understand what we see and, more generally,
experience. In fact, it even filters what we *see* in the first place. If you
believe that the world is the handiwork of a creator, you will probably
see a scene of mountains stacked behind each other receding into the distance as a revelation of the beauty of God. The convinced atheist is less
likely to see the scene in the same way. Someone who does not believe in
ghosts is unlikely to see one. Or, take my own experience of an Indian
street scene. People who believe in karma and reincarnation see a leper as
someone paying the price for past sins. As a result they will not show him
much pity. A Christian has a different worldview, and consequently sees
the leper differently: as someone unfortunate, as someone requiring help.
The word 'see' here is not necessarily used metaphorically. The mental
act of seeing already integrates sensation with value and meaning. We
do not first see neutrally, and then interpret. The leper is *seen as* unfortunate, as someone upon whom to show pity, or *seen as* a miscreant, as
someone to be reviled. Axioms operate at this very direct level as well as
in more discursive reasoning.
    Christian apologetics witnesses to a different sense of what is real.
Since these convictions are basic or axiomatic, we do not argue *to* them.
Instead, we show what difference it makes to think this way. As a consequence, it is useful for Christian apologetics to make an active demonstration of what it is like to interpret the world in a Christian way.
Apologetics is as much an invitation as an argument: an invitation to
'taste and see' what it is like to live and think differently.
    This issues a challenge to all of us: to live by our account of what is
most real (people not possessions, place not space, a world that is both
God's gift and understood in relation to a world that is to come and
so on). No doubt that calls in turn for attention to those disciplines by
which we co-operate with God in the renewing of our minds: daily prayer
and reading from the Bible, study of the Christian tradition, time apart
from the busyness of life, spiritual direction, participation in a community of Christian action, worship and thought.

The work of Christian apology is not exhausted by argument that certain things are true. The Christian faith also entails a different sense of what it means for something to be true. To give an example, Christianity recognized that Plato was on to something when he associated truth with goodness and beauty. Goodness, truth and beauty are facets of God; unified in him, they also have a certain unity in the world. Christian reason thinks about truth in close proximity to goodness and beauty. This sets Christian reason in sharp contrast, for instance, with the desiccated vision of reason typically upheld in British philosophy departments. There we find reason reduced to logic, severed from beauty and goodness as guides to truth. It is no accident that this account of reason exists – 'survives', perhaps – in faculties that are the most atheistic, or that argue that the question of God can and should be bracketed out of thought (which is equivalent to atheism when it comes to thinking).

My feminist colleague from my days at St Stephen's House, Lucy Gardner, uses a helpful distinction between 'thick' and 'thin' accounts of reason. 'Thin' reason is abstract and ahistorical; it is unimaginative, aspiring to the condition of pure mathematics. In contrast, for the 'thick' approach all reason involves history and story, imagination and desire. Thin reason is the work of a disembodied mind, or at least it could be. Thick reason is more bodily. This is more scientifically accurate, since thinking involves our heart rate and our blood pressure, adrenaline and testosterone, as well as the brain's lobes and neurones.

The contributors to this book argue that Christianity should work with a 'thick' account of reason. This affects not only *how* we offer the faith but also *what* we offer at any particular moment. Sometimes we will talk to someone who holds to an eviscerated account of reason. In those situations, part of what we offer with the Christian faith is a richer sense of what it means to think. We argue that this broader vision follows from the Christian message about God and the world.

On another occasion, we might be talking to someone so postmodern as to doubt the very possibility of reason. In this case, the Christian faith has a different gift to offer. We have the good news that we can believe in reason without having to betray the intuition that reality is untameably wild. God is *Logos*, reason itself, and therefore the world is reasonable. At the same time, the deepest mystery about the creation is a mystery about God. Because of that, our minds can never domesticate the world. Christian reason is part of the Christian proclamation. It is only part, but we should not underestimate its contribution in a world that operates with a variety of inadequate understandings of knowledge.

All thought begins somewhere, and there is more than one place to begin. There is more than one way to think, and no one way is conveniently marked out as better than all the others. Western philosophy came to see this over the course of the twentieth century. This was part of the collapse of the Enlightenment project, which had supposed there to be only one way to be rational, namely the enlightened way. This is a welcome collapse. It is a genuine advance to acknowledge more than one mode of rationality, as is the realization that all thought involves prior commitments.

Several consequences follow for Christian apologetics. The first is that no one view of the world can rest on its laurels. None of us can take it for granted that our particular worldview is better than all the rest, or that it is the 'natural' or 'obvious' way to understand things. No longer can any perspective claim to be neutral, supposing that all the others are biased. As the philosophers like to say, there is no 'view from nowhere'; thought involves presuppositions. That is not to say that no preconception is any better than any other, or more accurate. It simply means that there are always preconceptions.

As an immediate result, secular thought is not privileged over religious thought by means of some obvious and effortless superiority. Time and again, the Christian apologist will need to point this out. A certain secular worldview is increasingly prevalent, which we might call 'naturalistic'. It claims the natural sciences as its model and will not allow for anything to be real other than what the natural sciences can measure or discuss. It interprets the world on the basis that there is no God and that moral positions are human inventions. Every day we see, read and hear people assuming that this is the default option for reason and that it needs no justification.

Here the twentieth century's tectonic shifts over reason come to our aid. Because there is no thought without prior commitment to axioms, no way of seeing and thinking has automatic pride of place. Intellectually, if Christianity were in a culturally stronger position, this realization would serve to nudge us out of our complacency. That would be no bad thing. Since, however, the dominant mode of rationality in the West is not Christian but secular, the message that no stance is neutral, and automatically better than any other, works more strongly in the favour of the Christian apologist. Atheist rationality must state its case like any other. Naturalism is a faith commitment like any other. Indeed, it is a pretty incredible faith commitment, and one that naturalists deny in their daily lives and loves.

This is all old news. This particular light dawned some time ago, especially for anyone exposed to thinking from Continental Europe. It was a real breakthrough in understanding what it means to understand, but it came decades ago. That throws some light on the demographics of the New Atheists. It is no accident that they come, predominantly, from those few enclaves yet to have been affected by twentieth-century philosophy of a 'Continental' flavour. They are typically English or American, and from the old universities; they belong to one or other of two worlds least in touch with contemporary philosophy: the 'New Atheists' are lifelong scientists or neoconservative political writers.

Apologetics in a Post-Foundationalist World

The myth of neutral reason lives on in New Atheist polemic. As a sort of mirror image, this outdated and increasingly exotic approach to knowledge also turns up in certain forms of Christian apologetics. It lingers wherever we encounter a sharp separation between reason and revelation. An apologetic writer in this school gives to each its own domain. There is philosophy – this can demonstrate many matters concerning God with certainty, by its own methods. Then there is theology – in contrast with philosophy, this works with revealed information. In recent decades, some writers have begun to question this distinction and to ask whether it is so firmly rooted in the tradition as has been claimed. This has been a significant development for theology and for apologetics.

The distinction between reason and revelation is not nonsense: we know more or less what we mean by these two words and they do not mean the same thing. Nonetheless, the distinction between reason and revelation is unhelpful when pushed too far. We have already seen that it is impossible to keep theological convictions out of thought. Reason is theological: our axioms must take a stand one way or another on metaphysical questions of theological significance. Reason by its nature deals with matters that bear upon the territory of revelation. Pushing this further, all reason is by its nature a sort of participation in the divine mind and therefore already itself a sort of revelation. Revelation, for its part, must always involve reason. For revelation to communicate meaning at all, it must be received into a rational system. Reason and revelation are not so separate.

A sharp distinction between reason and faith lives on, however, in some more old-fashioned forms of Roman Catholic apologetics. Here it is still common to come across a commitment to neutral, uncommitted reason. This is the 'modern' – which is to say the enlightened – approach. These apologists risk being just as 'modern' as the atheists they take on.

In contrast to the position advocated in this chapter, and more widely in this book, this approach to apologetics does not celebrate any distinctive Christian account of reason as belonging to the Christian message. Indeed, these writers attempt to hide any distinctly Christian aspect to their arguments or motivation. Apologists in this vein claim to work with a reason-shared-by-everyone, Christian and non-Christian alike, prior to any religious commitments.

A particularly clear example of this approach to apologetics is to be found in Scott Hahn's best-selling book on apologetics, *Reasons to Believe*. The book has many merits, but on this point it perpetuates this unfortunate rationalist approach. As Hahn has it:

> I wish to cover just four brief points – four propositions that are universally accepted as true, and are practically undeniable. As such, they are the best starting points for dialogue or argument over God's existence.[4]

To look at these very briefly, they are:

> **the principle of non-contradiction:** 'Something (let's call it *A*) cannot be both *A* and *not A* at the same time and in the same way'
> **The general reliability of sense perception:** 'Our senses correspond to reality as it exists independently of our perceptions'
> **The principle of causality:** 'For every effect, there must be a cause'
> **The notion of self-consciousness:** 'I know that I exist, even if I try to pretend that I am uncertain about everything else'

Here we are presented with four supposedly universal principles of reason. Hahn claims that they are shared by everyone, independent of their religious position. This is an odd claim to make at the beginning of the twenty-first century. Fully respectable branches of mathematics, for instance, deny the principle of non-contradiction, as do various sorts of postmodern philosophy. Science and philosophy of all sorts qualify the reliability of sense perception, confirming a point already made in this essay: perceiving is already a work of interpretation; we have no access to 'reality' in an uninterpreted state. The principle of causality, as Hahn calls it, is particularly frowned upon today in philosophical circles. The populace at large may still think in terms of causation, but academics

---

4 Scott Hahn, *Reasons to Believe*, (London: Darton, Longman and Todd, 2007), p. 20. The examples in inverted commas that follow are from pp. 20–2.

have been trying their best to invalidate the category of 'cause' for centuries. Finally we have the 'notion of self-consciousness'. This is Descartes' classic method in the *Discourse on Method*: to reach firm foundations, we should doubt everything and everyone, except for one's own ability to think. In the history of philosophy, it is often called the 'turn to the subject'. It came under withering attack over the last century, not least because it presupposes that we can think in isolation. This is not true; we think in terms of words and concepts that we share as a group and which we have learned from the community to which we belong.[5]

Hahn's four features of neutral reason are a particularly clear example of *foundationalist* apologetics. He claims that there are at least four common foundations to thought that everyone accepts – you, me, the Regius Professor of Divinity, the person on the Clapham omnibus. If this were ever true, it is certainly not true now. The foundationalist approach sets apologetics up for a fall. No builder would assume to build on foundations that may not be there. Just as bad, this approach to apologetics sets out to hide the distinctively Christian coloration of Christian reasoning. It places under the bushel basket one of the very things we should be holding out as part of our good news: the strength and beauty of a Christian vision of reason.

We should spend a little time with Hahn's four foundations. The principle of non-contradiction stands as a cornerstone of logic. This brings us back to the question of what kind of reason Christian apologetics is to use – how 'thick' or 'thin' it is going to be. Certainly, the apologist will sometimes want to celebrate logic and a more steely form of rationality. It is part of the Christian approach to say that the world opens itself up to being understood. We should not yield this too easily, as something common and obvious to all. Not every set of preconceptions can make sense of the fact that the world makes sense. Of the many features of the world that call for an explanation of the sort we might call theological, the rationality of the world is one of the most remarkable. As Einstein is said to have put it: 'what is most incomprehensible about the world is that it is comprehensible'. In other words, why does the world make sense? What right have we to assume that it should? Christians can make sense of the universe's sense, saying that it is God's creation, made after the pattern of the Son, who is Word, Reason or *Logos*. There is logic because there is *Logos*; the world is open to reason because there is Reason in God.

---

5 Ludwig Wittgenstein, in particular, had it in for this sort of Enlightenment subjectivity. Fergus Kerr lays out his arguments clearly in *Theology After Wittgenstein*, second edition (Oxford: Blackwell, 1997).

The apologist need not yield ground over this logic or reasonableness so readily. It is part of the Christian faith that we have an account of why it is so.

There is a problem, then, with Hahn's use of the principle of non-contradiction. He cedes Christian territory too easily when he treats it as a neutral given. That there is logic can point us to God. At the same time, he may be too strongly committed to logic. Such a commitment is good as far as it goes, but we do not want to give the impression that Christian reason is cold or dry. For one thing, that can make apologetics sound detached and unrealistic. The world is by turns predictable and unpredictable, logical and strange. 'Something cannot be both *A* and *not A* at the same time and in the same way', claims Hahn. Maybe not, when it comes to logic but that leaves a great deal unsaid. Few matters really worth discussing are sufficiently clear-cut to be thought about in these terms. The subjects most worthy of human attention are a moving target when it comes to logic: people, purposes, fears, hopes and loves.

Hahn's first principle ignores the paradoxes we encounter throughout life. Christian theology contains paradoxes, and in the long run this goes in our favour. Our knottier or stranger doctrines do not *impose* paradoxes upon an uncomplicated reality; the paradoxes are there already. As every human being knows, life throws up mysteries and contradictions all the time.[6] The foundationalist approach to apologetics can easily seem out of touch with daily life when it suggests that human reason is at root something serene. When most people turn to consider the substrata of thought or reality, they encounter something far more complicated and unsettling. The approach to apologetics laid out in this book accepts this and treats it as something to work with, rather than as something to paste over or deny. Those who are faced with concerns about the world's intelligibility will be best served by Christian apologists willing to accept the world's problems, paradoxes and questions. Indeed, to those with little sense of these complications, it may sometimes be the apologist's task to point them out. In our sub-philosophical age, anaesthetized at least in the West by affluence and triviality, it may be the task of apologetics to make the world more of a problem or puzzle, and not less. Before anyone can accept God as the answer to the world's question, he or she must first perceive the world to be a question.

Hahn's further three examples of foundationalist apologetics can be dealt with more quickly, although they each provide a valuable lesson of their own. We are told that everyone accepts 'the general reliability of

---

6 I am grateful to John Milbank for making this point.

sense perception': that 'our senses correspond to reality as it exists independently of our perceptions'. The Christian might certainly agree that
there is something trustworthy about reason and sense. But again, that
is very much part of a Christian view of rationality, and not something
we should yield as a given for every approach to reason. For one thing,
the concept of 'reality' has all sorts of theological entailments. 'Reality'
is about as theologically loaded as any term we are likely to encounter.
Hard-line reductive Darwinism of the sort favoured by the New Atheists, for instance, offers no such reassurance that sense perception is
'accurate'. In that accurate senses favour survival and propagation, reductive Darwinism suggest that those senses should be *accurate*, but if
something other than accuracy favoured survival and propagation, those
senses might be otherwise: we might never know. One thing is for certain, that the Christian understands 'reality' to transcend sense perception (for all our only access is through sense perception) in such a way
that the atheist would surely deny.

Hahn's third example of universal reason is the principle of causation: 'for every effect, there must be a cause'. This an odd example of
something that everyone believes. Armies of philosophers have tried to
disabuse us of the notion of causality since the eighteenth century. Christians, admittedly, buck this trend. For example, theologians have often
explored the doctrine of creation rather brilliantly in terms of causation.
Christians believe in a creator who caused the world and who bestows
upon this creation the power to cause. It is part of the intellectual mission
of Christianity to uphold the robust sense of causation that most people
still possess, despite the best efforts of the philosophers. This is not because causation is something that everyone must take for granted; many
thinkers who consider themselves very clever scoff at it. Rather, causation falls into our lap because we believe in the God who creates.

Hahn's final example is the notion of self-awareness. This is Descartes'
cogito ergo sum: I think therefore I am. It is the idea that we can doubt
everything except for the conviction that we are thinking. As we have already noted, the subjectivity and individualism this introduced into philosophy have been widely excoriated and ridiculed over the past century.
Human beings cannot and do not think in isolation, not least because we
think with language, and language is a communal matter. We learn it and
exercise it within a much wider group.

We could go further and ask what this 'self' is, which Hahn holds to
be the common patrimony of all thinkers. There are a great many accounts of what it means to be a 'self ', and they are not at all mutually
compatible. The cluster of accounts we might most often encounter in

the West has profoundly Christian roots.[7] This is probably what Hahn had in mind. But, far from being neutral and unreligious, these ideas are profoundly Christian and tied up with Christian doctrines concerning creation and God, especially of God as Trinity. To adopt such an account of the person is already to have found something attractive and compelling that has unambiguously Christian roots.

We should also ask whether anyone other than Descartes is really as self-assured as Hahn supposes. The self is profoundly mysterious. Its existence will often seem more like a guttering wick than the solid entity Hahn has in mind. Who really understands him- or herself? Augustine of Hippo charted this territory better than anyone else, and in his *Confessions* he records the outcome: 'I have become a problem to myself'.[8] When Augustine excavated his own depths, he came across himself not as something solid but rather as something 'dispersed', to be brought together only by the 'continence' that is God's gift.[9] It is more the contingency and mystery of selfhood that points us to God than any sense of the self as stable and understood. It is not the attainment of self prior to knowledge of God that points someone like Augustine to God; it is our loss of self without him.

Holding out What Is Unfamiliar

The Christian apologist strives to speak clearly and to communicate the Christian faith as directly as possible. Part of this, however, is also to hold on to those central Christian ideas that may be unfamiliar to our culture. We should neither be ashamed of them nor water them down. Christian apologetics works between these two poles of clarity and unfamiliarity.

First clarity: the apologist, evangelist or preacher has the hard but rewarding task of finding ways to express the faith. This is a creative matter; it sometimes involves finding the right word, sometimes the right image or analogy. It is a task for which we can prepare. When we come across a particularly good or pleasing way into a Christian idea, we can write it down. On occasion, just the right example comes to mind in the cut and thrust of discussion. Pondering in advance is good preparation.

---

7 See, for example, Charles Taylor, *Sources of the Self: The Making of the Modern Identity* (Cambridge: Cambridge University Press, 1992).

8 Augustine, *Confessions* X.50, trans. by Henry Chadwick (Oxford: Oxford University Press, 1992).

9 For instance, *Confessions* X.40. I am grateful to Dr Richard Finn OP for drawing my attention to this passage.

By and large, we want to explain the faith in terms of shared and non-technical speech. That chimes with a proper understanding of language. Words mean what they are agreed to mean within the community in which they are used. I can talk about 'soteriology' within a theological community because it is a word we share. I cannot use it responsibly with a general audience because it is then not part of a shared language. If we claim that faith makes sense of things, we should be able to explain it in everyday language most of the time. Jesus sets this example with his parables, drawn from the agrarian culture of his hearers.

The demand for clarity should not, however, go so far as to blur the edges of Christian concepts. We avoid unnecessary jargon, but sometimes theological ideas demand theological words. If so, they need explanation, not elimination. There are times when we should replace a word such as 'sin' with something more instantly understood, such as 'rebellion', 'wickedness' or even 'selfishness'. There are other times where it is precisely the full-blown Christian doctrine of sin that is necessary or at stake. In that case, we had better also keep the word.

Clarity and familiarity are our guiding principles, so long as we are not accommodating our ideas to the culture in which we live. We should not give up on theological ideas because they are difficult or alien to the people to whom we talk. It is precisely those ideas that they most need to hear.

A good example of this comes from the fractious contemporary question of translating texts for the liturgy. Much of our Western liturgical tradition comes to us from Latin sources. For the Roman Catholic Church, the standard texts of all liturgies are in Latin. A new translation of these into English has been a long time coming. One reason is very close to the matter at hand in this section. I have it as an unconfirmed story from a reliable source that a certain sort of liberal-minded English-speaking bishop has resisted the use of theological words in the new translation. A good example is the word 'bounty'. We might encounter this word in phrases such as 'which you have given us of your bounty'. The bishops protested that people are unfamiliar with this word, and that it should therefore not be used in the new English liturgy. This is telling. People today are unfamiliar with the *word* 'bounty', beyond its use to name a chocolate bar, but that is because they are unfamiliar with the *concept* of bounty. This argues for holding on to such concepts, expressed with their proper words, even if they are unfamiliar. We should use the word 'bounty' in the liturgy, even if it seems a little unfamiliar and perplexing, because the message of God's abundance and largess *is* unfamiliar in a world of cut-throat capitalism. If 'bounty' perplexes people, that may be because it presents them with something wonderful and strange. In short, on occasion it is the task of apologetics to make things clear, and on other occasions it is the task of apologetics to cut through the vapid familiarities of our times and present something unfamiliar, glorious and true.

The approach to reason and apologetics given in this chapter, and in other chapters in this book, is both yielding and asserting. It yields that there are other forms of reason, which we cannot dismiss on a priori grounds. There is no mythical common and neutral rationality that we all share. Our approach acknowledges that there are other communities with religious faith (or of faith in disbelief). At the same time it is also asserting, saying that the Christian community and the Christian tradition have a distinctive and precious treasure. This is to be found in the way they think as well as what they think. We argue that Christian faith and Christian rationality are on to something distinctive: we have distinctive beliefs, distinctive forms of life and a distinctive history. Christian faith and thinking are not the only ones on offer. Because of that, neither are they the common possession of all humanity. Our Christian account of truth, our body of knowledge, our ways of life and our forms of community are not any old truth, knowledge, way of life or forms of community.

This is not to say that we have nothing in common with those outside the Church. We have a common humanity (although we can give an account of why that is so, and they may not be able to); we have the world in common (although the concept of a unified world may not make sense for those who do not believe in God, at least not if they follow that through to its logical conclusions). The approach outlined here does not stop us from trying to argue on someone else's terms. That is a jump that we will sometimes want to make. One good reason to enter into someone else's rationality is to point out its internal inconsistencies. It is just that when we do argue on another's terms, we should be careful to flag up that we are doing so. We are exploring someone else's territory, not yielding our own.

The principle of keeping Christian rationality in mind has another apologetic benefit, that of alerting us to a deeper and prior question. Often the best response to a question is to refuse to answer it in the terms in which it is presented. The way a question is formulated likely as not brings a certain rationality along with it, and it might be the rationality that is the problem. As an example, take a common objection to miracles: miracles are impossible because they violate the laws of nature. In its own way, this is a thoroughgoing attack. All the same, it rests upon the definition of a miracle as a violation of the laws of nature. The best response to this will be the most theological one, namely to deny this deist vision of the world and its relation to God in the first place. In this, as in other ways, apologetics shades into understanding and teaching the faith at its best and most fully theological.

The Communal Dimension of Apologetics and Christian Reason

In the last analysis, the Christian apologist, preacher or theologian is concerned with something that cannot be reduced to words. Consequently, unless it is also shown in action it is not adequately shown at all. Evangelism involves the whole person, will and action as well as intellect and thought. As John Keble put it, what matters is an encounter with 'speaking lives'.[10]

This is to endorse the Franciscan maxim 'preach the gospel; use words if necessary'. All the same, there is a danger here that it will be taken in an individualistic sense. It is the Christian *community* that is to use actions as well as words, and not only the individual. In this chapter we have explored a particular aspect of how the Christian community can speak intellectually: by embodying a particular 'faith' or worldview, by living out a particular account of what is real and what it means to think. These involve ideas but not only ideas. It is always also an invitation to join the community of the Church. In this final section we consider the link between a distinctive Christian rationality and a distinctive Christian community. Both are an important part of what we have to offer to those who are beginning to think about Christianity.

The twentieth-century philosopher Ludwig Wittgenstein pointed out the unbreakable bond between concepts and what he called 'forms of life'.[11] When a group of people share a common understanding of what words mean, they also share a common life, with a particular set of practices to which those words and concepts belong. 'Words have meaning only in the stream of life', as Wittgenstein put it.[12] As we have already considered several times, thinking requires language, and language is a

---

10 From his poem 'St. John Baptist's Day': 'So glorious let thy Pastors shine, / That by their speaking lives the world may learn / First filial duty, then divine' in John Keble, *The Christian Year*, second edition (London: J. Parker, and C. and J. Rivington, 1827), pp. 301–4.

11 'to imagine a language means to imagine a form of life' – Ludwig Wittgenstein, *Philosophical Investigations*, §19, quoted in Fergus Kerr, *Theology after Wittgenstein*, p. 29.

12 Ludwig Wittgenstein, 1980, *Remarks on the Philosophy of Psychology*, ed. by G. E. M. Anscombe, G. H. von Wright and Heikki Nyman, trans. by G. E. M. Anscombe, C. G. Luckhardt and M. A. E. Aue, 2 vols (Oxford: Blackwell, 1980), vol. 2, p. 687. Quoted in Kerr, *Theology After Wittgenstein*, p. 134.

communal matter. We learn it as members of a human community. What we must now add is that we learn through induction into common human practices. As Fergus Kerr puts this, we acquire a sense of what things mean through 'the practical exchanges that constitute the public world which we inhabit together'.[13] As an example, no one learns about forks in abstract isolation. We learn what a fork is by seeing forks in use, and by learning to use them ourselves. The same principle applies to everything else: cups, books and bicycles. In the same way, it is also by induction into practices and through communal interactions that we learn what it means to be a friend or an outsider, or what it means to forgive or to pray.

This insight of Wittgenstein's provides another reason why there is no neutral reason: what a community thinks and how it thinks is bound up with how it acts and lives. There are different forms of life and so there are different rationalities. His point is a general one; it applies to all communities and their ways of thinking. It is all the more important when a community has particularly distinctive ways of behaving, with associated distinctive ways of thinking. If our understanding of even common household items comes through practice, all the more does our understanding of concepts that are increasingly alien to our culture, such as prayer and forgiveness, the examples given above.

Prayer and forgiveness are part of what makes the Christian vision attractive. It is certainly possible to *talk* about prayer and forgiveness. They have rational theological content and this is something the apologist can explain. This does not mean, however, that we justify or argue for prayer or forgiveness from a more basic set of principles. In apologetics we are not so much trying to make sense of these practices as much as saying that these practices are what make sense of us and of our experience.

It may be that there are intimations of these disciplines in the thought and practices of the person to whom we are talking. If so, we can work with them. On the other hand, it may be that someone encounters the Christian practices of prayer and forgiveness saying 'they make no sense'. This can be an honest and therefore useful reaction. Approaching prayer or forgiveness with a non-Christian conception of reality, they may indeed make no sense. Our response in that case may certainly be to describe prayer or forgiveness even more carefully, but words are not likely to be enough. In the end, any account we give of prayer or forgiveness, or of anything like them, will need to become an encounter with the practices themselves: an invitation, once again, to 'taste and see'.

---

13 Kerr, *Theology After Wittgenstein*, p. 45.

Whatever the apologist might say about the Christian faith, it can only be incomplete without an introduction to a community where that faith is practised. Christian rationality is inseparable from Christian disciplines. They are woven into the life of the Church: in morning and evening devotions and the Sunday Eucharist, in the confession of sins, in the calendar. In her forms of life, the Church holds out a message about the nature of the human being. For instance the Christian community both rejoices deliberately and deliberately refrains from rejoicing; the Church both feasts and fasts. With the one we acknowledge the goodness of creation and the gift of human life and companionship; with the other we acknowledge our sinfulness and the waywardness of our desires. The Christian does not therefore simply talk about creation (and its goodness) and the human heart (and its selfishness); he or she joins with others to live out these ideas in practices and a form of life: Lenten or Friday abstinence, Eastertide and Sunday feasting.

The rationality of a community is bound up, as Wittgenstein says, with its structures of relation. The most profound structural orientation within the Church is an orientation beyond itself: to God as source and goal. This makes the Church a worshipping community. Similarly, the relation of the Church to God is one of grace. This makes the Church a community of thanksgiving. Thought and practice become fully Christian when awareness of this grace and gift becomes constitutive of what we think and how we think, of what we do and how we live. As Stephen Bullivant suggests in his chapter, healthy apologetics rests upon a healthy church.

The goal of apologetics is spelt out in the Letter to the Ephesians. It is to help people 'to comprehend . . . the breadth and length and height and depth, and to know the love of Christ which surpasses knowledge'. The Letter places this task in a communal setting. This 'comprehension' is a shared comprehension: it is 'with all the saints'; it is knowledge we can only attain in as much as we are 'rooted and grounded in love'.[14]

---

14 Ephesians 3.17–19.

Christian Apologetics and the
Human Imagination

3

Apologetics and the Imagination: Making Strange

ALISON MILBANK

The Christian apologist suggests that the world invites us to think of God. There are few more significant tasks for the apologist than this. When it comes to apprehending the world, however, so many contemporary attitudes of mind and heart leave us impoverished. New Atheist writers advance exactly such a vision of the world: one lacking an intrinsic transcendent reference or an innate moral dimension. They do this by making the natural sciences the sole arbiters for all legitimate questions. For Alison Milbank, this presents the Christian apologist with an important set of opportunities. The Christian faith offers a different way to understand the world, which discerns something valuable and mysterious in both the remarkable and the everyday aspects of life. People, things and events are seen and accepted as a gift; they are recognized as possessing a depth that gestures to God. Milbank invites the apologist to discover an almost liturgical potency in literature and the visual arts that can awaken a new sensitivity to the splendour and strangeness of the world. The fault line between Christian and atheist accounts of reality is seen to be one for or against the imagination. **A.D.**

It might indeed seem strange to include the imagination as a tool for apologetics, as this chapter will seek to do, because we associate apologetics with reasoned defence of belief, and in the wake of the Enlightenment imagination came to be seen as divorced from reason, belonging to the world of 'enthusiasm' and even superstition. In the influential *Encyclopédie*, edited by Diderot, the organization deliberately divided Reason/Philosophy from Imagination/Poetry.[1] This does not mean, however, that imagination was not important. For Hume it allows us to conceive of things outside our own mind, but this knowledge cannot

---

1 Denis Diderot (ed.), *Encyclopédie ou dictionnaire raisonné des sciences, des arts et des metiers* (Paris: Flammarion, 1973 [1751–72]).

be rationally grounded.[2] In Kant's philosophical system it is important because it belongs to perceptual experience as an organizing principle, which allows space and time to be apprehended, but these concepts themselves are rendered subjective.[3] I shall seek to demonstrate, however, that the imagination is a philosophical tool that helps us reason by providing an epistemology, a way of knowing, that is inherently religious. For in apologetics we do not just want to convince people of the rationality of what we believe as if it were a fact about the population of the Galapagos Islands: we want to make them understand in a *participatory* way. And what we believe has implications for the whole way of experiencing reality. Paradoxically, we need a religious imagination to give us access to the divine and to the reality and otherness of the world beyond the self.

Enlightenment disdain for the imagination, of course, is not the end of the story. Philosophers and poets of the Romantic Movement reasserted the power of the imagination but their response was prompted by the somewhat tragic situation that Kant's critical philosophy created. Kant argued strongly for a transcendent spiritual reality, but we have no access to it by means of our perceptions. He was fascinated by the claims of the visionary scientist, Emmanuel Swedenborg, who wrote of his conversations with angels and gave detailed descriptions of the afterlife. Yet Swedenborg could offer no rationale for how his supposedly substantial spirit world could impact upon our own. Kant comes to the conclusion that since spirit can only be penetrable, it can occupy no space and, even if real, is unavailable to our senses.[4] We are cut off, therefore, from the noumenal spiritual world, and metaphysics is the science of the *limits* of our understanding. This does not just mean we have no perceptual access to God but no access, indeed, to anything as it truly is in itself: the material objects of our perception such as flowers and tables also hide their depths of reality from us. Ernest Cassirer describes this outcome as 'resembling a tragedy of metaphysics' and rightly so.[5] It leads to a world in which the appearances of things are dead in that they are

2 See Gerhard Streminger, 'Hume's Theory of the Imagination', *Hume Studies*, 6 (1980), pp. 91–118.

3 Immanuel Kant, trans. by Norman Kemp Smith (London and Basingstoke: Macmillan, 1978 [1787, 2nd edn]), pp. 74–80, 142–9.

4 Immanuel Kant, *Dreams of a Spirit-Seer Elucidated by the Dreams of Metaphysics*, in *Theoretical Philosophy, 1755–1770*, trans. and ed. by David Walford and Ralf Meerbote, (Cambridge: Cambridge University Press, 1992 [1766]), pp. 301–60 (pp. 311–12).

5 Ernst Cassirer, *Symbol, Myth and Culture: Essays and Lectures*, ed. by Donald Verene, (New Haven, CT: Yale University Press, 1981), pp. 78–9.

wholly in our grasp by the senses, and the spiritual dimension is wholly unavailable.

At a recent debate at the ICA in London, the philosopher Slavoj Žižek claimed that reality today is like a computer game in which only the sections needed to play the game are finished, and can be engaged.[6] The rest of the images are flat, unfinished and one runs into a blank wall in trying to work with them. The Kantian world of dead objects is akin to this, and the metaphysical is similarly always coming up against a limit. This reality of a few densities and mainly flat objects is, however, very much the daily experience of contemporary Western existence, in which movement is primarily by vehicle, especially the car, and only a few sites in an area are actively engaged with. The virtuality of twenty-first century life is the result of multiple causes, but the philosophical impasse of the phenomena/noumena distinction is one of them: it is a distinction much debated but assumed by contemporary philosophy. In practical terms, it means we have lost heaven but also earth, the real and the ideal together.

As I have already mentioned, there was an immediate reaction to Enlightenment rationalism, in a Romantic response in which imagination played a key role. What is often underplayed here, however, is that this is not just an attempt to restore the value of our capacity to conceive the invisible and spiritual but equally to engage the world beyond the self, whether of material or spiritual objects, as truly real. As we shall see, this has implications for religion. These two projects are most ambitiously combined in the writings of the young German Friedrich von Hardenberg, whose pen name was Novalis, and who sought an integrated mode of knowledge that could revivify the dead world of objects. In his unfinished philosophical novel, *Henry von Ofterdingen* (1802), the hero goes seeking a certain blue flower, which represents a kind of homesickness that Novalis believes we all have: a homesickness for the ultimate truth.[7] This is not so much an idea as an experience: a homeland. To know the truth is to be, as D. H. Lawrence put it in his poem 'Pax', like a cat asleep on a chair, 'a creature in the house of the God of Life'.[8] The Romantic project of Novalis and those influenced by him, like the novelist George MacDonald, is to awaken in the reader this feeling of homesickness for the truth. And this, in my view, is the beginning of the apologetic task.

---

6 'The Return of Christ', 18 June 2009, Slavoj Žižek and John Milbank.

7 Novalis, *Henry von Ofterdingen: A Novel*, trans. by Palmer Hilty (Prospect Heights, IL: Waveland Press, 1990 [1802]).

8 D. H. Lawrence, *The Complete Poems*, 3 vols (London: William Heinemann, 1957), Vol. 3, p. 143.

Good evidence for its effectiveness may be found in the conversion of the critic and theologian C. S. Lewis, who purchased a copy of MacDonald's *Phantastes* from a second-hand bookstall in 1916, and described what he later called, 'a baptism of the imagination' through a story imitating Novalis in taking a young man on a journey in search of the good, the true and the beautiful.[9]

This task is not to 'sell' God as an object of credence so much as to offer a whole way of regarding our experience and beginning to reintegrate our experience. This is where Novalis's second project becomes important. He sought to counter that Enlightenment *Encyclopédie* with his own Romantic Encyclopaedia, which would not separate knowledge and nail it down so much as bring it alive. For Novalis nature is a 'magic petrified city', which lies as if under a spell, and it is the task of the philosopher-poet to bring this frozen entity back to life by means of his imagination. He wrote:

> The world must be made Romantic. In that way one can find the original meaning again. To make Romantic is nothing but qualitative raising to a higher power . . . By endowing the commonplace with a higher meaning, the ordinary with mysterious respect, the known with the dignity of the unknown, the finite with the appearance of the infinite, I am making it Romantic.[10]

Novalis called this poeticizing of reality 'magic idealism', whereby everything is revealed as a work of art and a symbol: 'the transformation of the visible world into the higher truth of the symbolic'.[11] This activity is rather like that of Adam naming the creatures; it is a priestly action whereby the chaos of nature is given meaning and value, and becomes a demonstration of divine creativity. In this way the natural world is no longer dead but revivified, and in the same action its relation to its divine origin is re-established. A modern popular analogy would be the transformation of science into 'potions' in the Harry Potter books. The natural world literally comes alive under the wand and the inert takes on a wonderful, even dangerous, activity.

---

9 See the introduction by Lewis to *George MacDonald: An Anthology* (London: Bles, 1946), p. 20.

10 *Novalis: Philosophical Writings*, trans. by Margaret Mahony Stoljar (Albany, NY: State University of New York Press, 1997), p. 60.

11 Bruce Donehower (ed.), *The Birth of Novalis: Friedrich von Hardenberg's Journal of 1797, with Selected Letters and Documents* (Albany, NY: State University of New York Press, 2007), p. 13.

The English poet, Coleridge, developed this idea of the imagination revivifying nature in a letter of 1802 in which he decries Greek poetry as the work of 'fancy' rather than imagination because it treats natural objects as '*dead* – mere hollow statues – but, there was a Godkin or Goddesling *included* in each', but commends the Hebrew poets for whom 'each Thing has a life of its own, and yet they are all one life. In God they live and move and have their Being – not had, as the cold system of Newtonian Theology represents, but have.'[12] The Prayer Book Psalter, which is the English version of the Psalms that Coleridge knew, preserves this particular effect very powerfully. It gives an effect of actual material presence and createdness: in examples such as 'He shall defend thee under his wings, and thou shalt be safe under his feathers' or 'the mountains skipped like rams and the little hills like young sheep' we have a wonderfully precise image of the divine embrace of the self that does not confuse but illuminate the natural nesting instinct of birds, and a landscape that is always ready to break into praise by intense activity. In the final chapters of the book of Job, God himself seems to wonder at his own bizarre creations, such as the Leviathan.

Poets can write like this, according to Coleridge, because of the creative nature of the imagination, which is 'the living Power and prime Agent of all human Perception' and 'a repetition in the finite mind of the eternal act of creation in the infinite I AM'.[13] Our ability to recognize forms and to accord meaning to phenomena has a Christological dimension. God works in us through the imagination: it is his instrument. When we consciously imagine, in the sense of making art or poetry, we engage in a similar, if lesser, act of re-creation, seeking meaning and unity in what we experience, dissolving only to re-create.

In the contemporary world, in which we are all at the mercy of global economic forces, distant decisions and the seductive glare of the market, our primary task as the Church is surely to awaken people to their own creative capacity, for in so doing we shall quite naturally awaken also the religious sense. Part of our problem in presenting the Faith is that our world deadens desire, and many people do not know that they are missing anything. The market orchestrates and channels desire in very limited directions, turning the transcendent into the commodity set so artfully in the shop-window or 'placed' by designer label showing in the Hollywood film. It is a desire always based around lack: once the object is achieved, the desire is only momentarily fulfilled. In theological terms it

---

12 S. T. Coleridge, *Collected Letters II, 1801–1806*, ed. by Earl Leslie Griggs (Oxford: Oxford University Press, 2000), p. 866.

13 S. T. Coleridge, *Biographia Literaria*, Book I (London: Dent, 1906 [1817]), p. 159.

lacks immanence, and there is no participation. In contrast, the religious sense does not just awaken a desire for the transcendent God, it gives us the world itself. As Luigi Giussani writes:

> How can this complex, yet simple, this enormously rich experience of the human heart – which is the heart of the human person and, therefore, of nature, of the cosmos – how can it become vivid, how can it come alive? How can it become powerful? In the *'impact' with the real*. The only condition for being truly and faithfully religious, the formula for the journey to the meaning of reality is to live always for the real intensely, without preconclusion, without negating or forgetting anything.[14]

The paintings of Caspar David Friedrich give us an insight into what this might mean in practice. A painter of the Romantic period, his work often shows human figures gazing at the world around and beyond them. In *Chalk Cliffs at Rügen* (1818), people are looking in various directions: down the cleft, out to the infinity of the sea, all enraptured by the otherness of reality and yet also participating in it. The woman's hand and arm imitate the waving action of the tree branches; a man on the right leans like a tree trunk. They perceive what lies beyond them and also participate in shaping what they see. The humans have their backs to the viewers, so that we too can enter the painting from behind and enter this experience. Even the tree framing our view seems to participate and to lean out over the abyss with delight. The painting is intensely real, giving us that 'impact' of which Giussani writes, but it also discloses a further reality, and opens that homesickness of the blue flower of Novalis. We do not need crosses or religious iconography to experience this as a religious painting because it gives us a religious sense of the mystery of the real.[15]

To encounter the real in this way is equally possible through the man-made and contemporary urban landscape, which can also be raised by the act of magical idealism. A character of G. K. Chesterton exclaims: 'wherever I see a red pillar-box and a yellow sunset, there my heart

14 Luigi Giussani, *The Religious Sense*, trans. by John E. Zucchi (Montreal: McGill-Queens University Press, 1997), p. 108.

15 The painting includes certain symbolic features. The woman wears red for charity, the central figure blue for faith and the man on the right green for hope, thus representing the three theological virtues. Friedrich, the central man, kneels in a kind of worship, with his hat off in humility before the sublimity of nature. The sea is sometimes interpreted as symbolizing death but the delicate blue colouring suggests rather being, the absolute or the transcendent – as in Novalis's *blue* flower.

beats!'[16] In Chesterton's *Autobiography* he waxes similarly lyrical about the Campden Hill Waterworks.[17] We can all remember how, in our own childhood, every aspect of reality of our own bedroom, house and street where we lived had a quality of intense reality: it seemed to mean more

16 G. K. Chesterton, *The Napoleon of Notting Hill* (New York: Dover, 1991 [1904]), p. 17.

17 G. K. Chesterton, *Autobiography* (Thirsk: House of Stratus, 2001 [1936]), p. 1.

than appeared, and even to have a life of its own. Getting up in the night as an adult can give one this same rush of reality: new sounds and creaks, objects that might move at any moment. Even our pet cat encountered in the dark is a mysterious new creature.

Chesterton was a master at writing stories in which ordinary sites like bus stops, fairgrounds and teashops are rendered eerie and strange. He notices the same skill in Charles Dickens, who describes a walk through foggy London in which an oval glass plate, lit from within, emerges out of the soupy air, spelling the mysterious words, MOOR EEFFOC. The strange language conjures up an entire exotic world and invitation to adventure. Viewed from within the building, the sign just spells out the prosaic 'coffee room', but the moment of mystery is never wholly erased, so that forever afterward, when Dickens sees the words 'coffee room' written up, he writes, 'a shock goes through my blood'.[18]

We are no longer in a world quite as divided as that of my own childhood, in which Brownies from downtown Portsea, taken on their first ever trip to the country, would be frozen in shock by the sight of a cow. We need estranging techniques if we are to shock people into engagement with reality, so that they may appreciate the religious sense and we can begin to explain the Christian faith at all. They need to be aware of 'being': that there is an 'Ens' to use the language of Thomas Aquinas. Art, music and poetry are all important here and they need not necessarily be explicitly Christian but merely art that gives us a sense of the real, whether of realistically presented objects or of colour and shape themselves. So Cézanne's apples, or children's art that revels in vivid blocks of abstract colour, would work equally well. I once gave a sermon based on the contents of our local ironmonger's shop, discussing in depth the solidity of tools, the smells of the wood-yard, the vast range of possible screws and fastenings. This language provoked a strong, positive response from the men listening, both believers and non-believers, who were enabled to reflect metaphysically upon the reality of their own experience as men who put up shelves and mended household items. For there is something very theological about a well-ordered tool shed. Ronald Knox once wrote a teaching-aid for parishes called *The Mass in Slow Motion*, and indeed, the Eucharist is not only our encounter and participation in Christ himself but also our encounter with the reality of the material and therefore the best teaching aid to shock us into the perception of the real. For bread and wine only become truly themselves when given back to God to be transformed into his body and blood. The Communion Service is one

---

18 G. K. Chesterton, *Charles Dickens* (Teddington: Echo Library, 2007 [1906]), p. 21.

long act of 'making strange' that restores the world and our own selves to us, divinized.

The community activities of parish life can be given an imaginative edge to engender this 'magic idealism' in the wider parish. Samuel Wells describes how one church invited a group of single mothers who used the hall to mount a photography exhibition of the life of the parish in all its aspects.[19] This made it possible for the women to imagine the area as a complex web of relations but also to unify it by the creative act of the photography itself and by its arrangement on the walls. In Coleridgean terms they were dissolving and analysing in order to reunite the various elements in the manner of the secondary imagination. It is not being postmodern to claim that community is a fiction: rather it is something we imagine together, and in so doing it becomes actual.

The model of imagination I have used so far, taken from Novalis and Coleridge, is idealist in the sense that the self is central to the construction of a world. I have tried, with my emphasis on encounter with the real, to allow a stronger role for the 'otherness' of reality. Another helpful model here is that given by J. R. R. Tolkien in his important essay, 'On Fairy-stories' (1947). One might assume that inventing a complete imaginary universe, as Tolkien does in *The Lord of the Rings*, is to have complete control over it, and indeed, to be idealist, but that is not how Tolkien sees it in this essay. He describes the functions of fairy tales as threefold: escape, recovery and consolation. Escape speaks to our desire to burst the limits of our ordinary experience by, for example, being able to converse with animals – and even with trees – as characters are able to do in *The Lord of the Rings*. The second function, recovery, returns us to our own world but seen in a new way: 'I do not say, "seeing things as they are and involve myself with the philosophers", though I might venture to say, "seeing things as we are (or were) meant to see them" – as things apart from ourselves.'[20] Tolkien argues here that a fairy tale takes us to a world of magic trees that walk and trees bearing golden apples that allows us to find a new quality in our usual experience of non-walking trees and green apples, whereby they now have the enchantment of the magic. It is as if endowing them with strange attributes allows us to see them for the first time. They are, importantly, no longer the dead objects of the Kantian with which we can do what we like but things set apart from ourselves. Whereas in magic idealism the stress was on the

---

19 Samuel Wells, 'How Common Worship Forms Local Character', *Studies in Christian Ethics*, 15 (2002), pp. 166–74 (p. 68).

20 J. R. R. Tolkien, 'On Fairy-stories' in *Tree and Leaf* (London: Unwin, 1964 [1947]), pp. 11–72 (p. 52).

recovery of human creative power, here the emphasis shifts to the objects themselves. Tolkien believed that his own fictional writing was a way of setting things free, like jewels rescued from a dragon's hoard, or like the white witch's captives in *The Lion, the Witch and the Wardrobe* released from stone statues to be themselves.

So Tolkien's Middle-earth is full of creatures that are different from us: Ents and wild men, talking eagles and elves. Even the hobbits, who share a Middle England love of pubs, gardening and fish-and-chips, are given huge hairy feet, two breakfasts and hobbit-holes to live in, so we do not think we know them completely. And Tolkien increases the hobbits' ontological independence by making them surprising and strange to other cultural groups within Middle-earth: they are just a legend to the Rohirrim, while Treebeard the Ent has no line for them in his Song of the Creatures.

One reason why a novel like *The Lord of the Rings* brings people to a religious perception of life, as I have often seen it do, is the way in which the reader is presented with an invented world of such intense richness and depth that, unlike the computer game with its abrupt cul-de-sacs, one feels as if one could go ever deeper. Some readers baulk at Middle-earth's resistance to our contemporary experience, and never read beyond the seeming cosiness of the hobbit birthday party in the first chapter; others are drawn in with delight to the alterity of a different reality. Giussani's words about reality generally are particularly applicable to Tolkien:

> This reality with which we collide releases a word, an invitation, a meaning as if upon impact. The world is like a word, a 'logos', which sends you further, calls you on to another, beyond itself, further up. In Greek 'up' is expressed in the word *ana*. This is the value of analogy: the structure of the 'impact' of the human being with reality awakens within the individual a voice which draws him towards a meaning which is farther on, farther up – *ana*.[21]

The Lord of the Rings presents a troubled world, riven with death and destruction, but totally credible within itself. And yet, despite this inner coherence, that is realistic enough to encourage people to learn the elvish languages and dress up on a regular basis as orcs or hobbits as if to live out the fiction – there are even occasional communal efforts to instantiate

---

21 Giussani, *The Religious Sense*, p. 109.

the Shire, as in Madrid recently – the novel calls the reader to something beyond itself: to an 'ana'.

The best example is the ambiguous ending of the novel. The wounded Frodo sets sail for the Blessed Realm of the elves:

> Then Frodo kissed Merry and Pippin, and last of all Sam, and went aboard; and the sails were drawn up, and the wind blew, and slowly the ship slipped away down the long grey firth, and the light of the glass of Galadriel that Frodo bore glimmered and was lost. And the ship went out into the High Sea and passed into the West, until at last on a night of rain Frodo smelled a sweet fragrance on the air and heard the sound of singing that came over the water. And then it seemed to him that as in his dream in the house of Bombadil, the grey rain-curtain turned all to silver glass and was rolled back, and he beheld white shores and beyond them a far green country under a swift sunrise.[22]

This journey is, of course, an 'ana', which takes Frodo further on and up into a world beyond the text. It is all the more effective because it merely gives the reader an anticipation, as Frodo's senses open out to its smells, and sights and sounds. That it goes beyond is indicated by the use of oxymoron in the glass being rolled back, which is impossible for a stiff substance like glass, and by the strangeness of a swift sunrise, as if the green country is being revealed and snatched away in one and the same gesture. As in Augustine's use of the spiritual five senses in his *Confessions*, our desire is awakened, our longing for the absolute: 'you have made us for yourself, and our heart is restless until it rests in you'.[23] But the reader can follow Frodo no further. Instead he or she is back with Sam, Frodo's companion, on his way home:

> At last they rode over the downs and took the East Road, and then Merry and Pippin rode on to Buckland; and already they were singing again as they went. But Sam turned to Bywater, and so came back up the Hill, as day was ending once more. And he went on, and there was yellow light, and fire within; and the evening meal was ready, and he was expected. And Rose drew him in, and set him in his chair, and put little Elanor upon his lap.
> He drew a deep breath. 'Well, I'm back,' he said.[24]

---

22 J. R. R. Tolkien, *The Lord of the Rings* (Boston: Houghton Mifflin, 2006), p. 1007.

23 Augustine of Hippo, *The Confessions*, I.1, trans. by Henry Chadwick (Oxford: Oxford University Press, 1991), p. 3.

24 Tolkien, *The Lord of the Rings*, p. 1008.

Here is reality as we know it: a fire in the hearth, supper, spouse, and a child on one's lap. And yet, long denied to Sam by his grim journey to Mordor with Frodo, these domestic details take on a new pellucid reality. Here is life as it should be lived, in relation with other humans but also with the inanimate world of chair and light. And even these simple elements of life lead us upward and further. If Frodo's ending gives us the opening to the transcendent, the blue flower of homesickness for heaven, Sam's opens to us the immanence of the real, and little Elanor is herself named for a flower in the magic forests of Lothlórien.

This opening of the religious sense is central to the theology and experience of the sacraments in which it is truly matter that takes us 'up'. A child baptism, for example, is a wonderful argument in itself for the religious dimension. Even apart from the putting on of Christ, dying to sin and regeneration at its heart, the simple fact that a family brings a baby to church is a religious act. They are seeing their child apart from themselves; like little Elanor she is truly real to them. To offer a baby for baptism is to affirm that she is more than a bundle of rosy flesh and a needy mouth. She means more than she seems. In a young infant we encounter reality and it leads us upwards.

People today are so lost to the meaning of our faith that we need to begin very basically indeed, and to find a language that can show people that they are *already* engaging in religious practice, and assuming implicitly that it is true. For to be human means to exceed ourselves: to go 'beyond'. In the words of Chesterton, '[man] seems rather more supernatural as a natural product than as a supernatural one'.[25] I once told a surprised congregation of golfers at a funeral that golf was religious. It accords form and meaning to swinging clubs about. To make rules and see a meaning in actions is to see significance beyond the merely physical. It takes us beyond the Dawkins world of chaos and randomness, to 'make a form shine upon a matter', as Jacques Maritain puts it in Thomistic terms.[26] As at a baptism, so at a funeral, people are according the dead person a similar significance. If we are only bodies, bundles of atoms, what would be the point of such an activity? All Christians are called, as part of the priesthood of believers, to recognize and affirm form and meaning wherever it may be found, and in their own lives to use their imagination to call the world into participation. We do this in acts of service, according meaning and

25 G. K. Chesterton, *The Everlasting Man* (San Francisco, CA: Ignatius Press, 1993 [1925]), p. 34.

26 Jacques Maritain, *Art and Scholasticism*, trans. by J. F. Scanlan (London: Sheed and Ward, 1930), p. 23.

value to the elderly, the disabled, the outcast. Such acts are equally activities of the imagination.

Frodo's ending in *The Lord of the Rings* is one in which lack and woundedness is opened to fullness and excess. And his destiny being hidden from the reader opens our desire. For me, the whole enterprise of presenting the faith convincingly is aimed at opening this desire in others, rather than offering pre-packaged answers. I write as a creedal, orthodox Christian but I hope that my confidence in the truth of Christianity allows me to be relaxed and generous, understanding that our creeds are forms of truthful speech, faithfully shaping the mystery of our understanding of God. Our use of Scripture similarly can no longer be that of earlier modes of apologetics, in which the miracles were presented as forms of evidence in themselves. Miracles even in the Gospels do not convince alone, but as signs of the divine at work. We can, however, point to the texts as mysteries in the manner described above in the discussion of Coleridge on the Hebrew poets. And we can convince people, paradoxically, by pointing to the *mystery* of Christ as something attractive and convincing.

The more I study and meditate upon the Gospels, the more distant and mysterious the figure of Christ becomes. I can imagine the places – Capernaum, Jordan, the Temple mount, Bethany – but I cannot imagine Christ in the same way. He often seems elusively too large for his setting. His words seem ironic and even sarcastic, strange and paradoxical. I come closest when Christ addresses an individual, such as the woman at the Samarian well in John or the man for whom he spits on some earth and places it on the man's eyes to help him see again. This may seem strange to those for whom Christ is as easily accessed as their best friend, but it is not strange to those outside the faith. Indeed, in my view this is a way to engage them in the behaviour, actions and words of a man whose importance is visible in the effects of his presence, and who never seems more himself, as Hans Frei argued, than when he is most powerless, in his trial and passion, and whose resurrection blows apart our tidy classification of the nature of the material and the spiritual realms. Pasolini's 1964 film, *The Gospel According to St Matthew*, in which only words from the Gospel are used for dialogue, works precisely in this manner of 'making strange'. Christ there is not an object, any more than he is in the Gospels, nor is he the cuddly toy he can too easily become. He is powerful, challenging and elusive, and one learns to see as he sees. For if Christ is the reality that takes us upward, we see through him, by means of him, with him. And in trying to convince others of his divinity, we should return, perhaps, to that Tractarian reserve of the early Oxford Movement in communicating religious truth. Christ is beautiful, especially when he is most disfigured, and if we are to convince others to follow him, we need to guard and gradually reveal that beauty.

To sum up, an apologetics of the imagination has two main aims. The first is to awaken what one might call the religious sense, that home-sickness for the absolute which Novalis sought in his blue flower, and which Caspar David Friedrich paints so powerfully. And it is to help those with whom we come in contact to recognize their own assumption of a religious depth to experience. The second is Novalis's 'magic ideal-ism' filtered through Tolkien's participatory realism by which we learn to share in divine creativity by awakening the world beyond itself to its own reality, and to be surprised by the 'thisness' of phenomena. We want non-believers to understand that Christianity is not narrow but a vision that includes everything, restoring the lost beauty of the world, whether the city streets or the natural world. We want people to understand that IT consultancy, bathing your children and tiling a bathroom are all cre-ative acts that participate in God's creativity through what I have been calling 'magic idealism'.

In fact, the priest's blessing of people and objects can itself become a mode of apologetics: it is the primary mode of Jewish prayer, which we imitate at the Eucharist in the 'blessed are You, Lord God of all creation' prayers over the gifts. We ought to imitate Jewish practice by blessing every activity and person. Children leaving school should be blessed, as should people moving house, starting a new job, starting to care for an aged relative. We should bless homes, workplaces, tools, paintings and stories. For in this way we demonstrate the outpouring of God's love that is always given, and also the value of the person or activity is con-firmed and reconnected to its divine source. It takes very little work to make this clear.

I began this chapter with Kant, to whom I attributed the post-Enlight-enment tragedy of a dead phenomenal world of perception and its con-verse, an inaccessible world of the spirit to which our experience cannot reach. Kant wrote also about the limits of Reason, which falls back upon itself in critique. The imagination I have described redeems this tragic separation of phenomena and noumena, and it also avoids being anti-rational. Indeed, as I have tried to demonstrate, it has a certain intellectual toughness. It suggests, however, that reason does need rescuing and we can do so by recasting the limit to understanding from a negation to an opening out to mystery. As Fr Giussani argues, reason discovers mystery: 'the summit of reason's conquest may reveal itself as a foothill' but this perception is *itself* a positive discovery that there is more: 'the existence of something incommensurable in relation to [Reason] itself'.[27] And it is imagination that helps reason to recognize the mystery *as* mystery. So let us use every imaginative tool at our disposal to awaken the religious sense, and then use reason to explain the difference this viewpoint makes to our experience of the whole of reality, which is restored to us, in all its fullness.

---

27 Giussani, *The Religious Sense*, p. 117.

4

Apologetics, Literature and Worldview

DONNA J. LAZENBY

Continuing the programme of previous chapters, Donna Lazenby works through apologetics in terms of worldview. Since this is always a matter of the imagination, contemporary literature gives us unparalleled access to prominent aspects of the worldviews currently in circulation. Drawing on examples from recent fiction, she finds that each one embodies a particular stance on a range of metaphysical (and therefore religious) questions. More than this, these novels also serve to perpetuate these visions of reality, or even to evangelize for them. The task of the apologist is twofold in response. She should pay careful attention to what our literary culture reveals about the desires and conceptualities of our time. She will then go beyond this analysis of these implicit worldviews to point out their inconsistencies, to show the roots in Christian history of much that is good in them, and to offer Christian faith and practice as what most truly satisfies the longings that these contemporary novels express. **A.D.**

One of the most important characteristics of the twenty-first century Christian apologist is an ability to read the signs of the times. When surveying contemporary culture, the apologist must be able to skirt the superficial, while grasping hold of deeper currents and working to interpret them. This captures a key step in the apologetic task. It is not possible to discover how the Christian faith, and the Church, can speak meaningfully into a secular world unless efforts have first been made to understand the shape of this world itself: its values, assumptions, prejudices, cravings; especially as these reveal where the veil is thinnest between secular and religious concerns, and where, in fact, the Spirit may be going before those who already belong to faith, made manifest in places beyond the confines of the institutional Church. Religious people cannot afford to be 'snobs' about their faith. They need to interpret, respect and respond to the prevailing cultural phenomena with which people are already engaged, rather than insisting that others must read what they read, act as they act or believe what they believe, before conversations can be had. It is not good enough to observe something like the Harry Potter phenomenon – into which millions of people of all ages have poured their yearnings for an experience of transcendence, redemption, miraculous events and a part in that epic battle between good and evil – and to dismiss this as a mish-mash of heretical hocus-pocus above which the Church should simply rise, with an indignant backward glance.

Since Christians have been commissioned to make disciples of all nations, to feed Christ's flock and minister to a broken world, they would do better to follow Saint Paul's model of mission, making efforts to understand the culture that is being witnessed to, and shaping Christ's message in ways that translate effectively into this world. Paul himself 'becomes all things to all people so that by all possible means I might save some' (1 Cor. 9.22). Before the philosophers at the Areopagus, he is able to utilize the language of philosophy to share the Christian gospel, that the 'unknown God' of the pagans has been revealed and identified in the person of Jesus Christ (Acts 17.23). It is in the language of the seventh-century BC Cretan poet Epimenides, well known by his philosophical listeners, that Paul describes a God in whom 'we live and move and have our being' (Acts 17.28). Paul is the archetypal Christian apologist: charged with the mission to communicate the Christian gospel, he knows the worth of being able to speak in the language of his audience, fully aware of the values, ideas and hopes that they hold dear.

Christian apologists must locate 'diagnostic spaces': places where the relationship between religion and the wider world is being clearly played out, and where this relationship can be studied. Contemporary literature is such a place. Literature that is especially popular offers itself as a cultural lens through which popular misunderstandings of religion may be located. It is also possible to discover, through this literature, what people are spiritually hungering for. This is a powerful tool for apologetics. If people are getting something from a certain kind of literature that they are not getting from the Church, the apologist needs to know what this is, and why the Church is not a place where people appear to be receiving it. As I am about to show, a study of certain contemporary literatures reveals that there is a very fertile ground on which the Church can minister. The task of apologetics is to learn how.

I will chart a path through two very different kinds of literature, currently gripping two very different audiences. This provides an ideal overview of how conversations about religion are emerging in different social places. The *second* of these will be the *Twilight* saga, arguably the biggest literary phenomenon since Harry Potter, which has gripped the imaginations not only of teenagers, but of people of all ages.

But first, I will consider what a study published in the early months of 2010 has identified as a new breed of 'New Atheist Literature'. In certain contemporary cases, literature has become 'weaponized': consciously constructed not purely to reflect, but to actually *promote*, a certain worldview, to advocate a particular set of values, to actively disparage others, and to urge a certain kind of society or vision for humankind. To be specific, works of literature have become prescriptive of the New Atheist worldview, tools for propaganda. One place where this has happened is in the highly contemporary, quite deliberate appropriation of the New Atheist creed into works of literature.

The 'New Atheist Novel'

'New Atheism' is the phenomenon that began with the appearance of several best-selling polemics against religion: Sam Harris's *The End of Faith* (2004), Daniel Dennett's *Breaking the Spell* (2006), Richard Dawkins's *The God Delusion* (2006) and Christopher Hitchens's *God is Not Great* (2007). These texts are united by the conviction that religious belief is not simply irrational but immoral and dangerous.[1]

Distinctive characteristics of New Atheism include its intellectual crudity and sheer polemical force; its failure to engage with religious ideas on their own terms while condemning religious thought absolutely; its failure to make any distinction between extremist, militant varieties of alleged religious expression and the codes of belief, behaviour and practice that the vast majority of believers actually hold to. In other words, in an ironic reversal, this New Atheism is the living embodiment of the very fundamentalist, intolerant, conceptually violent, neoconservative caricature of dogmatic faith that it claims to oppose. The New Atheists practise all the reductive, literalist thinking and de-contextualized readings of Scripture that inform the strongest versions of religious creationism. Indeed, they take it for granted that such readings of the Bible are the only legitimate ones, thereby themselves reproducing and underlining the reductive approach of the fundamentalists.

In their recently published study, *The New Atheist Novel: Fiction, Philosophy and Polemic after 9/11* (2010), Arthur Bradley and Andrew Tate

---

1 Arthur Bradley and Andrew Tate, *The New Atheist Novel: Fiction, Philosophy and Polemic after 9/11* (London: Continuum, 2010), p. 1.

identify a new literary genre. The 'New Atheist novel' *fictionalizes* the New Atheist belief in 'militant atheism, evolutionary biology, neuroscience and political Neo-Conservatism'.[2] Indeed, for Ian McEwan, Martin Amis and their contemporaries, 'the contemporary novel represents a new front in the ideological war against religion, religious fundamentalism and, after 9/11, religious terror'. Quite simply, the novel now 'stands for everything – free speech, individuality, rationality and even a secular experience of the transcendental – that religion seeks to overthrow'.[3] The New Atheist writers believe that literature *replaces* religion. Literature takes all that is best about religion – ideas of transcendence, redemption, a contemplative piety inspired by wonder for the universe – and leaves aside what is apparently equally integral to religion: its violence and delusions. However, what this literature *really* stands for is 'a disturbing aesthetic-political dogmatism': about science, reason, Islam and religion in general.[4] Meanwhile, the things that are claimed to be especially precious and redemptive about literature are actually recycled *religious* ideas. As I will show, the distinctly redemptive qualities of an apparently secular literature must be recognized, in the end, as requiring nothing less than an act of faith.

Ian McEwan

In his essay, 'End of the World Blues',[5] McEwan describes 9/11 as the ultimate failure of moral imagination: the terrorists could never have acted as they did if they had recognized their victims as real people. In his pre 9/11 novel *Atonement*, McEwan explores the idea of the novel as the optimum space through which people can experience the perspectives of others and therefore achieve genuine empathy.[6] By reading literature, we get into peoples' heads and see the world from their point of view. It is precisely because the character Briony fails to do this in *Atonement* – to see people as real – that she is able to precipitate such tragedy within their lives, falsely accusing young staff-member Robbie of committing rape. In her recognition of herself as a 'saviour' and her characterization of Robbie as evil personified, we find the New Atheist association of religious self-delusion with neurotic pathology. However, as critics such as Tate

---

2 Tate and Bradley, *The New Atheist Novel*, p. 11.

3 Tate and Bradley, *The New Atheist Novel*, p. 11.

4 Tate and Bradley, *The New Atheist Novel*, p. 12.

5 Ian McEwan, 'End of the World Blues,' in *The Portable Atheist: Essential Readings for the Non-Believer*, ed. by Christopher Hitchens (London: Da Capo Press, 2007), pp. 351–65.

6 See Ian McEwan, *Atonement* (London: Vintage, 2002).

and Bradley recognize, McEwan's *faith* in the power of the novel is tested to destruction by his own method: Briony is a writer, and it is precisely the narcissistic, solipsistic pretensions of this activity which leave her as much in bondage to self-absorption as any militant theism.

As Christian apologists, there is cause for a serious pause for thought here. If McEwan, and the New Atheists, identify religion with a failure of moral imagination, this is surely counteracted by the profound literatures of the Christian tradition that are precisely concerned with the development of a moral imagination. Take the Gospel parables: what are these *stories*, these narratives, if not powerful invitations to people to locate themselves within the situations of others, precisely in order to realize the moral landscapes of their life, so that they may develop their spiritual, empathetic and imaginative view of reality? The listener, or reader, is a prodigal son; a traveller fallen by the wayside. Whole spiritual traditions of imaginative reflection have developed around this understanding of Scripture as key to reality, and as helping the listener to see life from different perspectives. The Ignatian practice of imagining myself into particular scriptural situations, and into the lives of their characters, invites me, through regular and sustained exercises, to strengthen the organ of my moral imagination. The moral–spiritual practice of making an *examen*, of considering what, during the day, has brought life to ourselves and others – or conversely taken this life away – helps a person to develop a more consistent, day-to-day awareness of these dynamics so that their life may bear more spiritual fruit. A person becomes increasingly attentive to the invisible forces that shape their own, and others', lives. Similarly, the prayerful, contemplative reflection of *lectio divina* is a form of 'sacred reading' during which a piece of Scripture is repeatedly attended to: is read over and over again, is 'teased out', so that its depths, lessons and many interpretative layers can be discovered and explored. This exercise is not so much about the enquirer's questioning of the text, but rather about allowing the text to interrogate the enquirer: the process is precisely about opening the self up to a moral and spiritual reality so that this self might be transformed by the 'other'. These are but a few examples of specifically spiritual exercises that take place within the context of religious devotion, and are absolutely about the development of the moral imagination. The New Atheists, and their literary exponents, desire and revere just this kind of awakened moral imagination, and its achievement through works of literature: but they deny that this can be found in the Bible, or achieved through engagement with its Scriptures. This is ironic, given that the Bible, and the traditions guiding its use, in many ways constitute the historical archetype of such imaginative reading.

For the New Atheist, and his literary exponent, religion is characterized by moral blindness and a critical lack of empathy. What, then, of Christ's command to hold, as a central law of the heart, the conviction to love others, and to treat them just as we would wish to be loved and treated ourselves? This is essential Christian teaching. Taking into account only the fundamentals of any Sunday School child's religious comprehension, it is evident that the Christian believer aspires to a fullness of imaginative and moral vision for which the New Atheist gives no credit.

McEwan believes that the novelist asks the question that never occurs to the terrorist – and, for the New Atheist, never occurs to the religious person in general – 'what must it feel like to be a victim?' But again, for the Christian imagination, the ultimate victim is the person of Jesus Christ, around whom, and in relation to whose suffering, Christian theology is an announcement of the gift of freedom, grace and liberation. It is precisely on account of God's identity with humanity through Christ – this Son who was once a victim, but is now glorified – that there exists a 'redeeming love' beyond the bounds of which no one can fall. As a victim, a sufferer, a servant, Christ can identify with every broken human situation. Nothing, in Christ, lies 'beyond the pale': no sheep is *too* lost to be found. But this theology announces a moral imagination of such immensity, and a redemptive possibility of such scope, that the New Atheist's definition of religion is unrecognizable here. In the end, the best thing that they claim literature to be capable of achieving is revealed as what it really is: a borrowed Christian ideal. If the New Atheist persists that a notion of redemption exists independently of a religious framework, for example as a pre-Christian or even post-Christian idea, then the burden of proof remains on their side: for, as we will see, the transformative power of the redemptive events which they claim can take place through literature lacks the necessary metaphysical grounding which a religious context provides. Their reductive, secularist worldview cannot support such super-natural hopes or aspirations.

Saturday, McEwan's explicitly 9/11 themed novel, stages allegorically the war he saw waged on that day. The character Henry reflects that, 'out in the real world there exist detailed plans, visionary projects for peaceable realms, all conflicts resolved, happiness for everyone – mirages for which people are prepared to die and kill. Christ's kingdom on earth, the workers' paradise, the ideal Islamic state'.[7] Henry considers that, 'The primitive thinking of the supernaturally inclined amounts to what his psychiatric colleagues call a problem, or an idea, or reference. An excess

---

7 Ian McEwan, *Saturday* (London: Vintage, 2006), pp. 171–2.

of the subjective, the ordering of the world in line with your needs, an inability to contemplate your own unimportance. In Henry's view such reasoning belongs on a spectrum at whose far end . . . lies psychosis. And such reasoning may have caused the fire on the plane. A man of sound faith with a bomb in the heel of his shoe.'[8]

This description is saturated with New Atheist ideology. First, these writers claim that if Christians and other religious people believe in a supernatural deity at all, they are already on a road leading inevitably towards the psychotic solipsism and terrorism whereby, for them, other people simply cease to exist. Second, such terror is apparently committed by someone of 'sound faith' – there is no sense, again, of differentiation between extremist and mainstream belief. Third, militant behaviour is seen as the purest version of religious belief, rather than what almost all religious people see it to be: a disastrous aberration. Faith, as the now well-rehearsed caricature goes, is an excess of subjective feeling, a reading of the world in line with personal needs, whereas of course, as those of genuine faith know, religious belief frequently involves the opposite: a consistent and uncomfortable *re*-setting of personal preferences and prejudices in light of a new vision of the world which is revealed through that faith. The version of religion that the New Atheists believe to be definitive of all religion is a version that most genuine believers simply would not recognize.

In the end, as critics such as Tate and Bradley recognize, what McEwan believes literature is able to accomplish, in the place of religion, actually requires a spectacular leap of *faith*. The idea of 'literature as redemption' is tested beyond capacity at the end of *Saturday*, when a potential rapist is transformed into a lover when poetry is read to him. Believing the poetry to be written by the girl he faces, he suddenly 'sees' her as a real human being – again, we encounter the theme of the awakening of moral imagination. But this magic 'spell',[9] with which the book ends, shows that McEwan has simply committed the secularist rationalist error of assuming that he has no beliefs. Words alone cannot inspire this instantaneous change in a person, not least given its suddenness. The change is indeed miraculous. The redemptive potential of poetry, in this instance, requires a distinctly supernatural event, as a person is transformed, in an instant, from one kind of being to another. But this *power*

---

8 McEwan, *Saturday*, p. 17.

9 McEwan, *Saturday*, p. 278. 'Daisy recited a poem that cast a spell on one man. Perhaps any poem would have done the trick, and thrown the switch on a sudden mood change. Still, Baxter fell for the magic, he was transfixed by it, and he was reminded how much he wanted to live.'

in literature begs serious metaphysical questions which the New Atheist not only refuses to answer, but will not even permit to count as meaningful questions. McEwan has *faith* in the power of literature to achieve this moral transformation: but the precise dynamics of this transformation, and the way that literature achieves it, is not consistent with the New Atheist's reductive science. The potential rapist, transformed through the beautiful poetry's 'spell', will choose to 'live'. The kind of metaphysically loaded value judgement being made here is elsewhere dismissed by the New Atheist on evolutionary grounds. But, clearly, spirit lurks within this machine.

Martin Amis

In an article called 'The Voice of the Lonely Crowd', printed in *The Guardian* in June 2002, Martin Amis wrote that,

> The twentieth century, with its scores of millions of supernumerary dead, has been called the age of ideology. And the age of ideology, clearly, was a mere hiatus in the age of religion, which shows little sign of expiry. Since it is no longer permissible to disparage any single faith or creed, let us start disparaging all of them. To be clear: an ideology is a belief system with an inadequate basis in reality; a religion is a belief system with no basis in reality whatever. Religious belief is without reason and without dignity, and its record is near-universally dreadful.[10]

Like McEwan, Amis's understanding of religion bears all the hallmarks of New Atheist dogma. Faith is irrational. Faith tries to reduce the awe-inspiring mystery of the universe to some finite, exhaustive account; religious people have apparently missed the fact that reality transcends doctrine; the voice of believers is a droning monologue – they cannot think for themselves; they are unquestioning disciples of a reductive, naive, simplistic creed. What lies on the other side of religion, for Amis, is not atheism, but independence of mind. The religious mind, by contrast, is impoverished, straitjacketed by centuries of tradition. The cult of the literary instead worships a transcendental deity that actually exists: 'something boundless, beautiful and divinely bright'. It is impossible to miss the suspicious borrowing of religious language here.[11]

---

10 Martin Amis, 'The Voice of the Lonely Crowd' in *The Second Plane: September 11: 2001–2007* (London: Vintage, 2008), pp. 11–20 (pp. 13–14).

11 Amis, 'The Voice of the Lonely Crowd', p. 16.

Amis describes the distinctive value of literature as its resistance to historical attempts to turn it into an object for collective worship, an ideological tool or political weapon. But surely, this describes exactly what New Atheist literature aims to be. The worldviews espoused in this weaponized literature are extremely and indiscriminately intolerant of religious sentiments, and even a brief acquaintance with such literature betrays its strikingly ideological and propagandizing nature.

Rather as it did for McEwan, Amis's case for literature against religion begins to unravel when we examine what it is that literature is believed to achieve in religion's place. What we find, again, is a confidence in the capabilities of literature that can only be called an act of *faith*. Amis writes,

> True, novelists don't normally write about what's going on; they write about what's not going on. Yet the worlds so created aspire to pattern and shape a moral point. A novel is a rational undertaking; it is reason at play, perhaps, but it is still reason.[12]

The stories may not literally reflect actual reality: but they have an internal logic that renders their worldview meaningful.

An important question emerges here. If a novel can write about 'what's not going on', can create worlds which 'aspire to pattern and shape a moral point,' and yet is crucially still a 'rational undertaking'; if this novel is an exercise of 'reason at play', but is emphatically 'still reason'; then why cannot such generosity of spirit be extended to religious belief and theology? This must be asked not least on behalf of the worlds of Scripture, where just such a blend of literal events and imaginative possibility is described in order 'to pattern and shape a moral point'. A double standard is operating here. The New Atheist believes that the absence of absolute reductive literalism in religious statements is outright proof of religion's irrationality. At the same time, their own works, and those of their literary supporters, are permitted a great deal of imaginative scope without this being viewed as impairing the rational quality of their work. The New Atheists and their literary exponents draw the bounds of reason far wider for their own works than they will allow for either the Scriptures or the stories of the Christian tradition.

In the end, insofar as writers such as McEwan and Amis adopt the intellectual violence of the New Atheist anti-religious worldview, they are in danger of becoming as intolerant as the perspectives they attack. Their suspicious, fear-imbued reflections radically misunderstand and

---

12 Amis, 'The Voice of the Lonely Crowd', p. 13.

misrepresent the true nature of religious faith. Indeed, several inconsistencies are operating here. An imaginative reach is allowed for secular literature that is not extended to biblical and theological writing, even though the New Atheist writers adopt Christian categories to express their worldviews. There is an explicitly religious and spiritual quality to their treatment of the word, and its power, which they value, even while they refuse to accept the validity of the metaphysical questions begged by this power. Furthermore, while the texts of religious tradition are condemned as irrational by the New Atheists because they do not literally depict physical reality, the New Atheist literature draws the boundaries of its own rationality more widely, defining literary creativity as 'reason at play.' These double standards are the foundations upon which the New Atheists, and their literary compatriots, build their case against religion.

The *Twilight* Saga

A less high-brow but equally illuminating indicator of current popular attitudes toward religious and spiritual ideas can be found in the *Twilight* saga. The four *Twilight* books currently making up the series had sold over 17 million copies in 38 languages by November 2008. Three have been made into films, with the fourth on the way.

The story is a first-person narrative by 17-year-old Bella Swan, who moves to a small, gloomy town in Washington State to stay with her father. She epitomizes the classic teenage angst of feeling herself to be an outsider while actually making friends quite easily. She remains aloof at her new school, until being drawn strongly towards Edward Cullen. Edward, it turns out, is a vampire. He thirsts for Bella's blood and is so attracted to her that he attempts to maintain a distance for fear of killing her. Eventually they confess their love for one another, but Edward tries to put her off their relationship with the truth: 'I'm a killer.' However, Bella is too in love to be without him, and declares that, man or monster, she loves him and trusts that he will not kill her. The biggest challenge they will face involves sex: Edward cannot risk sexual relations with Bella for fear of losing control and killing her. So begins a powerful epic, revolving around the complexities of 'the agony and ecstasy of abstinence', as one critic has described it.[13]

---

13 Cosmo Landesman, 'Twilight', *The Sunday Times Review*, 21 December 2008, http://entertainment.timesonline.co.uk/tol/arts_and_entertainment/film/film_reviews/article5358921.ece (accessed 30 June 2010) (para. 6 of 9).

The *Twilight* saga has a huge appeal, not only for teenagers, but for people – especially women – of all ages. It is important to ask, what is it offering these people? There is, of course, the age-old delight of a story of star-crossed lovers, but the story's appeal *also* lies in its attendance to central life-questions, many of which have significant spiritual dimensions and, quite simply, give people an experience of transcendence. There is the question of the nature and possibility of immortality or some kind of afterlife, the idea of unconditional love, the supernatural, the occult, the nature of free-will and predestination. These are all questions to which the Christian Church is fully equipped to respond, and yet which millions of people are content to explore in the novels and films, we may assume, without the Church.

It is especially striking, and very likely symptomatic of our age, that there is no vision of heaven in *Twilight*. The options for Bella, for example, are either to remain human and simply die, or to gain immortality in the form of eternal damnation – what Edward calls 'an eternity of night' – by becoming a vampire. The novels seem to capture the essence of a secular age: there is no hope because there is no eschatology, and the only acceptable, palatable version of immortality is one clothed in horror. There is a reverberation of the New Atheist writer's world here: any light is too much light. The artist has become a necrophiliac, developing a necro-aesthetics:[14] for McEwan and Amis we live in nauseating worlds of suspicion, fear, murder and danger; in *Twilight*, we are literally thinking about making love to the dead.

What, in the *Twilight* saga, is distinctly religious in character? What aspects of this phenomenon are appealing to people's religious and spiritual sensibilities? Which distinctly religious and spiritual hungers are fed by the series? The first book opens by quoting Genesis 2.17: 'But of the tree of knowledge of good and evil, thou shalt not eat of it; for in the day that thou eatest thereof thou shalt surely die.'[15] There follows a story explicitly engaged with the idea of the freedom of the will: Edward has an original sin embedded within his nature – he constantly suffers the temptation to kill, even that which he loves – but he can make a choice whether or not to respond to this impulse. Bella tells him she believes he is dangerous but not bad: drawing something like a distinction between individual acts of sin and the possession of sin as an inescapable ontological state. As Dave Roberts writes in his study *The Twilight Gospel: The*

---

14 See Tate and Bradley on Martin Amis as 'a curious case study of the artist-as-necrophiliac' (*The New Atheist Novel*, p. 46).

15 Stephenie Meyer, *Twilight* (London: Atom, 2006).

Spiritual Roots of Stephenie Meyer's Vampire Saga (2009), the moral centre of the story is found in the interplay between the beliefs of Edward and another vampire, Carlisle. This moral centre is 'rooted in the familiar Judaeo-Christian narrative about God, creation, moral choice and our eternal destiny'.[16] Carlisle is a man of peace; a vampire who does not hunt humans. The son of a sixteenth-century Anglican clergyman, he was part of his father's vampire hunt when he was bitten. Carlisle's respect for his spiritual roots prior to being a vampire is a strong theme (he has a large wooden cross in his house). Carlisle tells Bella: 'Never, in the nearly 400 years since I was born, have I ever seen anything to make me doubt whether God exists in one form or another.'[17] Carlisle is aware that vampires do not qualify as candidates for the heaven of the Judaeo-Christian God. Bella struggles with this idea in the second novel and film, *New Moon*, telling Carlisle that if there is a heaven, surely he cannot be damned, since his goodness is almost saintly. Crucially, Carlisle says, 'By all accounts, we were damned regardless. But I hope, maybe foolishly, that we'll get some measure of credit for trying.'[18]

This is all, of course, strikingly at odds with that message of the New Testament contained in many places but perhaps most clearly in the Letter to the Ephesians: 'For it is by grace you have been saved, through faith . . . not by works, so that no-one can boast' (Ephesians 2.8–9). *Twilight* is a world without *grace;* at least without *redemptive* grace. There is no such gift: more just a pagan sense of fate. In light of this, Carlisle is even more admirably a peacemaker, a reconciler, a wise judge, who only kills according to a 'just war' philosophy; he has dignity, he shows tolerance and forgiveness; he is immensely selfless. He is absolutely unconcerned with domination. Bella reflects on this goodness when claiming of one vampire attacker that he does not understand real families who are 'in relationships based on love rather than just the love of power'.[19] At the heart of this world, a deeply sacrificial love is gestured towards, yearned for, sought after: it could be said to be an almost Christ-like love, which seeks no gain for itself, and, realizing the inevitability of its own crucifixion, is nevertheless unfailingly committed to building a world based on love. The tragedy is, of course, that most of the people reading these books believe that this possibility belongs to the world of pure fiction – and do not seem to be searching for it within the Christian Church.

---

16 Dave Roberts, *The Twilight Gospel: The Spiritual Roots of Stephenie Meyer's Vampire Saga* (Oxford: Monarch Books, 2009), p. 120.

17 Quoted in Roberts, *The Twilight Gospel*, p. 130.

18 Roberts, *The Twilight Gospel,* p. 130.

19 Roberts, *The Twilight Gospel*, p. 134.

Perverse though it may at first sound, there may also be a Christlike-ness about the vampire Edward that draws people towards wanting a relationship with him. Bella herself is frequently confused about whether he is more vampire-demon or archangel. She has Mary Magdalene's own yearning to touch her transformed lover's body. His smell, his presence, his beauty, his attention, his power are all thoroughly intoxicating. Simi-larly, Edward's response to her advances echoes Christ's own 'Do not touch me', albeit for very different reasons. Bella's intimacy with this man pulls her into a place where her deepest questions and longings about love, life, hope and the future are absolutely present and completely rel-evant. Vampires aside, it is a love that anyone would yearn for, and it is certainly possible that what pulls people towards these stories is the idea of being so wonderfully caught up in such a spiritually charged love.

For the Christian apologist, two strong lessons emerge from this study of contemporary literature. First, religion is misrepresented in literature in ways that inform the popular consciousness, and the apologist needs to find ways to respond to this. Second, these literatures, claiming either overtly, or inadvertently, to cast religion aside, are not giving genuinely non-religious alternatives for their readers, but are actually reconfiguring human desires, aspirations and passions on their own religious and spiri-tual terms. The apologist must find ways to expose this deceit, address-ing peoples' confusion around what the Christian faith is really about, while making it demonstrably clear that the Church has a response for the yearnings these literatures document. To achieve this, the Church may need to radically re-imagine the shape of its outreach, and the me-dia it uses to present the gospel. It may have to be daring and try things that feel improper. But as the religious leader William Booth once put it, when accused of the indecency of setting religious hymns to pub songs, 'Why should the devil have all the best tunes?' In our times, the Christian Church must ask again, 'Why should the devil have all the best tunes?' Moreover, 'Why should we let him steal ours?'

5

The Good Serves the Better and Both the Best: C. S. Lewis on Imagination and Reason in Apologetics

MICHAEL WARD

For C. S. Lewis, the imagination is our capacity to apprehend meaning. He saw this illustrated by his own conversion. It was not for Lewis a matter of coming to a new understanding of a few isolated 'religious' topics. Rather, the faith enlightened and enlivened his sense of the meaning of anything and everything. His conversion, in Lewis's own words, 'baptized' his imagination. This is to find in him a powerful advocate of the approach to apologetics encountered throughout this volume. So is a second feature of Lewis's journey: that conversion challenged him to think about the nature of reason in light of the Christian faith. He found reason broadened out to include a rationality of narrative as well as one of concept. This simultaneously both placed the Christian story at the heart of his imagination and paved the way for him to apprehend, and accept, some of these truths in other systems of thought and belief. In other words, his imaginative account of reason opened up a generous line of conversation, which could itself be a basis for apologetics. Beyond and alongside any of these considerations, he was also an 'imaginative apologist' in the sense that he engaged in apologetics through works of the imagination, primarily through fiction. Although this draws our attention to the dearth of contemporary literature in this vein, it also places before every Christian apologist the positive and more modest responsibility to become familiar with the wealth of analogy, simile and metaphor provided by the Christian tradition, and to do our part to enrich it ourselves. **A.D.**

C. S. Lewis is probably the most influential practitioner of Christian apologetics over the last 100 years. According to his Oxford contemporary, the theologian and philosopher Austin Farrer, Lewis was 'the most successful apologist our days have seen'.[1] Works such as *Mere Christianity*, *Miracles*, *The Problem of Pain* and *Surprised by Joy*, as well as his classic Chronicles of Narnia, have been read by millions of people round the world since they were first published in the 1940s and 1950s.

In this chapter I want to take a step back and look at the Lewis of the 1930s in order to examine some of the groundwork to his thinking that enabled him to become so effective an apologist. The titles I just listed are the famous flower of his life's work: in what follows we will inspect the stem and indeed the root. Our examination will show that Lewis's apologetics were successful not simply because the Christianity he presented was reasonable (although reasonable it certainly was, or at any rate was intended to be), but first and foremost because it was presented with imaginative skill and imaginative intent. Lewis had a profound respect for the imagination, and his thinking about and practice of imaginative apologetics constitute one of the main reasons why he is still a relevant, indeed a most timely, voice in the field. In a postmodern world, systematic or abstract or propositional apologetic strategies may often be of limited appeal because of suspicions about the supposed neutrality or utility of 'reason'. Lewis himself gave considerable thought to the relations between reason and imagination, and it is this that I propose to explore. As someone trained in literary history and criticism and equipped with talents as a poet and novelist, Lewis inevitably thought long and hard about the role of imagination, but he also taught philosophy at Oxford for a period and was a (non-professional) theologian of wide reading, so he gave considerable attention also to the claims of reason. When he turned to apologetics, that thinking about imagination and reason naturally informed his whole approach and only if we understand his thinking about both faculties and the way they interrelate with each other and with the life of faith will we gain a secure grasp of his effectiveness as an apologist.

Definitions

Apologetics is usually defined as 'a reasoned defence'. In Lewis's view, reason could only operate if it was first supplied with materials to reason

1 Austin Farrer, *Faith and Speculation: An Essay in Philosophical Theology* (London: A. & C. Black, 1967), p. 156. Cf. 'almost certainly the most influential religious author of the twentieth century, in English or any other language', according to Robert MacSwain, 'Introduction', *The Cambridge Companion to C. S. Lewis* (Cambridge University Press, 2010), p. 3.

about, and it was imagination's task to supply those materials. Therefore, apologetics was necessarily and foundationally imaginative.

In order to provide an easy – and amusing – introduction to Lewis's thinking on this subject, let me relate the following (untrue) story.

One day I took my car into the repair garage for its annual overhaul. At the end of the repair job, I collected the car and, as I was driving it out of the garage forecourt, realized I had forgotten to check on something, so I stopped and rolled down my window and called over my shoulder to Billy, the car mechanic, and asked, 'Is my rear indicator light working?' To which he replied, 'Yes. No. Yes. No. Yes. No. Yes.'

This little exchange neatly encapsulates Lewis's definition of imagination. 'Imagination' is a notoriously slippery term and different thinkers and writers define it in very different ways. According to Lewis, imagination is simply 'the organ of meaning'.[2]

Billy the car mechanic's 'organ of meaning' was sadly deficient. A flashing phenomenon, as far as he was concerned, could have only one possible meaning: electrical failure. He was able to see the raw data – light on, light off, light on – but was unable to discover the correct meaning of those brute facts. He had sight, but no insight. He focused on externals and failed to perceive their inner significance.

Not that Billy was entirely without the capacity to perceive meaning. He knew the basic meaning of electrical circuits. He knew that when a light shines a connection has been made and when a light goes out a connection has been broken. But he was unable to find a meaning in the *relationship* between a completed and a broken electrical circuit, imaginatively incapable of perceiving that, in this case, an intermittent light means 'indicator', not 'insecure connection'.

Lewis's definition of imagination as 'the organ of meaning' appears in an important but much overlooked essay called 'Bluspels and Flalansferes: A Semantic Nightmare', which was first published in 1939. (The odd title may have had something to do with why it has been so overlooked.) Mainly concerned with how metaphors are created and used, the essay also contains some larger scale epistemological observations. As well as defining imagination as the organ of meaning, Lewis defines the opposite of meaning as not error but nonsense. Things must rise up out of the swamp of nonsense into the realm of meaning if the imagination is to get any handle on them. Only then can we begin to judge whether their meanings are true or false. Before something can be either true or false it

---

2 C. S. Lewis, 'Bluspels and Flalansferes: A Semantic Nightmare', in *Selected Literary Essays*, ed. by Walter Hooper (Cambridge: Cambridge University Press, 1969), p. 265.

must mean. Even a lie means something, and a lie understood as a lie can be most instructive. Only nonsensical things mean nothing.

Back to Billy and the car. Not every flashing light on a car is meaningful. Sometimes there really are loose connections, whose occasional bursts of luminosity, flickering on and off in no particular rhythm, we should best describe as nonsensical: the connections are arbitrary, random, meaningless. If the connections were regular or patterned, however, we would be inclined to conclude that they were significant, meaningful. But what kind of meaning would they have? A true meaning, showing that the driver was about to make a turning? Or a false meaning, showing that the driver had forgotten to cancel the lever? It is human reason, in Lewis's view, that judges between meanings, helping us to differentiate those meanings that are true and illuminating from those which are false and deceptive.

To summarize his definitions: reason is 'the natural organ of truth'; imagination is 'the organ of meaning' and meaning itself is 'the antecedent condition of both truth and falsehood'.[3] Imagination is therefore, for Lewis, 'the prius of truth':[4] before something can be either true or false, it must mean.

Meaning appears to mean the relation between the physical and the psychic or psychological, 'the psycho-physical parallelism (or more)' which characterizes the universe,[5] linking bodies in space and time with spiritual realities ('spiritual' meaning not just psychological, but also rational and, ultimately, pneumatological). A true meaning would be a complete, unimpaired, healthy, fruitful psycho-physical relationship.

Imagination in Practice

Leaving definitions to one side, let us turn now to Lewis's understanding of Christianity and look at the role played by imagination in his journey towards acceptance of the faith. It is worth doing this because his theoretical understanding of the relationship between imagination and truth seems to be strongly related to his personal experience, insofar as we can reconstruct it from the history of his Christian conversion.

Lewis's own imagination was, he said, 'baptized' in a certain sense when, in the second half of his teens, he read a book called *Phantastes* by

---

3 Lewis, 'Bluspels and Flalansferes', p. 265.

4 C. S. Lewis, Letter to Owen Barfield, 27 May 1928, *The Collected Letters of C. S. Lewis, Volume I*, ed. by Walter Hooper (London: HarperCollins, 2000), p. 762.

5 Lewis, 'Bluspels and Flalansferes', p. 265.

the nineteenth-century Scottish writer George MacDonald. In his auto-biography, *Surprised by Joy*, Lewis explains how his early life had been haunted by powerful, fugitive sensations of longing and beauty, experi-ences which he labels 'joy', similar to what the German Romantics would have called *Sehnsucht* (yearning). The effect that *Phantastes* had upon him was somehow to make these moments less transitory. He writes:

> Up till now each visitation of Joy had left the common world mo-mentarily a desert . . . Even when real clouds or trees had been the material of the vision, they had been so only by reminding me of an-other world; and I did not like the return to ours. But now [as I read *Phantastes*] I saw the bright shadow coming out of the book into the real world and resting there, transforming all common things and yet itself unchanged. Or, more accurately, I saw the common things drawn into the bright shadow . . . In the depth of my disgraces, in the then invincible ignorance of my intellect, all this was given me without ask-ing, even without consent. That night my imagination was, in a certain sense, baptized; the rest of me, not unnaturally, took longer. I had not the faintest notion what I had let myself in for by buying *Phantastes*.[6]

We do not have time to go further into *Phantastes* or George MacDonald and investigate more precisely why this book and its author had such an impact on Lewis's imagination. We just need to note that it happened. What *Phantastes* did was to awaken Lewis's imaginative capacity for un-derstanding 'holiness', so he said. For the first time, he was able to attach some meaning to the idea of sanctification, the sanctification of all com-mon everyday things, not by throwing them out in order to make room for some transcendent but alien reality, still less by replacing them with an irrational, fantastic never-never land, but by changing their *meaning* from the inside, transforming them, illuminating them with a different light.

'That night,' Lewis records, 'my imagination was, in a certain sense, baptized; the rest of me, not unnaturally, took a little longer.' In fact, it took about another 15 years for the rest of him to be baptized[7] and for his whole outlook, not just his imaginative outlook, to be converted.

He became a Christian when he was 32 years old, and it is imperative to note that, at the decisive moment, it was his imagination that first

---

6 C. S. Lewis, *Surprised by Joy* (Glasgow, Collins, 1982), p. 146.

7 Lewis had been baptized as an infant (29 January 1899), so 'baptized' here does not mean the literal ritual, but the spiritual realization in Lewis's own adult consciousness of that ceremonial and sacramental washing.

had to be addressed; it was through his imagination that his reason and, ultimately, his will were transformed. The organ of meaning had to be enrolled before his 'natural organ of truth' could get to work; and both imagination and reason had to be satisfied before the core part of him, his 'command centre', the will, could turn about and receive supernatural truth.

The immediate human cause of his conversion was a long night-time conversation with two good friends, J. R. R. Tolkien and Hugo Dyson, on the subject of Christianity, metaphor and myth. In a letter to a third friend, Arthur Greeves, Lewis recounted the substance of the conversation, and it is clear that questions of meaning – that is to say, of imagination – were at the root of it.

Lewis's whole problem with Christianity, at that stage, was fundamentally imaginative. As he wrote to Greeves, 'What has been holding me back . . . has not been so much a difficulty in believing as a difficulty in knowing what the doctrine *meant*.'[8] Tolkien and Dyson showed him that Christian doctrines are not the main thing about Christianity. Doctrines are *translations* into concepts and ideas of that which God has already expressed in 'a language more adequate: namely the actual incarnation, crucifixion and resurrection'[9] of Christ. The primary language of Christianity is a lived language, the real, historical, visible, tangible language of an actual person being born, dying and living again in a new, ineffably transformed way.

When Lewis realized this, he began to gain an understanding of what Christianity really meant, because he was already fascinated – he had been fascinated from childhood – by stories of dying and rising gods. In many ancient mythologies there are stories of characters who die and go down into the underworld and whose death achieves or reveals something back here on earth: new life in the crops, for instance, or sunrise, or the coming of spring. Lewis had always found the heart of these pagan stories – he mentions those of Adonis, Bacchus, Balder, among others – to be 'profound and suggestive of meanings beyond my grasp even tho' I could not say in cold prose "what it meant"'.[10]

The difference between his attitude to Christianity and his attitude to the pagan myths was that, with the latter, he did not try officiously to explain them: these stories he considered to be fruitful enough in their own terms. They were myths that had to be accepted as saying something

8 Letter to Arthur Greeves, 18 October 1931, *Collected Letters, Volume I*, p. 976.
9 Letter to Arthur Greeves, 18 October 1931, *Collected Letters, Volume I*, p. 977.
10 Letter to Arthur Greeves, 18 October 1931, *Collected Letters, Volume I*, p. 977.

in their own way, not treated as a kind of allegory and translated into something less, something secondary, mere 'doctrines'. By accepting that Christianity too was primarily to be understood in its own terms as a story, *before* its translation into a codified doctrinal system, Lewis had moved, we might say, from an analytic to a religious perspective. *Analysis* means literally 'loosening up', while *religion* means something like 'tying back up' – re-ligamenting, if you like. Doctrines, though useful, are the product of analytical dissection; they recast the original, equivocal, historical material into abstract, less fully realized categories of meaning. In short, doctrines are not as richly meaningful as that which they are doctrines about. By coming to this conclusion, Lewis anticipated by several decades the turn to 'narrative theology' that would characterize much later twentieth-century theological thinking.

When Lewis understood that the story recounted in the Gospels, rather than the commentary upon and outworking of that story in the Epistles, was the essence of Christianity's meaning and that the Christ-story could be approached in a way similar to the way he approached pagan myths, it was a huge breakthrough for him. Christianity, he now saw, was a 'true myth' whereas pagan myths were 'men's myths'.[11] In paganism God expressed himself in an unfocused way through the images which human imaginations deployed in order to tell stories about the world; but in the story of Christ, Lewis located 'God's myth'[12] – the story in which God directly expressed himself through a real historical life of a particular man, in a particular time, in a particular place – Jesus of Nazareth, the Messiah, crucified under Pontius Pilate outside Jerusalem, circa AD 33. That there were certain similarities between pagan myths and the true myth did not lead Lewis to conclude, 'So much the worse for Christianity'; it led him to conclude, 'So much the better for Paganism.'[13] Paganism contained a good deal of meaning that was realized, consummated and perfected in Christ.

In a sense, Lewis had found in pagan myths what Christ himself had said could be found in the Old Testament story of Jonah. Jesus told the Pharisees: 'No sign will be given this generation except the sign of Jonah: for as Jonah was in the belly of the great fish for three days and nights, so the Son of Man will be in the heart of the earth for three days and nights' (Matthew 12.39–40). Jonah's descent and re-ascent are a meaningful prefiguration of Christ's own death and resurrection. For Lewis, pagan myths amounted to a similar sort of Christotypical prefiguration.

11 Letter to Arthur Greeves, 18 October 1931, *Collected Letters, Volume I*, p. 977.
12 Letter to Arthur Greeves, 18 October 1931, *Collected Letters, Volume I*, p. 977.
13 C. S. Lewis, 'Is Theology Poetry?', *C.S. Lewis, Essay Collection*, ed. by Lesley Walmsley (London: HarperCollins, 2000), p. 15.

A couple of weeks after his conversation with Tolkien and Dyson, Lewis passed from being nearly certain that Christianity was true to being certain, but the important thing to notice, for our present purposes, is that the first hurdle Lewis had to clear before he could accept the truth of Christianity was an imaginative hurdle; his 'organ of meaning' had to be attended to and satisfied. Although imagination, in Lewis's thinking, is a 'lower' thing than reason, it is not for that reason to be ignored; on the contrary, it is to be all the more honoured. 'The highest does not stand without the lowest' was a maxim from *The Imitation of Christ* that he greatly valued,[14] and rational assent to Christianity cannot occur unless there is some low 'stuff', some meaningful content, to which the higher faculty of reason may grant assent. Reason cannot operate *without* imagination.

The Pagan Imagination

And as reason casts about, looking for things that are not only meaningful but identifiably true, it inevitably finds a great many stories presented for its consideration, some of which are much more true than others, and very few that are completely untrue. This point was important to Lewis because, as a boy, he had been told by his schoolmasters that Christianity was 100% correct and every other religion, including the pagan myths of ancient Greece and Rome, was 100% wrong. He found that this statement, rather than bolstering the Christian claim, undermined it, and he abandoned his childhood faith 'largely under the influence of classical education'.[15]

Having discovered through personal experience that the first thing necessary for Christian faith is an apprehension of Christianity's meaningfulness, and not (not immediately, not primarily, in the order of explanation) its truth, Lewis was untroubled by the similarities between, for instance, the pagan Jupiter and the Hebrew Yahweh. The similarities 'ought to be there';[16] it would be a problem if they were absent. And so he takes pleasure in pointing out, in *Miracles*, that 'God is supposed to have had a "Son," just as if God were a mythological deity

14 See, for example, C. S. Lewis, *Reflections on the Psalms* (Glasgow: Collins, 1984), p. 75; *The Four Loves* (Glasgow: Collins, 1989) pp. 9, 14, 15, 20, 81, 94.

15 Letter to the Revd Henry Welbon, 18 September 1936 (unpublished, but available in the Wade Center, Wheaton College, IL).

16 C. S. Lewis, 'Myth Became Fact', *C.S. Lewis, Essay Collection*, p. 142.

like Jupiter.'[17] The resemblance needs to be present, given that God works through human myths as well as through his own true myth, the historical story of Jesus Christ. Since God is the Father of lights,[18] even the flickering lights of paganism could be attributed ultimately to him. Christians should feel no obligation to quench the smouldering wick burning in pagan myths: quite the reverse, they should do whatever they could to fan it into flame. Lewis, with Edmund Spenser, one of his greatest poetic heroes, believed that 'Divine Wisdom spoke not only on the Mount of Olives, but also on Parnassus.'[19] Of course, the Parnassian wisdom was not as complete as that offered in Christ – it was not sufficient or salvific – but it should be admired and respected as far as it went.

By acknowledging the wisdom of Parnassus, Lewis was following the example of Saint Paul. In the Book of the Acts, Paul preaches to the men of Athens, using the pagan gods to communicate his message. He says to the Athenians that God 'is not far from each one of us, for "In him we live and move and have our being"; as even some of your poets have said, "For we are indeed his offspring"' (Acts 17.27–8).

Paul gives two quotations there, but who is he quoting? Moses? Isaiah? One of the minor prophets? He is not quoting the Hebrew Scriptures at all, but rather Greek poetry, poetry about the pagan gods, in particular the king of the pagan gods, Zeus. The first quotation comes from Epimenides, a Greek poet and philosopher of the sixth century before Christ. Epimenides wrote a poem in which he refers to Zeus as the god 'in whom we live and move and have our being'. And the second quotation comes from Aratus, a poet from about 300 years before Christ, who again refers to Zeus, saying that 'we are indeed his offspring'.

Paul's example here is extremely interesting. Obviously he is not recommending that the men of Athens should worship Zeus: he is urging them to worship the true God, the Father of our Lord Jesus Christ. But notice how he goes about making this point. Rather than saying to the Athenians, 'You've got it completely wrong,' he says, 'You've got it partly

---

17 C. S. Lewis, *Miracles, A Preliminary Study* (Glasgow: Collins 1980), p. 72.

18 'I do believe that God is the Father of lights – natural lights as well as spiritual lights (James 1.17)'. Interview with the Billy Graham Evangelistic Association, reprinted as 'Cross-Examination', *C. S. Lewis, Essay Collection*, p. 555. Cf. Lewis's assessment of Richard Hooker, perhaps his favourite theologian, who thought that 'all kinds of knowledge, all good arts, sciences, and disciplines come from the Father of lights and are "as so many sparkles resembling the bright fountain from which they rise"', *English Literature in the Sixteenth Century, Excluding Drama* (Oxford: Clarendon, 1954), p. 460.

19 C. S. Lewis, *Spenser's Images of Life*, ed. by Alastair Fowler (Cambridge: Cambridge University Press, 1967), p. 14.

right. You're right that we live and move and have our being in God; you're right that we are God's offspring. You're wrong in thinking that that God is Zeus, but you're right in these other respects.'

In other words, Paul meets the men of Athens where they are, where they already have an inkling of meaning. He is not concerned to obliterate their traditions; he feels no need to denigrate their limited and incomplete religious knowledge. He works with it, corrects it, adds to it, sublimates it. He says, in rough paraphrase, 'You have something here, but there's a whole lot more, and that more is to be found in Jesus Christ.' He takes what they already possess, imaginatively, and baptizes it. And apparently he had some success. When the Greeks heard Paul, 'some mocked; but others said, "We will hear you again about this." So Paul went out from among them. But some men joined him and believed, among them Dionysius the Areopagite and a woman named Damaris and others with them' (Acts 17.32–3).

As an apologetic strategy, it only makes sense to meet people where they are. Where else, indeed, can they be met? Before people know the God and Father of the Lord Jesus Christ, they are not in a state of complete innocence or ignorance about the divine nature. Everyone after a certain age has thoughts and beliefs about what is of ultimate value in the universe, that is what is 'divine'. Those thoughts need to be recognized and responded to. Sometimes the response will consist in contradiction, but more often than not there will be something that can be responded to positively, that can be coaxed into a fuller life and a brighter light. This is why Lewis can say, 'the only possible basis for Christian apologetics is a proper respect for paganism'.[20] Paganism must be 'looked back at' – re-spected – in order for the Christian apologist to see whether or how much it needs opposition.

Imagination Is Necessary

So, although apologetics is 'a reasoned defence', its basis is necessarily imaginative, for reason cannot work without imagination. The high value that Lewis accorded to imagination is seen in an essay called 'Myth Became Fact', where he writes:

I suspect that men have sometimes derived more spiritual sustenance from myths they did not believe than from the religion they professed.

20 Letter to the Revd Henry Welbon, 18 September 1936 (unpublished).

To be truly Christian we must both assent to the historical fact and also receive the myth (fact though it has become) with the same imaginative embrace which we accord to all myths. The one is hardly more necessary than the other.[21]

Of course, it is not possible, in fact, to separate 'the one' (the imaginative embrace) from 'the other' (the rational assent), but it is occasionally worth doing a thought experiment on oneself to discover which of them one would prefer if (*per impossibile*) one were forced at the point of a gun to choose between them. There is little doubt which Lewis would have inclined towards. He writes, 'A man who disbelieved the Christian story as fact but continually fed on it as myth would, perhaps, be more spiritually alive than one who assented and did not think much about it.'[22]

Given that an imaginative embrace of Christianity is as necessary a response as rational assent, and given that rational assent cannot be given without imaginative content informing it, the only issue that the apologist has to settle is whether he is going to conduct his 'reasoned defence' in terms which are more imaginative or less imaginative. They are going to be imaginative at some level whether he likes it or not. The question to be answered is: to what extent will they approximate the lived language of the Christ story and to what extent will they render that language in more abstract categories?

Abstract categories have the value of clarity, but in other respects are less desirable, Lewis thinks. The less imaginative the terms in which an apologist couches his argument, the less they can actually communicate the thing under discussion. In a brilliant, though sadly incomplete, article entitled 'The Language of Religion', Lewis homed in on this problem:

Apologetics is controversy. You cannot conduct a controversy in those poetical expressions which alone convey the concrete: you must use terms as definable and univocal as possible, and these are always abstract. And this means that the thing we are really talking about can never appear in the discussion at all. We have to try to prove *that* God is in circumstances where we are denied every means of conveying *who* God is.[23]

---

21 Lewis, 'Myth Became Fact', p. 141.
22 Lewis, 'Myth Became Fact', p. 141.
23 C. S. Lewis, 'The Language of Religion', *C.S. Lewis, Essay Collection*, p. 261.

We have already observed how Lewis discovered, in the course of his own path to faith, that doctrinal language is less adequate to the reality of Christian truth than the lived language of the Christ story itself. As an apologist, he further discovered that controversial language (the language of debate, persuasion, demonstration) was even less adequate than doctrinal language because, in a controversy, one has to thin down one's language so that one can communicate with one's opponents who, by definition, do not posssess the imaginative embrace of the topic in hand necessary to a full appreciation of what one is saying. The apologist has to work, so to speak, at the university lecture podium or at the bar of the courtroom, all the while talking about something that goes on, in reality, at neither place, but rather in prayer, Communion, confession, the reading of the Scriptures – in the holistic life of faith. Apologetic language unavoidably uses 'the logic of speculative thought' instead of the more pertinent 'logic of personal relations';[24] it has to be univocal so that it is useful in contexts where Christianity does not, of its own nature, normally reside. The situation is akin to Mozart or Beethoven trying to prove their musicality not by conducting one of their symphonies in front of an orchestra but by standing gagged at a maths blackboard using only numbers.

This is what Lewis means when he talks about 'the great disadvantages under which the Christian apologist labours'.[25] The life of faith is best communicated in its own terms, namely 'life': the lived language of real human beings in real times in real places. Actions speak louder than words. If faith has to be turned into apologetic words, it is best to use words that tell a story, as in the Synoptic Gospels, or words that both tell a story and are richly resonant and connotative, like the mighty nouns of John's Gospel ('Word', 'Light', 'Life', 'Way', 'Water', 'Glory', 'Vine', 'Bread'). Such narrative or symbolic terms are more capacious than the attenuated metaphors characteristic of abstract arguments; they are therefore more able to contain the huge wealth of meaning that there is to carry.

Aware of the 'disadvantages' of abstraction, Lewis did not limit himself to the 'reasoned defences' of traditional apologetics. He also attempted more poetic and creative presentations of the faith in his fiction. His most notable attempt was, of course, the seven Chronicles of Narnia, and these stories have achieved more, perhaps, than any of his writings, by way of communicating the heart of his faith. Rowan Williams has said of the Narnia septet that 'more theological students ought to read it for a sense

---

24 C. S. Lewis, 'On Obstinacy in Belief', *C.S. Lewis, Essay Collection*, p. 215.
25 Lewis, 'The Language of Religion', p. 261.

of what classical orthodox theology *feels* like from the inside – a unique achievement at that level'.[26] Chad Walsh, author of the first study of C. S. Lewis, *Apostle to the Skeptics*, is of the opinion that 'In these books where his imagination has full scope [Lewis] presents the Christian faith in a more eloquent and probing way than ever his more straightforward books of apologetics could.'[27]

But this present essay is about apologetics in the sense of 'reasoned defence', where language cannot be as rich and redolent, and therefore true to life, as in a fairy tale. In non-fiction apologetics, language has to be univocal or, at any rate, 'as univocal as possible'. Lewis did not think it was possible to be utterly univocal, even in his 'reasoned defences', for he believed that all language, except for the most basic and elementary, was metaphorical, and even the highly desiccated metaphors are not verbal algebra.[28] So, he makes a virtue of necessity and, if one compares his *Mere Christianity* against other broad introductory apologetic works such as John Stott's *Basic Christianity*, N. T. Wright's *Simply Christian* or Timothy Keller's *The Reason for God*, one notices how much Lewis's book stands out for the wealth of imagery it employs. He constantly resorts to analogy, simile and metaphor in a way and to an extent that none of these three successor books does. His 'flotilla' metaphor has always struck me as especially helpful,[29] likewise the image of the statues in the sculptor's shop.[30] Other images, such as the Whitesmile's toothpaste that remains unused 'by a healthy young negro',[31] are now well past their use-by date; the famous 'poached egg'[32] simile is also perhaps too colourful for its own good. But Lewis's working principle is sound, whatever the particular faults one may identify in his practice: apologetic language benefits from being vivid, sensory and chosen with poetic, not just abstractly rational, intent.

Lewis aims, then, to lead his readers along the road he himself trod. Apprehension of meaningfulness was, as we have seen, the first step in

---

26 Rowan Williams, 'A Theologian in Narnia', address to the Oxford Lewis Society, 9 November 1999; speaker's own notes (copy in this author's possession).

27 Chad Walsh, 'Impact in America' in Jocelyn Gibb (ed.) *Light on C. S. Lewis* (London: Geoffrey Bles, 1965), p. 116.

28 'When we pass beyond pointing to individual sensible objects, when we begin to think of causes, relations, of mental states or acts, we become incurably metaphorical. We apprehend none of these things except through metaphor.' Lewis, 'Bluspels and Flalansferes', p. 263.

29 C. S. Lewis, *Mere Christianity* (Glasgow: Collins, 1990), p. 67–70.

30 Lewis, *Mere Christianity*, pp. 135–6.

31 Lewis, *Mere Christianity*, p. 175.

32 Lewis, *Mere Christianity*, p. 52.

his conversion, and so it became, in due course, the customary first step in his apologetic method. If one looks at the rhetorical strategies informing Lewis's apologetics, one almost always finds that he begins, in the very first paragraph, by immersing the reader in a meaningful situation, whether it be quarrelling (as in *Mere Christianity*), despairing (as in *The Problem of Pain*) or doubting (as in *Miracles*). When, in *The Four Loves*, he introduces the first of the loves, *storge*, he aims first of all to establish 'the meaning of the word':

> The image we must start with is that of a mother nursing a baby, a bitch or a cat with a basketful of puppies or kittens; all in a squeaking, nuzzling heap together; purrings, lickings, baby-talk, milk, warmth, the smell of young life.[33]

The method is poetic, rather than polemic. There is no question, at the outset, of whether these various images or situations are good or bad, true or false, beautiful or ugly. They just *are*: rational judgements about their value can wait. We know that they mean something and they resonate with our experience or our observations of the world. Having thus engaged our imaginations, Lewis then proceeds to his next step. But as he proceeds, he does not leave imagination behind and exit into some purely 'rational' realm. His strategy is imaginative all the way along: it has to be, given his understanding of how reason works. There is no question of discarding imagination and emerging into a neutral, reliable, 'scientific', disinterested region, which must perforce command the assent of all objective observers. Lewis is not willing to reduce himself or his readers to mere 'thinkers' in a sort of ultra-Cartesian move, which plagues so much inferior apologetics and so many earnest undergraduate late-night discussions. It is no good arguing for 'God' or 'Christ' or for 'the atonement' or even for 'truth' until the apologist has shown, at least at some basic level, that these terms have real meaning. Otherwise they will be just counters in an intellectual game, leaving most readers cold. Likewise, apologetic arguments for the authority of 'the Church' or 'the Bible' or 'experience' or 'reason' itself, must all be imaginatively realized before they can begin to make traction on the reader's reason, let alone on the reader's will. Before we act or think, we understand meaning, in Lewis's view, and so the provision of meaningful images becomes the hallmark of his apologetic method.

---

33 Lewis, *The Four Loves*, p. 33.

But although Lewis accords imagination a high place, it is not the only or the highest place. There is also reason, and reason is important – indeed, essential – if imagination is to serve its proper purpose.

Imagination Is Insufficient Without Reason

Lewis distinguishes between 'imaginary' (bad) and 'imaginative' (good).[34] Pagan myths, howsoever meaningful, were ultimately untrustworthy as a final guide to life because their meanings were imaginary rather than imaginative. Without the controlling and clarifying effects of reason, imaginative efforts at apprehending God are always apt to lose themselves and turn unreliable or even rotten.[35] In *The Pilgrim's Regress* it is because their imaginative 'pictures' are not supplemented by the truthful 'Rules' of the Shepherds that the Pagans 'become corrupt in their imaginations'.[36] Likewise, it is because its resulting play of imagination is undisciplined that awe at the universe's size can be taken as an argument against God; this is 'matter spiritualized' in the wrong sense, the psychophysical parallelism (wherein meaning resides) mishandled.[37] Lewis is almost Feuerbachian here. As Feuerbach considered imagination to be the engine of religion and ground of its falsity, so Lewis would have said that it stoked the engine of religion and was a potential ground of its falsity.

To prevent imagination running amok it must be properly related to reason, and both to the will. Lewis sometimes pictures the human person as three concentric circles, the outermost being the imagination, the middle ring being the reason and the core being the will.[38] Although imagination is the most exposed of these three rings and the one most naturally inclined to deceive, it is nevertheless indispensable to the two higher or more central levels. Images provide reason and the will with the very stuff

---

34 See, for example, letter to Eliza Butler, 25 September 1940, *The Collected Letters of C.S. Lewis, Volume II*, ed. by Walter Hooper (London: HarperCollins, 2004), p. 445.

35 Hence the phrase 'only imagination' is always meant pejoratively in Lewis's works. This independent imagination is his target when, for example, he opposes 'faith and reason on one side and emotion and imagination on the other' (*Mere Christianity*, p. 120).

36 C. S. Lewis, *The Pilgrim's Regress* (Glasgow: Collins, 1980), p. 195.

37 'If ever the vastness of matter threatens to overcross our spirits, one must remember that it is matter spiritualized which does so. To puny man, the great nebula in Andromeda owes in a sense its greatness': C. S. Lewis, 'Dogma and the Universe', *C. S. Lewis, Essay Collection*, p. 121.

38 For example, C. S. Lewis, *The Screwtape Letters* (Glasgow: Collins, 1982), p. 37. Screwtape, the senior devil, advises Wormwood to evacuate his patient's will and intellect of virtues, locating them entirely in his fantasy or imagination: 'No amount of piety in his imagination and affections will harm us if we can keep it out of his will' (p. 70).

of conscious life: 'I doubt if any act of will or thought or emotion occurs in me without them.'[39] Thus, imagination, which is good, serves reason, which is better, and both serve the will, which is best of all. We will look briefly at the will in the final section of this essay, but before we come on to that subject, let us say a little more about how reason works on the meanings supplied to it by imagination.[40]

Reason, in Lewis's scheme, is much more than the faculty of bald ratiocination. The sort of understanding of Reason that Lewis appears to be working with is that 'Practical Reason'[41] which was accepted by 'nearly all moralists before the eighteenth century'.[42] It is difficult to say exactly how much of the detail of that pre-eighteenth-century understanding of Reason Lewis adopted in his own thinking, but there is a general harmony between the idea of the tripartite 'Rational Soul' that he outlines descriptively, from the literary historian's point of view, in *The Discarded Image*, and the model of man that he presents argumentatively in *The Abolition of Man*, *Mere Christianity*, 'Bluspels and Flalansferes', 'On Ethics' and elsewhere.[43] Reason, the defining part of the Rational Soul, consists of *intellectus* (the ability to see self-evident truth) and *ratio* (the ability to arrive at truth which is not self-evident). In this twofold capacity, Reason obviously has a moral element (it is 'the organ of morality'[44]) because certain self-evident truths are moral axioms.[45] That these understandings of Reason still linger in our concept of morality is shown, Lewis believes, by the fact that, when we would recall a person to right conduct, we sometimes say, 'Be reasonable'.[46] The Rational faculty guides and governs the Sensitive Soul and its five inward 'wits' (including the imagination). In doing so, Reason chooses between the meanings presented to it by the imagination, distinguishing true meanings from false and, where a choice of expressions is available, choosing the one most suitable for the desired meanings to be communicated.

---

39 C. S. Lewis, *Prayer: Letters to Malcolm* (Glasgow: Collins, 1983), p. 87.

40 Lewis practised his theory of disciplining his imagination from young adulthood onwards. For example, see his resolution not to let 'things I really don't believe in and vague possibilities haunt my imagination', diary entry for 26 January 1927, *All My Road Before Me: The Diaries of C. S. Lewis, 1922–1927* (London: HarperCollins, 1993), p. 439.

41 C. S. Lewis, *The Abolition of Man* (Glasgow: Collins, 1984), p. 29.

42 C. S. Lewis, *The Discarded Image* (Cambridge: Cambridge University Press, 1964), p. 158.

43 Such as the epistemology that structures his approach in *Mere Christianity* (p. 16), for instance, which broadly reflects the categories of Rational, Sensitive and Vegetable Soul described in *The Discarded Image*, pp. 152–65.

44 Lewis, *The Discarded Image*, p. 158.

45 See, for example, Lewis, *The Abolition of Man*, pp. 23, 28.

46 Lewis, *Miracles*, p. 39; cf. *The Discarded Image*, p. 161.

One of the reasons, I think, why Lewis has become so long-lived as an apologist, and why some passages from his apologetics have become veritable anthology pieces, is this very point: that his logical, reasoned argumentation is informed by a sensitive poetic intelligence. His choice of image, metaphor and analogy is controlled by an alert imagination and, as a result, charges what he says with a pleasing appropriateness, even sometimes a superfluity, of meaning. His apologetic writing, at its best, becomes rich and enjoyable for its own sake, almost regardless of whether one actually agrees with the conclusions he arrives at. This carries its own dangers, of course. As Austin Farrer remarked, with respect to *The Problem of Pain*, 'We think we are listening to an argument, in fact we are presented with a vision; and it is the vision that carries conviction.'[47] But the dangerousness is an indication of the method's power and, when used aright (for instance, the image of the great 'dive' in *Miracles* as a picture of the incarnation,[48] or the 'myth' of Lewis's own devising in the chapter on *agape* in *The Four Loves*),[49] the vision does not overpower the argument but supports and indeed enables it.

Imaginative Reason Is Also Insufficient

Thus the good imagination serves the better reason, which allows readers to understand a good deal about their human situation and even a certain amount about God. But only a certain amount. We have already pointed out imagination's deficiencies; reason also is insufficient for the full knowledge of God. Reason, for Lewis, we must remember, was not the organ of truth but 'the natural organ of truth',[50] it could not rise to the supernatural in its own strength.[51] Though a self-confessed 'rationalist',[52] Lewis was a great deal more than merely a believer in the power of 'Enlightenment' ratiocination. Reason depends not only on what we might call the ground floor (imagination) but also on the basement (physical sensation)[53] in order to be supplied with its raw materials. Considered

47 Austin Farrer, 'The Christian Apologist', in Jocelyn Gibb (ed.), *Light on C. S. Lewis* (London: Geoffrey Bles, 1965), p. 37.

48 Lewis, *Miracles*, pp. 115–16.

49 Lewis, *The Four Loves*, pp. 116–28.

50 Lewis, 'Bluspels and Flalansferes', p. 265.

51 'Human thought is not God's, but God-kindled', Lewis, *Miracles*, p. 33.

52 'Bluspels and Flalansferes', p. 265.

53 'Man's reason is in such deep insolvency to sense': C. S. Lewis, 'Horrid Red Things', *C. S. Lewis, Essay Collection*, p. 129. Lewis is quoting Robert Bridges, *The Testament of Beauty* (Oxford: Clarendon Press), Book I, line 57.

alone, then, reason is nothing special: 'gnawing, peasant reason', as the young Lewis calls it.[54] It is helpless unless equipped by imagination (and sensation); and even thus equipped it cannot reach into the heavens. To his friend Harwood, Lewis wrote in 1926: 'No one is more convinced than I that reason is utterly inadequate to the richness and spirituality of real things: indeed this is itself a deliverance of reason.'[55] And he never resiled from this position, as many of his later writings, most notably *Till We Have Faces*, demonstrate.[56]

So, his religion is not merely rational, any more than it is merely imaginative. But it would be a mistake to conclude that his religion was composed merely of an imaginatively informed rationality: imagination and reason together work not to serve themselves but to serve the will. The good serves the better and both serve the best. The best is the will, the heart of a person, and this must be reorientated by a meeting with the divine. However much an apologist may labour with imaginative and rational tools to defend the faith and persuade sceptics to accept its claims, nothing can be achieved 'without the intervention of the super-natural', because only the supernatural can bring about 'an alteration of the will'.[57] How then, can the apologist hope for supernatural inter-vention in the imaginatively rational process of Christian apologetics?

Imaginative Reason Serves a Purpose

There are two ways by which the supernatural may intervene. One method of supernatural revelation is *by means of* natural revelation. The creative Word of God sustains the 'natural virtues'[58] among which we may include the good use of fallen imagination, no less than the good use of fallen reason, for God is the Father of lights. The divine light enlightens all human minds, not just those which are already Christian, so that certain examples of 'imaginative perception' can be argued to be real approaches, however rudimentary, to the 'idea of God', approaches

54 'The Philosopher', C. S. Lewis, *Collected Poems*, ed. by Walter Hooper (London: HarperCollins, 1994), p. 186–7.

55 Letter to Cecil Harwood, 28 October 1926, *Collected Letters, Volume I*, p. 670.

56 In this, Lewis's last novel, there is a character called the Fox, a rational teacher, who comes to learn at the end of the story that mere reason is 'glibness . . . a prattle of maxims . . . all thin and clear as water', C. S. Lewis, *Till We Have Faces* (Glasgow: Collins, 1985), p. 306.

57 C. S. Lewis, 'The Decline of Religion', C. S. Lewis, *Essay Collection*, p. 182.

58 Letter to Brother George Every, 12 October 1940, *Collected Letters, Volume II*, p. 448.

that operate 'beyond our own resources'.[59] Imagination, like all created things, including reason,[60] properly understood, reflects something of its Creator.[61] It is this sort of imagination which Lewis told T. S. Eliot he believed in as 'a truth-bearing faculty'.[62] To think otherwise would be to embrace the 'negative theology' of the modern 'German Protestant' kind, of which Lewis, with his deep-rooted belief in natural law, disapproved.[63] 'I am inclined,' he wrote, 'to distrust that species of respect for the spiritual order which bases itself on contempt for the natural.'[64] The natural exercise of imaginative reason may, up to a point, be a revelation of (and therefore an intervention by) the supernatural.

However, even this is insufficient. The rationally imaginative explanations and defences of Christianity provided by the apologist (and supported by the divine) can only take one so far, and it is at the point where they fall short that the divine intervention already seen in the exercise of natural faculties may be supplemented, God willing, by divine *supervention*. The internal presence of God in the human subject may meet the external presence of Holy Spirit in direct illumination, or, as may be, mediated through the more normal channels of preaching, sacrament, Scripture, prayer, absolution, fasting or other forms of askesis.[65]

The apologist is thus a John the Baptist figure, preparing the way for

---

59 Letter to his brother, 24 October 1931, *Collected Letters, Volume II*, p. 7.

60 'Where thought is strictly rational it must be, in some odd sense, not ours, but cosmic or super-cosmic. It must be something not shut up inside our heads but already 'out there' – in the universe or behind the universe . . . a rationality with which the universe has always been saturated': C. S. Lewis, *'De Futilitate', C. S. Lewis, Essay Collection*, p. 676.

61 'I do not think the resemblance between the Christian and the merely imaginative experience is accidental. I think that all things, in their way, reflect heavenly truth, the imagination not least. "Reflect" is the important word. This lower life of the imagination is not [that is not necessarily and by its own nature: God can cause it to be] a beginning of nor a step towards, the higher life of the spirit, merely an image', Lewis, *Surprised by Joy*, p. 135–6.

62 Letter to T. S. Eliot, 2 June 1931, *The Collected Letters of C. S. Lewis, Volume III*, ed. by Walter Hooper (London: HarperCollins, 2006), p. 1523.

63 See Lewis, *The Discarded Image*, p. 70. It is not known how much of Karl Barth's work Lewis read (he was not sure himself, see letter to Corbin Scott Carnell, 13 October 1958, *Collected Letters, Volume III*, p. 980), but his references to it are invariably unfriendly. He coined 'Barthianism' as a loose term to cover 'a flattening out of all things into common insignificance before the inscrutable Creator', Lewis, *English Literature in the Sixteenth Century*, pp. 449, 453. Cf. *The Pilgrim's Regress*, p. 18; 'Why I Am Not a Pacifist', *C. S. Lewis, Essay Collection*, p. 292; letter to his brother, 18 February 1940, *Collected Letters, Volume II*, pp. 350–2.

64 C. S. Lewis, *The Allegory of Love: A Study in Medieval Tradition* (Oxford: Clarendon, 1936), p. 267.

65 I take it that those who read apologetic works and who are in need of their help may include many whose religious practice is already significantly developed.

the One who comes after. Apologetics serves a vital ancillary function and this is its main justification, for although reasoned defences do not of themselves create conviction, the absence of them makes belief much harder to engender or sustain. As Farrer wrote, 'What seems to be proved may not be embraced; but what no one shows the ability to defend is quickly abandoned. Rational argument does not create belief [not even rational argument most richly and sensitively supplied by imagination], but it maintains a climate in which belief may flourish. So the apologist who does nothing but defend may play a useful, though preparatory, part.'[66]

Divine supervention takes us away from the field of pure apologetics into evangelism and soteriology. The indispensable role Lewis found for divinely imparted faith both in the acquistion and retention of Christian belief[67] is not something we can here address, though it is a subject worth exploring.[68] Let us therefore conclude with what Lewis wrote in 'The Decline of Religion':

> Conversion requires an alteration of the will, and an alteration which, in the last resort, does not occur without the intervention of the super- natural. I do not in the least agree with those who therefore conclude that the spread of an intellectual (and imaginative) climate favourable to Christianity is useless. You do not prove munition workers useless by showing that they cannot themselves win battles, however proper this reminder would be if they attempted to claim the honour due to fighting men. If the intellectual climate is such that, when a man comes to the crisis at which he must either accept or reject Christ, his reason and imagination are not on the wrong side, then his conflict will be fought out under favourable conditions.[69]

66 Farrer, 'The Christian Apologist', p. 26.
67 See, for example, Lewis, *Mere Christianity*, pp. 119–29; 'Religion: Reality or Substi- tute?', *C. S. Lewis, Essay Collection*, pp. 131–7.
68 See, for example, my 'Escape to Wallaby Wood: Lewis's Depictions of Conversion', in Angus J. L. Menuge (ed.), *C. S. Lewis, Lightbearer in the Shadowlands: The Evangelistic Vision of C. S. Lewis* (Wheaton, IL: Crossway, 1997), pp. 143–67.
69 Lewis, 'The Decline of Religion', p. 182.

Being Imaginative about Christian Apologetics

6

Atheism, Apologetics and Ecclesiology: *Gaudium et Spes* and Contemporary Unbelief

STEPHEN BULLIVANT

Apologetics calls for us to be imaginative in many ways. In this chapter Stephen Bullivant draws inspiration from a generation of Roman Catholic theologians who had the imagination to ask 'what is it about Christianity that puts so many atheists off the faith?' Having been brave enough to ask the question, they were then able to suggest responses. This relates apologetics to other tasks for the Church, here primarily the need to be active in the works of mercy and the urgent demand to think carefully about what marks the Church out in both theory and practice. At the heart of the problem is a need for Christians to be convinced by the faith they seek to hold out to others. The best apology for the faith is to be found in Christians whose imaginations are as much captured by the faith as they hope those will be to whom they offer their message. **A.D.**

Many [today] subscribe to atheism in one of its many different forms. They parade their godlessness, asserting its claims in education and politics, in the foolish and fatal belief that they are emancipating mankind from false and outworn notions about life and the world and substituting a view that is scientific and up to date. This is the most serious problem of our time.

[Nevertheless,] we observe them, driven by a demanding and often a noble concern, . . . dreaming of justice and progress. . . . They are sometimes endowed with great breadth of mind, impatient with the mediocrity and self-seeking which infects so many aspects of human society in our times. We see that they expertly employ sentiments and expressions brought forth from our gospel. . . . Surely some day we

shall be able to lead the cries of today, by which good morals are signi-
fied, back to their obviously Christian sources?[1]

These words, written over 45 years ago, are taken from Pope Paul VI's
debut encyclical *Ecclesiam Suam*. Promulgated in August 1964, it came
at a crucial point in the Second Vatican Council. The rise and prominence
of modern atheism, both in the West and the East, had for several decades
been a major theological, pastoral and missiological concern within the
Catholic Church.[2] In the Council's official, preparatory consultations,
the need for a new and sophisticated treatment of modern unbelief, beyond simple denunciation, was frequently raised.[3] Despite this, even a
relatively late version of Schema XIII (what would eventually become
Gaudium et Spes, the 'Pastoral Constitution on the Church in the Modern World') merely mentions, in passing and without comment, 'errors
which spring from materialism, especially from dialectical materialism or
communism'.[4] As we shall see, both the Pope's own initiatives, and the
interventions of the Council Fathers themselves, dramatically changed
all this. These resulted in *Gaudium et Spes* §§19–21, a text which, in the
future Pope Benedict XVI's 1969 opinion, 'may be counted among the
most important pronouncements of Vatican II'.[5]

Evangelization is an urgent and daunting task for the Church today. Indeed it must always be, in whichever 'today' the Church might find itself:
'Always be ready to give your defence to anyone who demands from you
an accounting for the hope that is in you' (1 Pet. 3.15). But apologetics, in
itself, is not enough. Rather we must be aware of, and sensitive to, the social and cultural 'background' against which our 'accounting' takes place.
This too is necessary for a genuinely *imaginative* apologetics. It is this idea,
through focusing on certain aspects of *Gaudium et Spes* §§ 19–21, that I
wish to pursue in this chapter. Obviously, this magisterial document was
promulgated over four decades ago. Since then, Christianity and atheism

---

1 Paul VI, *Ecclesiam Suam*, arts. 99, 100, 104. Official English translation available at:
http://www.vatican.va/holy_father/paul_vi/encyclicals/documents/hf_pvi_enc_06081964_
ecclesiam_en.html (accessed on 22 February 2010).

2 See, for example, Stephen Bullivant, 'From "*Main Tendue*" to Vatican II: The Catholic
Engagement with Atheism, 1936–65', *New Blackfriars* 90 (2009), pp. 178–87.

3 James L. MacNeil, *A Study of Gaudium et Spes 19–22: The Second Vatican Council
Response to Contemporary Atheism* (Lewiston, NY: Edwin Mellen, 1997), pp. 16–18.

4 Quoted in Peter Hebblethwaite, *The Council Fathers and Atheism: The Interventions
at the Fourth Session of Vatican Council II* (New York: Paulist Press, 1967), p. 25.

5 Joseph Ratzinger, 'Pastoral Constitution on the Church in the Modern World: The
Dignity of the Human Person', in Herbert Vorgrimler (ed.), *Commentary on the Documents of Vatican II*, vol. 5, trans. by W. J. O'Hara (London: Burns and Oates, 1969),
pp. 115–63 (p. 145).

have changed – as also has the fault line, or interface, between the two. Nevertheless, it is well worth revisiting, especially if we are simultaneously sensitive both to its context, and to our own. The structure of this chapter will be as follows. I shall begin by introducing *Gaudium et Spes* §§ 19–21's history and development at the Council. I shall then focus, in detail, on three specific passages (relating, respectively, to the meaning, the causes and the remedies of atheism). Finally, I intend to cast a necessarily tentative eye on the contemporary British – and by extension, western European and (increasingly) North American – situation.

Introducing *Gaudium et Spes* §§ 19–21

The draft version of Schema XIII, quoted above, was distributed to the bishops in Autumn 1964. Since Pope Paul's encyclical had already been published that August, its dismissive approach to atheism was already obsolete. This fact did not go unnoticed in the Council's Third Session. On the very first day of debate, for example, the Archbishop of Santiago, Chile, spoke 'on the need for dialogue with contemporary humanism', urging that 'The Church must try to comprehend atheism, to examine the truths which nourish this error, and to be able to correspond its life and doctrine to these aspirations.'[6] The following day, the Belgian Cardinal Suenens complained:

> The schema does not speak enough of a widespread and characteristic feature of our time, namely, the open profession of militant atheism in all its forms. Atheism is certainly a terrible error, but it would be too easy simply to condemn it. It is necessary to examine why so many men profess themselves to be atheists, and whom precisely is this 'God' they so sharply attack. Thus dialogue should be begun with them so that they may seek and recognize the true image of God who is perhaps concealed under the caricatures they reject. On our part, meanwhile, we should examine our way of speaking of God and living the faith, *lest the sun of the living God is darkened for them.*[7]

For these and other reasons, the entire draft was rejected, and sent to be rewritten. The new version of Schema XIII – the so-called 'Ariccia

---

6 *Acta Synodalia Sacrosancti Concilii Oecumenici Vaticani II* (hereafter AS) III/viii, p. 796. For full translations of the conciliar interventions on atheism, see Hebblethwaite, *Council Fathers and Atheism.*

7 AS III/v, p. 271 (emphasis added).

text' – was distributed in June 1965, and contained a much longer and improved treatment of atheism. Yet this too failed to satisfy the Council Fathers, and the subject was again a frequent topic in the Fourth Session debates that September. In the most powerful intervention, Cardinal Saigh, the Melkite Catholic Patriarch of Antioch, warned that atheists 'are often scandalized by the sight of a mediocre and egoistical Christendom absorbed by money and false riches'. He added: 'is it not the egotism of certain Christians which has caused, and causes to a great extent, the atheism of the masses?'[8] The same day, Cardinal König of Vienna, voicing similar concerns, suggested that a new text be written, entrusted to the Vatican's newly formed Secretariat for Non-Believers,[9] of which König was the president. The proposal was duly accepted, and the Secretariat, or rather a small team of its associates (including, not insignificantly, the theologians Henri de Lubac and Jean Daniélou)[10] created what, in less than three months, formed part of the final version of *Gaudium et Spes*.

The Meaning(s) of Atheism

The word 'atheism' designates phenomena that differ very greatly among themselves. For whilst God is expressly denied by some, others believe that man is able to assert nothing at all about him. Still others bring such a method of examination to the question of God that it would seem to lack all meaning. Many, unduly transgressing the limits of the positive sciences, either contend that all things can be explained by scientific reasoning, or, on the contrary, avow that there is no such thing as absolute truth. Certain people exalt man so greatly, that faith in God becomes weakened; they are more inclined, it would appear, to affirm man than to deny God. Yet others portray God to themselves in such a way, that this figment, which they deny, is in no way the God

---

8 AS IV/ii, p. 452. Since Saigh spoke in French rather than Latin, he is quoted here from Hebblethwaite, *Council Fathers and Atheism*, p. 81.

9 Another initiative of Pope Paul's, the Secretariat's foundation was quietly announced in the 9 April 1965 issue of *L'Osservatore Romano*. For further details on its history and work, see Peter Hebblethwaite, *The Runaway Church* (London: Collins, 1975), pp. 135–63; and Franz König, *Open to God, Open to the World*, ed. by Christa Pongratz-Lippitt (London: Burns and Oates, 2005), pp. 104–16.

10 Peter Hünermann, 'The Final Weeks of the Council', trans. by Matthew J. O'Connell, in *History of Vatican II. Vol. V: The Council and the Transition. The Fourth Period and the End of the Council. September 1965 – December 1965*, ed. by Giuseppe Alberigo and Joseph A. Komonchak (Maryknoll, NY: Orbis, 2006), pp. 363–483 (p. 398).

of the Gospels. There are others who never raise questions concerning God; who seem not to experience religious disquiet, nor see why they should concern themselves with religion. Not rarely, moreover, atheism arises either from a violent protest against evil in the world, or from the fact that certain human values are unduly adjudged to be themselves absolutes, so that these are established in the place of God. Contemporary civilization itself, not intrinsically, but inasmuch as it is too engrossed with the things of this world, can often make it more difficult to approach God. (*Gaudium et Spes* §19)[11]

I admit that this passage might seem an odd choice to focus on here. After all, it simply lists different types of, or in some cases motivations towards, unbelief. It is not attempting to offer any systematic taxonomy; it is not advancing any theological interpretation or critique. But what it *does* do is make the important and often overlooked point that 'atheism' is a very broad, varied and diffuse phenomenon.

The standard and most obvious definition of an 'atheist' is a person who believes that there is no God. I believe that this is how most people would understood the word, and this definition has a long history. Others – many others – might say that, actually, it goes a bit further than that: a *real* atheist is one who consciously *rejects* the existence of God. For them, the word 'atheist' implies a certain level of conviction about the subject. Both, related meanings of the word have much to recommend them: not only are they popular in common speech, but they are also well-attested in rigorous, scholarly treatments of the subject.

But whatever its virtues, such a narrow definition of atheism was not recognized by Vatican II. If we take *Gaudium et Spes* §19 at its word, then certainly, Richard Dawkins and Bertrand Russell are both atheists. But so too are (among many others) agnostics; logical positivists; postmodernists; promethean humanists; and the religiously indifferent. For *Gaudium et Spes*, an atheist is not someone who believes that there is not a God, but rather one who is *without* a belief that there is.

Now on *this* definition, 'the most serious problem of our time' becomes not only more serious, but vastly more problematic. In Britain itself, the number of strong, 'capital-A' atheists has never been huge. According to figures from the 1999 European Values Survey, for example, only 5% of Britons described themselves as a 'convinced atheist' (although I expect figures from the next wave of the Survey, soon to be released, will show a

---

11 AS IV/vii, p. 743.

marked increase).[12] Membership of the British Humanist Association and the National Secular Society, although recently growing quite rapidly, is not large. Between 2004 and 2008, the BHA's membership doubled to just over 7,500.[13] Membership of the NSS, I understand, currently stands somewhere between 3,000 and 4,000. (By contrast, the Royal Society for the Protection of Birds has over one million members.) However, again according to the 1999 European Values Survey, when asked, as a simple yes or no question, 'Do you believe in God?', 28.2% of Britons said 'no' (although again, I expect the next round of statistics to show a marked increase).[14] Even those who *do* tick the 'belief in God' box on surveys, very often, when probed, assert only the vaguest possible affirmation of there being 'something there'.[15]

Such statistics imply that something important is lost – from a pastoral, apologetic, evangelistic standpoint – when we think of 'atheism' in only, or even primarily, a too-narrow sense. At the time of Vatican II, Marxist atheism was the hot topic. And indeed, a significant minority of the Fathers wanted the Council's treatment of atheism chiefly to be a denunciation of communism. But this was resisted, and the final text makes quite clear that one specific form of atheism, however vocal or voguish, should not be concentrated upon to the exclusion of all others. Today, of course, the so-called 'New Atheism' – Dawkins, Harris, Hitchens, Dennett et al. – is attracting headlines and book sales. It is vital that the Christian communities have an intelligent and sensitive response, and that this response incorporates, to a significant degree, apologetics. But engaging with atheism, and engaging with the New Atheism, are not coextensive. And it must be remembered that a large proportion of even strong, 'capital-A' atheists are not Dawkinsians. Indeed, even in its narrower sense, '"atheism" designates phenomena that differ very greatly among themselves'. It is worth mentioning here, though, that for the Church's engagement with other, subtler, more widespread forms of atheism and indifference, the New Atheism may well prove to be rather more a help than a hindrance. This is a point to which I shall return.

12 Loek Halman (ed.), *The European Values Study: A Third Wave* (Tilburg: University of Tilburg, 2001), p. 86.

13 Personal communication from Bob Churchill, BHA Membership Manager, 11 December 2008.

14 Halman, *European Values Study*, p. 86.

15 See Steve Bruce, *God is Dead: Secularization in the West* (Oxford: Oxford University Press, 2002), p. 137; and David Voas and Alasdair Crockett, 'Religion in Britain: Neither Believing nor Belonging', *Sociology* 39 (2005), pp. 11–28 (p. 24).

The Causes of Atheism

> Certainly, those who wilfully try to drive God from their heart and to avoid religious questions, not following the dictate of their conscience, are not without blame [*culpae expertes non sunt*]; however, believers themselves often bear a certain responsibility for this. For atheism, considered as a whole, is not something aboriginal, but rather arises from diverse causes, among which are indeed included a critical reaction to religion and moreover, in some regions, especially the Christian religion. Wherefore in this matter, believers can have no small part in the rise of atheism, since by neglecting education in the faith, teaching false doctrine, or through defects in their own religious, moral or social lives, they may be said rather more to conceal than reveal the true countenance of God and of religion. (*Gaudium et Spes* §19)[16]

Here, I think, we come to the most significant aspect of Vatican II's understanding of atheism. It begins by stressing, gently but firmly, the 'salvifically precarious' nature of atheism. Note especially the phrase 'not without blame' (or 'fault' – *culpa* in Latin). *Lumen Gentium*, the Council's 'Dogmatic Constitution on the Church', had been promulgated the previous year. Famously, article 16 formally admits the possibility of salvation for various categories of non-Christians. Included among these, are those who are 'without blame (*sine culpa*), ignorant of the Gospel of Christ and his Church', and who also 'without blame (*sine culpa*), have not yet arrived at an express recognition of God'.[17] Likewise *Ad Gentes*, 'the Decree on the Missionary Activity of the Church', affirms that 'in ways known to himself God is able to lead men who are, without fault of their own (*sine eorum culpa*), ignorant of the Gospel to that faith without which it is impossible to please him'.[18] Building on these statements, *Gaudium et Spes* §19 points out that the atheist's being 'without blame' in this regard is by no means a foregone conclusion. Later on, in §21, the dangers of atheism (salvific or otherwise) are further underlined, with reference to 'those pernicious teachings and actions, which contradict reason and common human experience, and which cast man down from his innate [state of] excellence.'[19] These considerations are, however, strongly mitigated the above-quoted passage, beginning with the striking *nostra culpa* that: 'believers themselves often bear a certain responsibility for

16 AS IV/vii, p. 743.
17 AS III/viii, pp. 796–7.
18 AS IV/vii, p. 677.
19 AS IV/vii, p. 744.

this' (that is, for the atheists' trying to drive God from their hearts, and/or avoiding religious questions).

Before pursuing this further, it is worth giving a bit of back story. As I mentioned earlier, this point was raised several times in the conciliar debates surrounding Schema XIII. But the idea has a slightly longer prehistory. Beginning in the 1930s, the French Catholic Church was faced with both the rise to political and intellectual prominence of atheistic – and primarily Marxist – ideas and the realization that vast swathes of the proletariat had, effectively, abandoned the Church. They were, as a Dominican priest-worker put it in the mid 1940s, 'a pagan people with Christian superstitions'.[20] Yet these two trends were not – at least, not by the most sophisticated writers – explained in terms of 'this sinful and adulterous generation'. Let me give three examples. First, Yves Congar, in a 1935 article on 'The Reasons for the Unbelief of Our Times', observed:

> This social character not only of present unbelief, but of its causes and its origins, seems indeed to be one of the dominant data to be retained from the enquiry. If one has not got faith it is because the 'environment' removes it, it is because one has entered into an order of values which, far from demanding it, excludes it, *it is because the attitude taken by the Church with regard to modern life has put the very possibility of believing altogether out of the question . . .* [21]

Congar thus cites *both* secularizing social factors *and* the Church's inadequate response to them – in his words, 'she fell back upon her positions, put up barricades and assumed an attitude of defence'[22] – as the primary reasons for widespread unbelief and indifference. To counter this, Congar primarily turned his attention not outwards, to apologetics and evangelization, but inwards, to a renewal of the Church itself. Referring back to this article in the early 1960s, Congar commented: 'It seemed to me that, *since the belief or unbelief of men depended so much on us*, the effort to be made was a renovation of ecclesiology.'[23]

---

20 Jacques Loew, *Mission to the Poorest*, trans. by Pamela Carswell (London: Sheed and Ward, 1950 [1946]), p. 93.

21 Yves Congar, 'The Reasons for the Unbelief of Our Times, Pt. 1', *Integration: A Students' Catholic Review* 2.1 (1938), pp. 13–21 (p. 14). Emphasis added.

22 Yves Congar, 'The Reasons for the Unbelief of Our Times, Pt. 2', *Integration: A Students' Catholic Review* 2.3 (1938), pp. 10–26 (p. 19).

23 Yves Congar, 'The Council in an Age of Dialogue', trans. by Barry N. Rigney, *Cross Currents* 12 (1962), pp. 144–51 (pp. 147–8). See also Gabriel Flynn, *Yves Congar's Vision of the Church in a World of Unbelief* (London: Ashgate, 2004).

Second, three years later, in 1938, Henri de Lubac published *Catholicism* – a book which, as Fergus Kerr recently put it, 'Many, including Congar, Balthasar, Wojtyla and Ratzinger, considered . . . as the key book of twentieth-century Catholic theology, the one indispensable text.'[24] In his introduction he refers, not to social factors, but to intellectual ones. He presents quotation after quotation from contemporary atheists and freethinkers, giving their *mis*understandings of Christian doctrine as essentially individualistic, concerned only with securing one's own salvation. Naturally, de Lubac disagrees with them:

> We are accused of being individualists even in spite of ourselves, by the logic of our faith, whereas in reality Catholicism is essentially social. It is social in the deepest sense of the word: not merely in its applications in the field of natural institutions but first and foremost in itself, in the heart of its mystery, in the essence of its dogma. It is social in a sense which should have made the expression 'social Catholicism' pleonastic.[25]

'Nevertheless', he continues:

> if such a misunderstanding has arisen and entrenched itself, if such an accusation is current, is it not our own fault? . . . if so many observers, who are not lacking in acumen or in religious spirit, are so grievously mistaken about the essence of Catholicism, is it not an indication that Catholics should make an effort to understand it better themselves?[26]

De Lubac, it may be remembered, was one of the principal drafters of *Gaudium et Spes* §§19–21.

Third and more briefly, in the late 1940s, Jacques Maritain argued that 'absolute atheism', that is, 'a refusal of God, a fight against God, a challenge to God' (atheism with a very big capital A), is largely due to the prevalence of what he calls 'practical atheists' – that is, so-called Christians 'who believe that they believe in God (and who perhaps believe in Him in their brains) but who in reality deny His existence by each one of their deeds'.[27] Or, as he also puts it, 'Christians who keep in their minds

---

24 Fergus Kerr, *Twentieth-Century Catholic Theologians* (Oxford: Blackwell, 2007), p. 71.

25 Henri de Lubac, *Catholicism: A Study of Dogma in Relation to the Corporate Destiny of Mankind*, trans. by Lancelot C. Sheppard (New York: Mentor-Omega, 1964 [1938]), p. xi.

26 De Lubac, *Catholicism*, p. xi.

27 Jacques Maritain, 'A New Approach to God', in *The Range of Reason* (London: Geoffrey Bles, 1953 [1947]), pp. 86–102 (pp. 97–8).

the settings of religion, for the sake of appearances or outward show, . . . but who deny the gospel and despise the poor'.[28] A little later, Karl Rahner would agree with this basic point, describing practical atheism as 'a lifestyle in which no (discernible) conclusions are drawn from the (theoretical) recognition of the existence of God'.[29]

Now, all three of these Christian *self*-critiques concerning the rise and apparent plausibility of atheism are evidenced in the claim of *Gaudium et Spes* that: 'believers can have no small part in the rise of atheism, since by neglecting education in the faith, teaching false doctrine, or through defects in their own religious, moral or social lives, they may be said rather more to conceal than reveal the true countenance of God and of religion.' This recognizes a profound fact: *that widespread atheism –* religious forms of atheism, such as Buddhism, excepted *– is a near exclusive feature of Christian, or by now post-Christian, societies.* This is a hard fact. *Prima facie*, atheism is caused not by Christianity being absent, but by it being present – and, in some cases, perhaps – all too present. (And indeed, recent scholarship by Michael J. Buckley and others, on the intellectual origins of modern atheism, suggests that this is also true on levels other than those identified by Vatican II.)[30] For these reasons, as I mentioned earlier, apologetics, while indispensable, is not enough. Certainly, the finding of intrinsically plausible, philosophically robust presentations of the Faith – and finding new and effective ways to communicate these – is of crucial importance. But in countering contemporary atheism and indifference, intellectual arguments alone, however sharp and persuasive, will not work. 'They may indeed look, but not perceive; and may indeed listen, but not understand.' (Isa. 6.9). Yet it is not God who has hardened their hearts, but rather – as *Gaudium et Spes* readily admits – 'in no small part' Christians themselves.

---

28 Maritain, 'A New Approach to God', p. 99. See also Jacques Maritain, 'On the Meaning of Contemporary Atheism', *Review of Politics* 2 (1949), pp. 267–80 (p. 268).

29 Karl Rahner, 'Atheismus II. Philosophisch – III. Theologisch', in Michael Buchberger, Josef Höfer and Karl Rahner (eds), *Lexikon für Theologie und Kirche. Band 1: A – Baronius* (Freiburg: Herder, 1957), pp. 983–9 (p. 983).

30 See especially Michael J. Buckley, *At the Origins of Modern Atheism* (London: Yale University Press, 1984); and Gavin Hyman, 'Atheism in Modern History', in Michael Martin (ed.), *The Cambridge Companion to Atheism* (Cambridge: Cambridge University Press, 2007), pp. 27–46. For a somewhat similar argument regarding the rise of Russian atheism, see Mikhail Epstein, 'Post-Atheism: From Apophatic Theology to "Minimal Religion"', in Mikhail Epstein, Alexander Genis and Slobodanka Vladiv-Glover (eds), *Russian Postmodernism: New Perspectives on Post-Soviet Culture*, trans. by Slobodanka Vladiv-Glover (Oxford: Berghahn Books, 1999), pp. 345–93.

But this is not, you may be heartened to learn, *Gaudium et Spes*' final word on the subject.

The Remedies of Atheism

> The answer to atheism is to be sought in the fitting exposition of doctrine, and in the entire life of the Church and its members. For the Church's function is to make God the Father and his incarnate Son present and, as it were, visible, through unceasingly renewing and purifying itself, led by the Holy Spirit. This is chiefly accomplished by the testimony of a living and mature faith, one namely that is educated so as to be able clearly to perceive difficulties, and to overcome them. Many martyrs have borne, and bear still, an excellent witness to this faith. This faith should manifest its fruitfulness by penetrating the entire life, even the worldly activities, of believers, and by moving them to justice and love, especially towards those in need. The fraternal charity of the faithful – who work together in a unanimous spirit for the faith of the Gospel, and exhibit themselves as a sign of unity – contributes greatly to revealing the presence of God. (*Gaudium et Spes* §21)[31]

The passage is quite clear on the necessity of 'fitting exposition of doctrine'. By that, I assume, is meant the apologetic and evangelistic mission of the Church. But note that the rest of this paragraph on countering atheism is directly concerned not with those 'outside', but rather with the Church and its members. This, again, would seem to suggest the wise counsel of de Lubac. The idea seems to be, to put it a little crudely, that we need first to get our house in order (or at least to begin doing so), before we start inviting people inside. I would like to make two, fairly lengthy, main points in this regard.

The first concerns the emphasis in *Gaudium et Spes* on Christian living. As we have seen, 'defects in [Christians'] religious, moral or social lives' were earlier identified as one of the *causes* of atheism. Here, one of its primary *remedies* may be found in the 'entire life of the Church and its members', and a faith that shows 'its fruitfulness by penetrating the entire life, even the worldly activities, of believers, and by moving them to justice and love, especially towards those in need'. The text also points specifically to the Christian martyrs, whose very lives are lived out as

---

31 AS IV/vii, p. 744.

witnesses to the Faith. A somewhat similar suggestion was made, a little after the Council, by Hans Urs von Balthasar. Commenting not on atheism itself, but instead on the late 1960s' crisis of Christian confidence, he suggests that what is needed are:

> Not mere decrees, much less the institution of new study commissions, but saintly figures to serve as beacons by which we can find our bearings. . . . It is not true that we can do nothing to get saints. For example, we ought at least to try, though a bit belatedly, to become something like them ourselves. 'Better late than never.'[32]

Balthasar is quite right about 'saintly figures to serve as beacons'. Take, for example, the following story. In the early fourth century in Egypt, a young, devout pagan by the name of Pachomius was forcibly conscripted into the Roman army. He and a number of other recruits were transported, closely confined and badly treated, down the Nile to Thebes. When they arrived, a group of strangers began ministering to them, caring for them as if they were their own relatives, and giving them food and money. Astonished, Pachomius is said to have asked his companions: 'Who are they? Why are they so good to us when they do not know us?' To this, his companions replied: 'They are Christians; they treat us with love because of the God of Heaven.' Pachomius was deeply impressed, and as soon as he was permitted to leave the army, he enrolled as a catechumen, received baptism, and went on to become one of the great founders of Christian monasticism.

I quote that story, not (just) as piously wishful thinking, but as encapsulating something that is still constantly going on, the world over, albeit – usually, at least – in rather less dramatic ways. Needless to say, there are a great many reasons that people have for not only ignoring the claims of Christianity, but for rejecting them outright. Sometimes these are intellectual ones. But the most potent, perhaps, are moral and social ones. There are no shortage of moral failings, and even atrocities, with which Christians can rightly be charged. Joachim Kahl, not wholly implausibly, once said that 'the history of Christianity is the best school for atheism'.[33] Equally, it is not uncommon to hear religion in general, and Christianity in particular, still dismissed as 'the opium of the masses' – especially, for some reason, by people who have never read Marx, and certainly have never read the rest of the paragraph from which those words are taken.

---

32 Hans Urs von Balthasar, *The Moment of Christian Witness*, trans. by Richard Beckley (San Francisco, CA: Ignatius Press, 1994 [1966]), pp. 154–5.

33 Joachim Kahl, *The Misery of Christianity: A Plea for Humanity without God*, trans. by N. D. Smith (London: Pelican, 1971), p. 27.

The immorality and disutility of religion, and again Christianity in particular, is a dominant theme for the New Atheist authors.

But then we come to a Saint Francis, a Blessed Pier Giorgio Frassati, an Albert Schweitzer, a Dorothy Day or a Blessed Teresa of Calcutta. And such figures prevent Christianity being written off quite so easily. They hint, not only to us but to the *world*, that in among all the chaff, there is some wheat after all – and wheat that (if you will forgive my mixing of gospel metaphors) 'bears fruit and yields, in one case a hundredfold, in another sixty, and in another thirty' (Matt. 13.23). I am not saying that such saints, in themselves, are the key to countering atheism (although they have, by their example, converted a great many individuals). My point is rather that they prevent people from *completely* dismissing Christianity as ethically moribund and socially useless. As such, they offer an invaluable corrective to the more strident (and, to a point, sometimes justified) attacks on the Church and its members – *not* as incorporated into a meta-ethical, apologetic argument, but simply through undertaking the works of mercy and inspiring other Christians to do the same. The famous injunction, normally attributed to Saint Francis, to 'preach the gospel at all times; use words if necessary', like many timeworn phrases, contains much that is true.

This fact is, I think, not lost on the New Atheists. Mother Teresa, especially, is clearly a thorn in their side – a seemingly obvious and glaring exception to their claims. Christopher Hitchens led the charge in 1995, with his short book *The Missionary Position: The Ideology of Mother Teresa*, in part contrasting her unfavourably with 'freethinking humanists, who scorned to use the fear of death to coerce and flatter the poor'.[34] Richard Dawkins, in *The God Delusion*, deems her 'sanctimoniously hypocritical', and disputes her deservingness of the Nobel Peace Prize.[35] And Sam Harris, in *Letter to a Christian Nation*, regards her as: 'a perfect example of the way in which a good person, moved to help others, can have her moral intuitions deranged by religious faith'.[36] Comparatively generous in his assessment, Harris concedes:

Clearly, she was moved by the suffering of her fellow human beings, and she did much to awaken others to the reality of that suffering. The problem, however, was that her compassion was channelled within the rather steep walls of her religious dogmatism.[37]

---

34 Christopher Hitchens, *The Missionary Position: The Ideology of Mother Teresa* (London: Verso, 1995), p. xiii.
35 Richard Dawkins, *The God Delusion* (London: Bantam, 2006), p. 292.
36 Sam Harris, *Letter to a Christian Nation* (London: Bantam, 2007), p. 35.
37 Harris, *Letter to a Christian Nation*, p. 35.

According to Harris, it was Teresa's (albeit only partial) commitment to liberal humanist values which, despite her Christian faith, accounts for any good she may have done. This is indeed, as Terry Eagleton recently observed, 'rather like arguing that any advances made by feminists are due entirely to the benign influence of their fathers'.[38]

Although I have focused on the Teresas and Francises of this world, I do not mean to imply that this kind of witness to Christ and his Church – such 'living as though the Truth were true'[39] – is the preserve solely of the saints. In fact, that is not my point at all. Every day, countless charitable acts are performed by Christians, motivated by their faith. These, often very modest actions, individually and collectively, all play their part in stopping Christianity being wholly dismissed. I will give just one example of this, drawn from my own experience. Saint Francis House in Oxford is a community of the Catholic Worker Movement, which was founded in New York during the Depression by Dorothy Day and Peter Maurin. Every Monday evening, members and friends of the House take out hot drinks, sandwiches, cake, fruit – and in winter, extra clothing – to the homeless around Oxford city centre. When offering these to people whom they have not met before, it is fairly common for them to be asked, *not* – like Pachomius – 'who are you, and why are you doing this?', but instead 'what *church* are you from?' Evidently, at least some Christians, some of the time, must have been doing something right. Now these encounters themselves are not, nor should they be, opportunities for evangelization. But according to *Gaudium et Spes*, they are nevertheless an important form of *preparatio evangelica*, of 'preparation for the gospel'. This is true, not only of those to whom the works of mercy are administered (as again with Pachomius), but moreover to society at large.

My second point concerns the stress in *Gaudium et Spes* §21 on the need for Christians themselves to possess 'a living and mature faith'. Again, recall that §19 cited Christians' neglect of their own 'education in the faith' as playing a role in the rise of atheism. It is for this reason that arguably the most urgent evangelistic task facing the Church in Britain is not towards atheists and non-believers, but is instead to Christians: especially those who, for the time being at least, know that they do – *just about* – believe, but are not quite sure what, or more importantly, *why*. For some time now, the hallmark of British (and indeed, western

---

38 Terry Eagleton, *Reason, Faith and Revolution: Reflections on the God Debate* (New Haven, CT: Yale University Press, 2009), p. 97.

39 A phrase used by, and of, Dorothy Day. See, for example, Daniel Berrigan, 'Introduction', in Dorothy Day, *The Long Loneliness* (New York: Harper & Row, 1981), p. xxiii.

European) socio-religious culture has been *indifference*. This is so even among many who would call and consider themselves to be Christians, who profess belief in God and an afterlife (not necessarily conceived in orthodoxly Christian terms), and who perhaps even pray regularly. As recently as 2004, Cardinal Poupard, then President of the Pontifical Council for Culture (into which the Secretariat for Non-believers was gradually amalgamated away), could write:

> The Church today is confronted more by indifference and practical unbelief than with atheism. Atheism is in [decline] throughout the world, but indifference and unbelief develop in cultural milieus marked by secularism. It is no longer a question of a public affirmation of atheism, with the exception of a few countries, but of a diffuse presence, almost omnipresent, in the culture.[40]

Obviously, the New Atheism's rise to prominence would today lead us somewhat to qualify these comments. But it must not blind us to the fact that religious indifference, rather than vocal atheism, is dominant in contemporary Britain. And again, this is something to which the New Atheists are well-attuned. It is just these people to whom *The God Delusion*, in particular, is directed. On the very first page, Dawkins writes:

> I suspect – well, I am sure – that there are lots of people out there who have been brought up in some religion or other, are unhappy in it, don't believe it, or are worried about the evils that are done in its name; people who feel vague yearnings to leave their parents' religion and wish they could, but just don't realize that leaving is an option. If you are one of them, this book is for you.[41]

I mentioned earlier the possibility that the New Atheism may, to a certain extent, *benefit* Christian evangelization. What I mean is that, with the high media and popular profile of the New Atheists, religion, and its *significance*, is suddenly a hot topic. Religiously indifferent Britons are being told, by Dawkins and company, that, actually, *whether* and *what* one believes is extremely important. Now, as one might expect, this will almost certainly result in a significant increase in people who, having

---

40 Paul Poupard, *Where Is Your God? Responding to the Challenge of Unbelief and Religious Indifference Today* (Chicago, IL: Liturgy Training Publications, 2004), p. 12.

41 Dawkins, *God Delusion*, p. 1. See also Robert B. Stewart, 'The Future of Atheism: An Introductory Appraisal', in Robert B. Stewart (ed.), *The Future of Atheism: Alister McGrath & Daniel Dennett in Dialogue* (London: SPCK, 2008), pp. 1–16 (p. 7).

now – perhaps for the first time – thought about such things, no longer regard themselves as 'Christians', or indeed believers. But for others, this prompting to consider their religious convictions will lead to a stronger, more thoughtful, more committed faith. This much is clear from the large numbers of books *responding* to the New Atheism. They must be selling, or publishers would not keep producing them. But to whom? An interested atheist, perhaps, might read one or two – especially by one of the 'big-name' philosophers or theologians, such as Alister McGrath or Keith Ward. But they are surely not buying them *all*. My own, I think uncontroversial, suspicion is that these are being bought by Christians themselves, who though they may feel challenged by the New Atheists, nevertheless believe (or hope) that satisfactory answers can be found. Thus the reinvigoration of apologetics occasioned by the New Atheism is, to a large degree, having most effect not on unbelievers, but on Christians. If Vatican II is correct regarding the effects of 'a living and mature faith, one namely that is educated so as to be able clearly to perceive difficulties, and to overcome them', then the Christian reaction to the New Atheism may not be such a bad, long-term groundwork for countering atheism more generally.

Conclusion

I have titled this chapter 'Atheism, Apologetics and Ecclesiology' because I believe it captures the fact that, in facing contemporary atheism, the Church must simultaneously look both outwards ('apologetics') and inwards ('ecclesiology'). These two cannot, in fact, be separated. On the one hand, we must preach the gospel – argue for Christ; constantly finding new, intellectually robust means of doing just that. But equally we must look to ourselves and strive, individually and collectively, to provide a fitting 'backdrop', against which this proclamation will get a hearing, and seem plausible. Those who wrote and approved §§19–21 of 'the Pastoral Constitution of the Church in the World of *This Time*' (as it literally translates from the Latin) were well aware that the Council was not making any definitive, 'for-the-ages' pronouncement on atheism. Indeed, the statement itself stresses the necessity of further investigation and 'a dialogue that is sincere and prudent' – both of which were, of course, integral to the newly begun work of the Secretariat for Non-believers. Today, the study of atheism, indifference and unbelief – theologically, philosophically, historically, sociologically, psychologically, anthropologically – are vital tasks, both for academic scholarship itself and for the

Christian communities. There is, and will continue to be, a great deal of work to be done in this area. But on a slightly different note, I would like to leave you with the final sentences of *Gaudium et Spes* §21:

> The Church knows fully that its message is in harmony with the most secret desires of the human heart, when it champions the dignity of the human vocation, restoring hope to those who now despair of anything higher than their present lot. Its message, far from belittling man, secures the light, life and freedom of his development. Nothing other than this can satisfy the human heart: 'You have made us for yourself,' Lord, 'and our heart is restless until it rests in you.'[42]

---

42 AS IV/vii, p. 745.

7

Christian Ethics as Good News

CRAIG HOVEY

This chapter encourages us to take an imaginative, but sadly little used, approach to apologetics: to consider how the message of Christian ethics may be part of the Good News. This simultaneously reorientates both apologetics and Christian ethics, to the benefit of both. Indeed, no 'ethics' that is not 'good news' is worthy of the Christian faith from which it claims to spring. The association of ethics with apologetics represented in this essay widens the contention found in this volume that the Christian faith recommends itself because it makes sense of things, or at least begins to do so. This is usually worked out in terms of truth; here Hovey invites us to think it through in terms of goodness. Christian ethics makes sense of human life from a moral perspective, presenting us with a vision of what it means to be a flourishing human person. Christian ethics suggests a path to a full-blooded and worthwhile life. It doing so, it simultaneously redefines, in countercultural ways, what such a 'successful' human life would look like. **A.D.**

My experience with apologetics is twofold and I suspect reveals some of the tensions that this volume seeks to address. On the one hand, as an American Christian growing up in the 1970s and 1980s, I associated apologetics with the quasi-legal defences of a certain sort of self-confident Protestant who went around armed with a hundred and one proofs for Jesus rising from the dead. It always seemed to me that the only people this convinced were those who already believed it. But if this is the case, then the enterprise hardly seems worth the trouble. I do think it is important for Christians to come to rational and persuasive terms with what they confess to believe, but then we probably should not call it apologetics. On the other hand, theological training has put me in touch with the early Church's efforts to defend the faith against misunderstanding from their pagan neighbours. They were under no illusions that their neighbours might still reject the gospel; they only wanted it to be the true gospel that they rejected if they did.

If I am not mistaken, these really are two different understandings of what apologetics is all about; they at least point to two very different emphases. Timothy Radcliffe OP wrote a book called *What is the Point of Being a Christian?*[1] It is a good book, but I simply want to focus on the title, with its provocative question. My unease with the proof version of apologetics stems from my suspicion that if we set this question to the proof-apologists, they might respond that the point of being a Christian is to be right or to be rational. Now, I want to be right and rational too. But wanting to be these things does not really answer the question very well. Instead, appropriately attending to the question about the 'point' of being a Christian ought to send us into the realm of morality, since it is really a question about what is *good* about it.

It is certainly the case that it is good to believe true things and so, in a sense, there is no further need to commend the goodness of something for having a point beyond the mere fact that it happens to be true. If the resurrection of Jesus is true then it would be a good thing to believe it. But not every true thing is good in any way other than this surface sense. As Robert Jenson says, the goodness of the event depends on *who has been raised*: ' "Stalin is risen." would not be good news for most people. "The unconditional friend of publicans and sinners is risen" is good news to anyone willing to try those shoes on; "the chief keeper of the gulag is risen" would be good news to very few.'[2]

In this chapter, I consider what is good about the kind of living that is enabled, obligated, permitted and promised for Christians. Whether it is good in any sense other than that it pertains to us will be my focus. In short, what does the Christian moral life have to do with the news that the Church proclaims as good? What can we say about its goodness? Answering questions like these is a crucial project for contemporary Christianity, particularly if we hope to enrich and enliven the debates with the New Atheism, as some authors in this volume are doing more directly. There is surely more to say than to argue the existence of a god that, however provable, may or may not be good news to us. (A great deal of philosophy has devoted itself to the question of whether the existence of god can be proven, which makes one wonder what these philosophers take to be more important – the god or being successful in proving it.) Despite its pompous and malicious title, Christopher Hitchens is nevertheless right to raise in his book *God is Not Great* at least the prospect that just because a god

---

1 Timothy Radcliffe OP, *What is the Point of Being a Christian?* (London: Burns & Oates, 2005).

2 Robert W. Jenson, 'Identity, Jesus, and Exegesis', in Beverly Roberts Gaventa and Richard B. Hays (eds), *Seeking the Identity of Jesus: A Pilgrimage* (Grand Rapids, MI: Eerdmans, 2008), p. 43.

exists does not mean we might not be justified in rejecting it.[3] Nietzsche's swagger is no less self-assured. My point is that these questions are much more interesting and closer to Christianity's original apologists than questions that simply concern themselves with proving that God exists.

I will argue four interrelated points. The first is that Christianity countenances the goal of Christian ethics to be the faithful and obedient living of Christians rather than the production of scholarship on Christian ethics. This is a point that academics probably need to hear more frequently than do clergy. The second is that Christian ethics restores the original and proper functioning of our full humanity. Whatever else such living may demand of Christians, it is fundamental to Christian confession that it does not take us away from who and what we are as human beings. It is in fact sin that does the latter, not righteousness. Third, I show how the Christian moral life continually encounters – and disables – the demand to justify itself extrinsically, according to some kind of good or benefit other than it inhabits through its own exercise. Like joy – in fact as nothing other than joy itself – this moral life is released from the constraints of being instrumental in attaining any extrinsic goods. But, finally, I consider that the joy of the Christian moral existence is anything but obvious or immediately apparent. This, I believe, calls for the most seriously apologetic imagination, since even what Christians defend as being forthrightly good news often cannot easily escape (without contradiction) the charge that it is, in fact, anything but.

How you teach something ought to depend on what it means for you to learn it. You learn the countries' capitals by memorizing them, by setting your mind towards categorizing the relevant facts. And while quite a lot falls into this kind of model, Christianity has followed an older tradition of Greek reflection on the nature of the moral life by insisting that the manner of learning it goes much deeper. It goes far beyond the accumulation of information and more closely resembles formation.

In particular, a great deal of Christian reflection has been devoted to expanding on the goal of Christian ethics understood as the formation of character and the ability to make prudent judgements. That is to say, confronted with a situation in which one was not specifically trained, the moral person will show sound judgement in negotiating the unknown. There is no specific and particular way to prepare for it; there are only the habits and dispositions that the tradition has typically called the virtues. If I visit

---

3 Christopher Hitchens, *God is Not Great: How Religion Poisons Everything* (New York: Twelve Hachette, 2009).

a foreign country, I will try to learn what I can ahead of time. But what will serve me the best is if I can work towards being a 'seasoned traveller', someone who, quite apart from the specific knowledge of a place, can take the unfamiliar in my stride, with patience, grace and poise.

When thought of in this way, the goal of ethics lies beyond knowledge, properly speaking. Rather, it issues in action. While it may yield concepts, ideas and principles, these are merely steps along the way rather than the end itself. Christian ethics may help us conceive what moral existence looks like and, for example, how to make faithful decisions. But even this will include a picture of the life of faith that the Christian person will come more closely to resemble the more she comes to grasp it and live by it. Only on the basis that there exists such a thing as competency and skill in living a particular way is it possible for anyone to reflect on Christian ethics as a knowledge or discipline in the traditional sense.

Imagine what you would have to do if you wanted to learn to juggle. Even though there are books devoted to the question of how you do it, reading them will only get you so far. The reason is that juggling is a skill. You would not claim to 'know' juggling if all that you could do was give instructions to others about it. Your knowing juggling would be, quite simply, the way we would talk about the fact that you could juggle. In fact, it is impossible to imagine anyone writing *How to Juggle* if there did not exist people who have mastered the skill. There would literally be nothing to write about, if there did not first exist the expertise.

This implies that among the most important things to consider when it comes to gaining the skills of Christian living are things like discipline, physical actions, training and practice. It involves the body as much as the mind.

Now, if Christian ethics is about training the body more than producing a body of academic literature, then it will be clear that it is also a drawn out process that involves a considerable amount of hard work. This is precisely the aspect of the whole enterprise that thinkers such as Immanuel Kant focused on, indeed made into a virtue on its own. According to Kant, the moral person is one whose actions are able to overcome the reluctant will. Our human desire for living abides easily and in utter repose within the craven person, unchallenged, as it is, by an intellect that might otherwise challenge it to rise above itself. The craven person saunters past the beggar unperturbed. But the moral person is troubled by her conscience and her moral knowledge – what she knows she ought to do – even though she does not feel compassion. '[T]he will is a faculty of choosing only that which reason, independently of inclination, recognizes as practically necessary, i.e., as good.'[4] The moral person is moved to act in opposition to her desires. Her acts of mercy are not affective but instead demonstrate how the intellect overcomes the baser inclinations of the will.

In this way, ethics (for Kant) is at odds with our humanity. In fact, it is a singular measure of moral triumph when our will is beaten down by our more resolute commitment to do the work that we are duty-bound to do. This is bad-news ethics. Not because it is bad to act in contradiction to our emotions and will, but precisely the opposite. On this view, what is morally good is necessarily bad for these other faculties since it requires their suppression and not their flowering and flourishing. For this view, ethics is a matter of restraint and discipline, of careful management, restriction and keeping things in check.

In contrast, while Aristotle agreed that 'it is hard work to be excellent', he extends the scope of the things to which moral excellence truly applies, so that it includes things that Kant excludes, such as the will-as-desire and emotions.[5] Aristotle, we might say, significantly raises the bar in his determination to go beyond a mere consideration of moral actions. After all, what is most difficult is not necessarily the exercise of moral acts but submitting to the long-term formation of the disposition necessary to be able to own such acts flowing from your own will. 'So also getting angry, or giving and spending money, is easy and everyone can do it; but doing it to the right person, in the right amount, at the right time, for the right end and in the right way is no longer easy, nor can everyone do it. Hence doing these things well is rare, praiseworthy, and fine.'[6] The insight that we must aim higher than merely *acting* morally is dear to the Christian tradition. Saint Anselm prayed, 'Lord, make me taste by love what I taste by knowledge; let me know by love what I know by understanding.'[7] He might also have prayed not only that he might be kind to strangers, but feel compassion and have tenderness of heart towards them.

Following Aristotle, Thomas Aquinas, though he wrote centuries before Kant, markedly surpassed Kant in his account of the moral person.

---

4 Immanuel Kant, *Foundations of the Metaphysics of Morals in Critique of Practical Reason and Other Writings in Moral Philosophy*, trans. by Lewis White Beck (Chicago: University of Chicago Press, 1949), p. 72.

5 Aristotle, *Nicomachean Ethics*, 2nd edition, trans. by Terence Irwin (Indianapolis: Hackett, 1999), 1109a–b.

6 Aristotle, *Nicomachean Ethics*, 1109a–b.

7 *The Prayers and Meditations of St. Anselm*, trans. by Benedicta Ward (New York: Penguin, 1973), p. 237.

Thomas agreed that we should refer to someone who overcomes baser desires in order to do what is morally right as a moral person. Yet he envisioned a moral state that lies beyond this. As one's character over time is more and more shaped by and evinces the virtues, moral inclinations and emotions will be less and less in conflict with choosing the good. The one who acts morally *according to* her inclinations is more morally mature than the one whose moral acting can only come about by opposing them. In other words, with the development of character, you will less frequently experience a crisis of conscience. Instead, you will approach a serene compatibility between desire and act as both are conformed to what is good. The moral life, in short, will truly be doing what you want to do. The transformation of 'what you want to do' is one of the great insights Thomas borrows from Aristotle.

Theologically, we can identify two conceptions of humanity at work in this distinction between Kant and Thomas. While Kant envisions the moral person having to overcome humanity, Thomas sees the moral person coming more fully into his own as human. The twentieth-century Dominican theologian Herbert McCabe sided with Thomas in showing how this implies that Christ is the most human of all of us. Of course, 'fully human' is an orthodox Christian confession about Christ. In the Church's rejection of historic Christological heresies it was not affirming that Christ is less than or more than human, but just the opposite. We are to take our cues for what constitutes a fully human life from the life and person of Jesus Christ rather than apply to him, as theological measures, our prior notions of what it means to be human. McCabe explains the way that virtue enhances our humanity: 'Virtue, whatever else it means, at least means being more human; it would not be virtuous if it did not. Sin, whatever else it means, means being less human, more still, cold, proud, selfish, mean, cruel, and all the rest of it.'[8]

It is worth noticing what this says about our humanity. It certainly says that our humanity is typically less than it should be: we are less patient and more guarded, less caring and more self-centred, less loving and more estranged from each other than is humanly good for us. But in all of this, crucially, we are *less than human* rather than *less for being human*. Our problem is not that we are material and long to be released from the weight of bodies. Nor is it that we are creatures and long to be gods. The problem is that we are sinners. This important insight follows from theology's long-standing emphasis on evil as privation of the good, which has its parallel in identifying sin as failure. It is something that is

---

8 Herbert McCabe, *God Still Matters* (London: Continuum, 2002), p. 96.

lost – the space opened up by the loss itself – rather than something that has positive existence on its own.

Our addressing the failure of our full humanity does not mean coming to terms with the limitations that are characteristic of our being human (since, after all, God declared our humanity to be 'very good'). There is nothing about being human that itself keeps us from being fully righteous and good, indeed completely without sin, as Jesus Christ was. After all, Christianity does not teach that Christ's sinlessness owed to his divine nature winning out over his human nature. Rather, Christian ethics is the overcoming of our sinful condition; it amounts to our return to everything that God's creatures were intended to be when they were created. We do not transcend or exceed our status as creatures any more than we yearn for something that was not originally ours in our creatureliness. Whatever the final blessedness entails, it will not make us post-human. Salvation is material. 'We should help people to become more fully human', writes Archbishop Desmond Tutu. 'Become what you are.'[9] More fully human is what Christ is. The human rebellion against God is also, just so, a departure from our true nature.

Where have we got to? Simply this: Christian ethics is the name given to the therapeutic restoration of our full humanity in Christ. (Although by therapeutic, I do not mean to reduce this work to mere human achievement. It is no doubt, like many Christian things, a complex mixture of both the divine and the human.) It seeks to identify the completion of what is lacking. It is therefore not at odds with our nature. Rather, it is fundamentally not only compatible with our nature, but is nothing other than the manner in which coming into our own as humans is realized. Even stronger, it is the realization itself. But it is also a work of grace and is thereby a free gift that rebuffs efforts to describe it in terms that see it as a means to an end, as ways of accomplishing other good things. I argue this last point in what follows.

All of this means that the moral formation that Christian ethics enacts is good news for human creatures. No matter what else it may end up being good for, it is good for our humanity since it invites us to the life for which we were created, restoring what we lose of ourselves when we reject God, or in choosing evil, reject ourselves. If we were to consider the benefits or outcomes of Christian moral existence, this on its own ought

---

9 Desmond Tutu, 'Becoming More Fully Human', in Eddie and Debbie Shapiro (eds), *Voices from the Heart: A Compassionate Call for Responsibility* (New York: Jeremy P. Tarcher / Putnam, 1998), p. 277.

to be enough. There is no need to look for the extrinsic benefits of moral living as utilitarianism does. It is an astonishingly audacious Christian claim that the moral life need not benefit the world, save lives, protect the innocent or bring about justice in order for it to be called good.

Of course, Christianity also expects that what is good for those who live moral lives, which count to us as being more fully human, will also bring about benefits for others. In Luke's Gospel, Jesus begins his ministry by declaring that he will bring 'good news to the poor'. And Christians have long noted that following what Jesus taught would, among other things, enact a radical redistribution of wealth that will directly benefit the poor. There was, for ancient Israel, to be no permanent underclass, but instead a periodic and ongoing cancelling of debts, return to ancestral lands that had needed to be sold off owing to some misfortune and release of debt-slaves (see Lev. 25). Coinciding with this is the larger vision of the Sabbath over which Jesus frequently sparred with religious leaders (for example, Matt. 12; Mark 3). What is good news for the poor was not categorically good for everyone, particularly the rich who failed to see how their participation in the actions of God might be a joyful sharing in divine goodness, glory and plenty. The rich man goes away sad because he hears the good news as bad news (Mark 10.22).

We should note that the way Christianity singles out particular groups (the poor, vulnerable and so on) at once sets it at odds with the moral schemes of the Enlightenment. For example, Kant tried to find a universal foundation for morality that did not depend on the *content* of particular convictions (such as, presumably, God being on the side of the poor). Instead, he sought to found a universal ethic on the *form* of convictions and thereby developed his famous categorical imperative: 'We must be able to will that a maxim of our action become a universal law.'[10] In other words, what is moral can be deduced through this mental exercise of imagining actions to which everyone can reasonably assent. One example he gives is that we should never make deceitful promises.[11] Such principles are unshakable rules that ought always to be followed as a matter of duty, regardless of the consequences. But to achieve this level of uniformity, Kant's method also strives to be universal in the sense of not depending on the convictions of particular groups, religious communities, sacred texts or revelations. It is equally unconcerned in its method with questions about any results that following the rule might bring about. In this last sense, there is something eminently Christian about the steadfast

---

10 Kant, *Foundations of the Metaphysics of Morals*, p. 82.
11 Kant, *Critique of Practical Reason*, Book 1.

fidelity to acting morally no matter what. But notice that Kant's fidelity is *formal*, in the sense of being ultimately more committed to the form of our convictions than their content. Holding fast is more important than that to which you hold! In contrast, Christian ethics has been concerned with people, situations and actions, not primarily ideas or even duties and laws. Kant worried that these former things (people, situations and actions) would always be too variable and, besides, you could not possibly know them without looking. This means that what Kant had to say about making sincere promises has nothing to do with the content of the promises themselves nor the character of the promise-maker. And it is more praiseworthy to keep a promise because our reason tells us to than because we have the will to do so.[12] Promises simply *as such* (and kept out of duty to reason and not the will) are the kinds of things that only make sense as being what they are when they are made with sincerity.

The many ways that the Christian moral tradition has responded to Kant are obviously more complex than I can do justice to here.[13] However, for our purposes, let us notice that his radical separation of form from content was an attempt to situate morality on a surer footing than the hit-and-miss persuasiveness of what Kant saw as the more straightforwardly religious claims that Christianity makes – that Jesus Christ is the Son of God, that God is good and the like. Since the latter are unlikely to result from the exercise of 'pure reason' (unaided by revelation through Scripture, for instance), he thought it best to rescue the means of deriving moral laws and principles from such particular claims. Actually, Kant took pains to show that things like the existence of God manifestly could not be proven, which is, in a sense, all the worse for moral schemes that stand or fall according to God's existence. Putting the matter simply, Kant hoped we could all agree on morals even if we could not all agree on God.

I have been making the point that Christian goods are not easily judged by their extrinsic effects even though the connection to what they affect is part of Christian conviction about God who is able to bring good things out of very little and even out of nothing. At the same time, the logic that binds the good news with the poor does not flow in the other direction, as though everything that is obviously good for the poor is, strictly speaking,

---

12 Kant, *Foundations of the Metaphysics of Morals*, pp. 92–3.

13 Moreover, there is more to say about Kant on dispositions connected to the will – such as emotions – which, as Nancy Sherman shows can, for Kant, play a role in motivating acts that accord with the duties that reason dictates. See Nancy Sherman, *Making a Necessity of Virtue: Aristotle and Kant on Virtue* (Cambridge: Cambridge University Press, 1997), pp. 141–58.

everything that the Christian gospel is. We may therefore generalize a critique of an ethics of utility: a straightforward reading of the Christian good news does not reveal the understanding that a good action is identical with the action's effects. There are a few aspects to this.

One aspect is that it is very difficult to know where a single action begins and ends. It would be very peculiar if it is the case that I do nonmoral things most of the time and only on occasion engage in moral acts. Moreover, it is unclear when we should start assessing the effects of an action. I may do something that only years later makes sense of the good others will want to attribute to it. Some things may not bear fruit, as it were, until those responsible for it are long gone. This is not to say that moral judgements on actions are unconnected from the actions; it is only to acknowledge that the business of judging something good does not easily conform with most theoretical accounts. And finally, there are those actions that, no matter the timescale, quite simply seem to benefit no one. We may even recognize that the benefits we seek could only be accomplished through means that we feel compelled to judge as immoral even though we may not be able immediately to produce the grounds for this.

Even so, Christianity is certainly not unconcerned about effects. In fact, part of the skill of the Christian moral life – of growing in the virtues – surely lies in the ability to recognize what is happening when you see the hungry being filled with good things and not too quickly separate what is good for you from what is good for others. But we will never be able *only* to point to benefits or exchanges and declare that these are things that make the gospel good. After all, as Christians become more and more fully human – sanctified, to use the theological language – they will face the onslaught of everything that sets itself with great determination against the things of God, everything in rebellion against God's good order and every institution that derives benefit from enacting gross injustice on some. The goods of justice may attend to the efforts of those who pursue it, but it is just as likely that those who pursue justice will themselves become injustice's most notable victims.

This means that there is a crucial disconnect between ethical living and the good, real-world effects that may otherwise be cited as its justification, as if they easily followed on one from the other. Loving your enemies may or may not convince enemies that there is a better way. If the Church organizes its common life such that it refuses to make an important decision until it has heard from its weakest member, the world may look on with puzzlement, awe or hostility. There are no guarantees that reactions will be one way rather than another. But the ability to persist in the way of the gospel is itself part of the gospel's promise to those who endeavour to live it. Christian martyrs, for example, are those who refused to compromise, when it became apparent that the tide of public opinion was not going to go in their favour. How are they able to refuse?

For one thing, they are not limited by considering short-term results. To do so would make martyrdom quite impossible. Instead, identifying one's death with the death of Christ radically qualifies all talk of effects, outcomes and benefits. And this disconnect between faithfulness and its benefits is good news. But notice how it depends a great deal on faith and trust. The martyrs can die joyfully, even blessing their killers, because they trust that their deaths are sharing in the death of Christ; and if God could raise him from the dead, he can raise the martyrs too.

An ethics of utility requires too much of human responsibility and too little of God. But then, relieved of making ethics conform to the need to make things come out right, the Christian is set free for joy. Joy is keyed to this non-instrumentality. When you do something for the joy of doing it, you may also have other reasons for it even while the joy is likely to trump them. And if you imagine an activity – like dancing, perhaps – that you do for no other extrinsic benefits save the sheer pleasure of doing it, you have a sense of how closely joy really is keyed to non-instrumentality.

It is not a coincidence that loving falls into this category. It is part of the human experience of love and loving that we do not love for a *reason* or with an eye to outcomes. When it is true and genuine, love tends not to ask what can be gained by it or what it can achieve; it finds joy, rather, in its sheer exercise. But not all loving is manifestly and obviously for the joy of it. In fact, unrequited love is notoriously the stuff of tragedy and despair. Love is exercised as movement in its back-and-forth quality; it is given for the joy of it in a giving that exposes you to the possibility that it will go unmet. Even so, it is not genuinely love if it is done in order to elicit a loving response. Everyone recognizes this as manipulation and insincerity. There are many ways of trying to get what you want, but there is something about love that falls outside of this kind of scheming, something about scheming that disqualifies it from being called love. Which means that unmet love is fairly different from other instances of not getting what you want from other people (such as a pay rise, a movie contract or a free lunch).

Love is a desire that, in a sense, devotes itself to being understood only by the inner logic of loving, of being understood only in the way that those who also love can do. It is a feature of things like love that it is impossible to appreciate their fullness through descriptions of what they are about. You can gather as much information about love as you want to, but if you have been deprived of love all of your life, this information will not do much. In fact, to ask the question 'why love?' is already to make clear that you misunderstand what love is all about.

I have hazarded this brief excursus on love in order to be able to claim that Christian ethics is very similar to it. The joy of its exercise exceeds all talk of demands, outcomes, obligations and duties. Each of the latter yields a truncated moral existence that Kant, unfortunately, not only would have recognized, but would have thought exemplifies the best we can morally achieve. But just as the will to love regardless of the consequences – and even positively in the face of overwhelming tragedy and vulnerability for doing so – is itself the perfection and flourishing of love, so also the more one's will to the good is transformed out of love for God, the more we can say that morality is truly coming into its own. If this is a description of acting in accordance with the fullness of our humanity, then we are yearning to come back into the rest that is the fullness of our life as God's creatures. But saying this is not the same as offering a reason or justification for it. Rather, we are pushed towards loving without limits. Christian moral existence contradicts our natural tendency to hold ourselves back from making of ourselves full gifts to others and our natural inclinations to police our vulnerability before them.

Of course, Jesus was killed on account of living this way. So while a life lived more fully human may at some level be keyed to joy, we will only be able to hold on to this by complicating it.

It would be a mistake to conclude, based on the foregoing, that the Christian moral life is the key to well-being in anything like a straightforward sense. Becoming a Christian may ruin your life, lose you your friends, estrange you from family members, frustrate your career path and lead to a premature death. To insist on calling it good news requires that we face with honesty how a facile and glib happiness fails to get at the heart of Christian existence. I want to conclude by looking into this since any apologetics needs to take care lest it confuse its salutary goals with *winning*. As I insinuated earlier, the proof-style of apologetics probably wins only on the rare occasion. But its typical modus is to help those who engage in it feel *as though* they are winning. I want to keep us from that.

It is true that happiness is a concept that Christian moral theology has traditionally reached for in order to explain what is involved in living a more fully human life. But in doing so, it has not sought to evade the profound disruption and disorientation that such a life produces and, in a sense, even requires when it is most authentically what it claims to be. The more seriously deformed the setting (politically, socially), the greater the cost a moral existence is likely to exact. This is nothing new to a church that is skilled in remembering those who suffered for the faith. So what are we to make of happiness? Only that it must refer to the kind of well-being or contentment that, despite everything else, is able to look back over a life of faith and obedience and call it good. The fact that others may have to do this for me once I am gone merely demonstrates how the Church, rather than the individual, is the locus for this looking back.

Furthermore, as I said above, the disconnect between faithful living and its effects does not lie in faithfulness somehow being at odds with our human nature. It is rather a function of the fact that the world we have made for ourselves is a crucifying world that routinely rejects God's offers to it.[14] The seeming prosperity of the wicked – a question so poignant in the Psalms and in Job – has nothing to do with anything intrinsic about wickedness, but with the fact that the world is so thoroughly disordered that it is, in fact, aligned with the actions and designs of the wicked. The Bible is not only concerned with the fact that, as humans, we are sinners; it also shows that sinners are perfectly at home in a sinful world, with structures, institutions and modes of exchange that run on sin and even positively reward it. Dissonance and disruption are thus normal for those who refuse to live by them.

Most sobering of all, though, is the thought that even arguments such as I have laid out (that the joy of Christian existence is its release from being instrumentalized for some purpose) are bound to undo themselves if Christian ethics really is more about living than arguing, loving rather than knowing and making disciples rather than having debates. We will never be able to say anything more true than the claims our living make. This is the main problem with proof-apologetics. In this mode, arguments threaten to take the place of living in truth and so will surely refute themselves in exact proportion to their success. The more they win, the more they concede. The more convincing a proof-apologist is, the less convincing the Church needs to be through its existence as a people formed by the gospel. I take it that the latter is what Christianity means by *witness*. And the temptation to direct the query about goodness on to something other than the life of the Church is nothing other than the hope to evade the necessity of ourselves embodying the gospel's truth. Put starkly, if Christians cannot point to Christianity's goodness, they should refrain from claiming that, despite all appearances to the contrary, it really is quite true. Because it seriously affects Christian claims about goodness,

---

14 Herbert McCabe, *Law, Love, and Language* (London: Continuum, 2003), p. 132.

the sex-abuse scandal currently plaguing the Roman Catholic Church really does threaten the truth of the gospel. We need either to stake the gospel's truthfulness on its goodness or not at all. This means that what I have been narrating as a promise also points to how Christians are involved in a high-stakes game. The promise that the true gospel is good for the livers of it does not simultaneously allow Christians to prevent the inverse: that the gospel's truthfulness depends on our lives.

I think therefore that Christians ought to conceive of the apologetic task as a subset of witness. Just as witnesses do not dare to point to the truth of something without themselves displaying the life that issues from that conviction, so also all of their arguments are secondary to their doing so. The American theologian Jonathan Tran observes that this does not mean that arguments have no place. Arguments, Tran claims, 'help us make sense of martyrdom, namely, why in the world someone would die for God. In the absence of disciples who die for God, we offer arguments.'[15]

In other words, ethics may very well be part of the problem if it conceives of itself primarily as a knowledge, since it will invariably draw us away from life and discourage us from being more human rather than less. Nietzsche worried that this is what philosophy does, and precisely (he thought) by way of being too Christian: it tempts us away from living and towards a purer and more abstract form of existence than we actually have. (It is worth reminding ourselves that, while Christianity has surely fallen into this time and again, what is most striking about Christianity's notion of transcendence is how it plunges us more deeply into the world rather than mounts our escape from it. Jesus prays along these lines in John 17.) And if this is the case, then the answer to these tensions is not primarily a people armed with the truth, but a people whose goodness lies partly in their determination not to allow the truth they proclaim to outpace their single-minded devotion to its display in their common life. The language that Christians have usually adopted for this is *Church*, just as their native language for this display is *joy*.

---

15 Jonathan Tran, unpublished paper on Christian analytic philosophy of religion.

Situating Christian Apologetics

8

Cultural Hermeneutics and Christian Apologetics

GRAHAM WARD

In order to speak to people about Christ, the apologist must be able to speak their language. Christians should be confident in their identity 'in Christ' so as to be willing to become fluent in reading the signs of the times. It pays to be able to do this well, as the Christian claim is only one of a variety of cultural critiques claiming to offer a persuasive interpretation of the world. This requires skill in what Ward calls 'cultural hermeneutics'. Proficiency here will help the Christian to understand both what is well and what is ill about the societies in which we live, and why this might be so. Here attention to works of the contemporary imagination is important. The apologist can ask what literature and film reveal about the inchoate theological stirrings of our times. As an example, to understand how these are worked out in relation to place will help the Church to make more of her sacred buildings. Knowledge of the yearnings of our age will help the Christian to present the faith as it should be: as something both known and unknown, both recognizable as answering to the desires of the human heart, but also as utterly surprising: the depths of our own hearts are beyond our understanding, and all the more so is the response of God. **A.D.**

We have to begin with a fundamental question if we are to understand the importance of doing Christian apologetics, and that is 'from what position does the theologian speak?'[1] Beginning here we are presupposing that it is the task of all Christians to speak, and that the mission given to each one of us in such speech is the proclamation of the gospel of Christ. This proclamation is at the heart of the scriptural injunction not only to

---

1 Readers are referred here to Graham Ward, *Cultural Transformation and Religious Practice* (Cambridge: Cambridge University Press, 2005) not only for a more detailed examination of this foundational question but also for a more developed account of cultural hermeneutics and the role they play in the Christian proclamation of the gospel.

go out into all the world but to give that world an account of the hope of redemption that we have in Christ. And although there is a calling to be a teacher, as there is a calling to specific ecclesial roles, to the extent that this proclamation is enjoined among all who are faithful believers then we are all, to some extent, theologians. We are all, after Mary, bearers of the Word.

So our foundational question immediately situates the Christian theologian in the Church and the continuing formation that the Church is there to offer: through participation in its liturgies (particularly the Mass), tradition and the reading of Scripture. But the Church is not a ghetto or a walled city; just as it is not, primarily an institution among any number of other modern institutions. The Church is a living body; continuously active, continuously performing Christ in the myriad contexts within which it operates. It comprises those conformed to Christ in the past, being conformed to Christ in the present and who will be conformed to Christ in the future. As such, it is a body open to extension as all things are brought in subjection to Christ. The open-endedness of the Christian community is emphasized in the gathering around the Eucharistic elements, the distribution that proclaims that though we are many we *are* one body and the final sending out into the world. For that is where we live and make our own proclamation of the gospel – in the world. The answer then to the question 'from what position does the theologian speak?' is that the theologian stands at the western door of the Church, looking back at the baptismal font and beyond that the east-facing altar and, simultaneously looking out across the city where the work of Christ is to be undertaken.

The world is not an alien place, even in the depths of its godlessness (and modern secularity is only the most recent form such godlessness can take); for it is the particular and material place of our human abiding. It is here where, to cite an old advertisement for Mars bars, we work, rest and play. We may belong to a kingdom that has not yet fully come, a kingdom realized in heavenly places, but while we live we are sown into the very fabric of social existence as it is governed and manifests itself in this particular locale. We are on electoral rolls, we vote, we invest, we have payroll numbers and national insurance numbers; we have passports, medical cards, library cards, even clubcards; we are enrolled on this course; we are members of this gym, that union, this political party, that society of friends. We participate profoundly, without belonging.

This is essential to grasp if we are to understand apologetics as a form of 'culture critique' (I will return to that idea in a moment, because it has a specific provenance). There is a form of apologetics that wishes to find ways of accommodating Christian truths with aspects of secular culture. This apologetics was made famous by theologians like Paul Tillich and has been called 'correlational', because it wishes to co-relate the universal truth of Christian theology with the contingent truths expressed in certain cultural forms. So if Christianity questions the ultimate ground of our being, then there are more contemporary cultural forms which are also attempting to grasp a similar truth: Jean-Paul Sartre's classic, *Nausea*, for example, or Alejandro Gonzálaz Iñárritu's film *21 Grams*. Let me say now that I am not advocating a correlationist apologetics and there are at least three reasons why. First, in seeking similarities, it cannot articulate adequately the differences between, in short, Christ and culture. It cannot take up the position of the other voice that is so necessary for critical distance and genuine questioning. Second, the levelling of truth claims with respect to Christ and culture means that the space for transformation or conversion of the social and the cultural, and that is what the gospel is concerned with, is severely limited. The ongoing work of apologetics might suggest certain amendments to Christian theology; it cannot, however, tear up theology's own constitution and require a radical rethink of priorities. Third, and most importantly, the sovereignty of God cannot be compromised – even for the best of human reasons like tolerance, an ongoing conversation between Christ and the world or the continuing relevance of theology in a secular landscape.

To return then to what I mean by our participating in the world but not belonging to it. While the interwovenness of our lives with our cultural and historical contexts cannot be overleapt, as Paul wrote: 'Our lives are hid with Christ in God.' Put in metaphysical terms, existentially we participate fully in the world, but ontologically we live 'in Christ'. *En Christo*, as a dative of location, is a favourite Pauline phrase. As such our apologetics can be critical, for they articulate God's Word within human words – a Word that can never be reduced to human words since it is in response to that Word from which all our language arises. Without this theological difference, our cultural critique would lack prophetic bite; it would be only one more exercise in cultural criticism of the kind sociology or critical theory provide. Indeed the notion of cultural critique arose among social theorists, most famously those associated with the Frankfurt School, Theodor Adorno and Max Horkheimer. Theologians like myself are only borrowing the term, and some of the tools honed in the methodology informing its practice, when we engage in cultural hermeneutics from a Christian theological perspective. The borrowing is important, as I will go on to demonstrate.

Right now there is a more pressing need to understand that our immersion in the world requires reflective analysis if we are critically to engage the cultures that contextualize us. We can call this reflective analysis
'cultural hermeneutics' because our cultures are composed of systems of
interpretable signs, gestures and behaviours, and what we are involved
in is a process of understanding them. On a very basic level, ordinary
living requires us constantly to interpret the world. We wouldn't be able
to cross the road, drive a car, order a beer or recognize when someone
is attracted to us if we were not continually reading the signs around
us, and acting accordingly. These signs and how to interpret them are
culturally and historically specific. I have learnt what a mouse is with
respect to a computer; and I have learnt how to use one. I know what
the piece of plastic issued by my bank means for paying bills and getting
cash from cash-machines; and I understand the difference between a card
that says 'Debit' on it and a card that says 'Credit' on it. None of these
signs and how to interpret and employ them technically was available
to the Victorians. But then if I order 'porter' at my local hostelry, as
the Victorians could, I would be given blank looks – for the sign can no
longer be interpreted. As human beings we create and manipulate signs
and, through practice, learn both what these signs mean and how to
behave accordingly. We are, then, as human beings, cultural hermeneuts –
those who have to interpret the furniture of our environments. The better
our learning skills and the more accurate our interpretation, the better
we can adapt in ways that take advantage of the knowledge gained. I remember 13 years ago sitting next to a director of the computer firm IBM
at a dinner. He told me then what at that time seemed unbelievable –
that very soon there would be another class of poverty altogether; the
technically impoverished, who had no access to the Internet or a mobile
phone. Cultural hermeneutics, then, as I am employing the term, is only
a more complex and nuanced form of an activity that goes on at the
most basic survival levels in all animals. As the signs proliferate, as the
technologies for their proliferation and dissemination become ever more
pervasive and sophisticated, so a conflict among interpretations becomes
inevitable. Take as an example, that system of signs which had developed concerning vampires. Vampires are everywhere today – in books,
in films, in interactive media, record albums, online games, etc. As a system they began to emerge in the late eighteenth and early nineteenth
century. Given that, as far as I am aware, no one believes vampires exist
as creatures of this world, why do they appeal to our imaginations? The
cultural analyst is involved in trying to answer that question; trying to
understand what they are signs of such that, at times, they become more

or less popular. It might be suggested that the vampire is/was a figure for nascent capitalism (they are frequently very wealthy) or a bourgeois critique of aristocratic privilege and feudal politics (vampires frequently refer to their noble roots) or symbols of a desire to be immortal, remain young for ever and remain beautiful for ever (vampires recently are good-looking twenty-somethings) or perhaps they are characteristic of a new cultural ideal in which a highly charged eroticism is combined with a bar against sex (and so they appeal to anorexic teenagers) or maybe they signify a need for control and supernatural strength (and so one of the most popular vampiric scenarios involves leather-clad women). It may well be that the vampire is a sign bearing very different values in one age than in another: that Coleridge's Christabel, Bram Stoker's Dracula and the vampires in the novels of Anne Rice and Stephenie Meyer invoke quite distinct responses – because their appeal, and ability to be employed effectively in various forms of fiction, changes over time. But cultural analysts (and literary criticism is one form of cultural analysis) will argue with each other in attempts to understand a certain set of related cultural phenomena and how it relates to the society who, in employing and consuming them, finds significance in them.

We need to ask: what are cultural analysts doing when they engage in such interpretative practices? Well, they are attempting to understand the cultural context, the kind of societies that produce (and reproduce) these systems of signs and the relationship between cultural expressions and social relations. Put simply, such interpretative practices tend towards one of two objectives (though sometimes both objectives are the goal of the analysis). The first practice examines certain semiotic systems that would suggest all is well in the social body or systems that could well suggest an underlying malaise that might be corrected. The sight of young teenagers drunk and about town late at night is an indication, for example, that things are failing in the social body. Though where that failure lies will take more analyses, the results of which may not go uncontested. In this first kind of practice, cultural hermeneutics function like biopsies: they are testing beneath the surface of the social skin to see what the prevailing conditions are and, in offering a diagnosis, suggest a prognosis as well. The second practice of cultural hermeneutics, particularly practices that arose in the light of the work of Marx and Engels, is concerned with accessing and assessing social ills that result from certain ideologies, or levels of false consciousness, such that what appears to be benign is in fact an elaborate veil masking more profound oppressions and exploitations. Adorno wrote a famous piece of cultural hermeneutics along these lines, looking at horoscopes in Los Angeles newspapers, for example.[2] He was exploring the role the cultural industry has on social relations, and, in doing so, demonstrating that culture and society do not operate as separate and autonomous realms; they impact upon each other profoundly. Advertisements that play upon the glamour and allure of certain alcoholic drinks, and are targeted at certain audiences, are intent upon changing patterns of social behaviour within those targeted groups. The first interpretative practice collects empirical data and works on the statistics; the second examines phenomena and examines the ideas expressed within them. Marx, in *Capital,* did both: he worked with a theory of money, class, labour and its alienation from what it produced (developing notions such as fetishism) and he also treated *in minutiae* the prices of goods and the wages of those who laboured to produce them. Both practices, put in psychoanalytical terms, are explorations of the social unconscious or what I have termed the 'cultural imaginary'. Where 'imaginary' is a psychoanalytical term concerning the magma of images that composed what can be imagined as a possibility within any given culture – the stuff, if you like, of collective, social dreams.

As should now be evident, just as our contemporary society is diverse and complex, so too are the cultural signs, gestures and behaviours it gives expression to. No one can examine all the signs. In the plethora of signs that any society produces and reproduces, some sets of signs become more important than others for determining the character of that society. In the same way, as theologians, when we examine the history of Christian teaching in any given period some doctrines become the focus for more analysis and controversy than others. Pre World War Two Western theology was much taken on understanding the Eucharist; in the post World War Two context, the suffering Christ drew much attention, then the social dynamics of the Trinity and, most recently, critical analysis has turned to religion and politics, the role of the messianic, eschatology and the apocalyptic. Each of these emphases points to the character of a society as a collective body (its ideals, its hopes, its aspirations, its fears, etc.) and what it deems significant. To go back to what I said above, what is under the critical microscope is 'the society who, in employing and consuming them [these systems of signs], finds significance in them'. Hence, in my example above of vampires, I was not choosing a system of signs at random – as a cultural phenomenon vampires demonstrate their social significance because of the popularity

2 Theodor W. Adorno, 'The Stars Down to Earth: The *Los Angeles Times* Astrology Column', in *The Stars Down to Earth and Other Essays on the Irrational in Culture,* ed. by Stephen Crooks (London: Routledge, 2002), pp. 46–171.

they can elicit. It is their very popularity that draws the attention of the cultural analyst to them.

Let's get back to theology and apologetics. As human beings we are immersed in the social and the cultural, but we are also advised by none other than Jesus himself to understand our societies and cultures. Matthew 16.1–4:

> And the Pharisees and Sadduccees came, and to test Jesus they asked him to show them a sign from heaven. He answered them, 'When it is evening, you say, "It will be fair weather: for the sky is red." And in the morning, "It will be stormy today, for the sky is red and threatening." You know how to interpret the appearance of the sky, but you cannot interpret the signs of the times. An evil and adulterous generation asks for a sign, but no sign shall be given to it except the sign of Jonah.'

There are a couple of relevant observations we can make of this passage. First, there seems to be a difference between Jesus and the Pharisees and Sadduccees; a difference issuing from the fact that the Pharisees and Sadduccees are not being honest. They are seeking to test him in a similar way to the Devil's second temptation of Jesus in the wilderness when he transported him to the pinnacle of the Temple: 'If you are the son of God, throw yourself down . . .' (Matthew 4.6). The sign they seek, as Jesus pointed out to the Devil in that earlier situation, is actually attempting to tempt God. They use the word 'sign' but really they mean 'offer us proof'. A demonstration of proof is not a sign; though their need for such a proof is itself a sign of an inability to believe the God they serve – a symptom of a perversity with respect to the divine, which does not offer itself as part of the finite furniture of the world (except in Christ). As Jesus reminds them with reference to the weather, a sign is more oblique than a proof; from the token x (a red sky at night), an inference can be drawn: 'It will be fair.' But the inference is indirect because the sign might be misread. I recall travelling to northern Israel in the early 1980s and arriving at kibbutz Tal. On hearing explosions I asked the receptionist what rock was being mined in the vicinity, only to be told that what I was hearing was the war on the Golan Heights and the use of explosives! The inference I had drawn from what I heard, but had not seen, was wrong. That is the risk that every interpreter of signs understands: a sign is not a proof of anything. Having given the Pharisees and Sadduccees a quick lesson in a science now called semiotics, from the Greek for 'sign', Jesus moves on to the need to 'interpret the signs of the times'. The work God was doing in the world through Christ was at that time evident if these people could read the signs. After all, they were the same signs the disciples of John the Baptist presumably reported back to the prophet when he sent his disciples to Jesus with the question:

> 'Are you the one who is to come, or are we to wait for another?' Jesus answered them, 'Go and tell John what you hear and see: the blind receive their sight, and the lame walk, lepers are cleansed, the deaf hear, the dead are raised, and the poor have good news brought to them.' (Matt. 11.2–5)

For John, and hopefully his disciples, that was enough; not so the Pharisees and Sadducees.

The operations of God within the world continue, through the work of Christ's Spirit, and the Church must continually strain to understand the signs of this working amid the signs of the work of godlessness: like discerning the wheat from the tares. The Christian, then, as a theologian has to take what is a very human condition – we are as creatures not only makers but interpreters of signs – one step further in discerning the theological issues that these signs point towards. This is especially so at the moment; for Western culture is undergoing something of a sea change with respect to religion. The contemporary scene is saturated with religion to the extent that former champions of the secularization thesis – like Peter Berger – are admitting that the sociologists got it wrong. The secularization process is reversing as a new visibility of religion sweeps through the public realm.[3] In a contemporary situation in which Gnostic mythologies of good versus evil, vampires, werewolves, zombies, angels and magicians abound; where advertising is referring to religious themes; where films wish to explore issues such as the afterlife, the messianic and the apocalyptic; where there is not one single newspaper that is not reporting daily on events involving religion; and where religious events like the death of Pope John Paul II elicit far, far more attention than could possibly have been anticipated, then it is even more incumbent upon Christian theologians, in the development of their apologetics, to examine critically the world in which they are immersed. The gospel is not an archive in the past, but an operation across past, present and future. To preach the gospel now (which is at the forefront of the apologetic task, for *apologia* spearheads evangelism) demands good readings of the signs of these times.

---

3 See Michael Hoelzl and Graham Ward (eds), *The New Visibility of Religion* (London: Continuum, 2008).

How are good readings of our cultural situation best facilitated? Having outlined what cultural hermeneutics is and its theological significance for apologetics, we need to turn to the very practical aspects of interpretative engagement. As I said above, there are a lot of signs out there. Which ones require a Christian theological examination and how do we best undertake that examination? We can gain some advice here from the practice of those early apologists faced with a pagan Hellenized culture antithetical to the gospel – figures such as Justin Martyr, Tertullian and Irenaeus. Two steps are evident in their tactics: they courteously present their adversaries with detailed readings of their own work, while exposing the heresy announced with respect to Christian teaching; then they correct their teachings while also learning from and adopting some of their ideas. There is a rule of thumb: for the theological critique to be heard by or even be acceptable to a secular audience then certain expertises need to be acquired. If the cultural phenomenon being examined is film, then Christians need to learn how someone in film studies would read film; if it is a book or a set of books, then the expertise drawn upon would come from the field of literary studies, etc. The critical examination of cultural trends requires learning how the secular critical theorists might approach such an examination themselves: whether that trend is political, economic, social, media-related, etc. These critical theorists can provide a toolkit for the apologist – recognized by the professionals, if you like.[4]

Let us take one example from social theory. One of the 'tools' I have found particularly helpful in understanding the nature of the Church with respect to other sites in a city is Michel Foucault's notion of 'heterotopia'.[5] In thinking about cityscapes, Foucault draws attention to those places that are marginalized or 'othered' in some way with respect to the more official and public sites. We might think of a cemetery or a fairground, for example. What Foucault examines is how behaviour changes in these places because they are not surveillanced in the same way. By 'surveillance' Foucault is not referring to the use of CCTV but the internalized surveillancing that fashions each subject into a citizen of the city: the dos and don'ts of a legally bound society. Heterotopias are spaces where different forms of behaviour manifest themselves rather than the forms of behaviour that pertain to living with others in civil society more generally. And these behaviours express different ways of relating to

---

4 For a resource you might look at Graham Ward, *Theology and Contemporary Critical Theory*, second edition (Basingstoke: Macmillan, 2000).

5 See Michel Foucault, 'Des espaces autres', in *Architecture, Mouvement, Continuité*, No. 5 (October, 1984), pp. 46–9; an English translation is available on the Internet.

space. These relations can be illicit (like those involved in 'cottaging') or border on the illicit (like those involved in the chance meeting of someone in the heady party atmosphere of a fairground) or be more personal and intimate (like visiting a grave in a cemetery). Relations in these spaces tend towards being more intensive, even if only temporarily. One might then take the analytical tool that Foucault has forged and develop a notion of the parish or cathedral church with respect to the more public topography that surrounds it; examining the behaviours and relations such spaces foster; examining what it might mean existentially to cross a threshold into a 'heterotopia'. Such examinations might then develop into a theology of the sacred place, which would distinguish both the use and nature of that place from the more public institutions like a library or a school. And so an ecclesiology begins to emerge that points, on the one hand, to the way the church belongs to a specific location while, on the other hand, transcending that location by being 'other'. Such an ecclesiology can then be used apologetically with respect to conversations with local councils or shopping malls or residential units or hospitals. It may facilitate a better theological understanding of the local church as different; itself an incarnation in the very contingencies of material reality of the divine.

Other interpretative tools might include Marx's analysis of reification with respect to goods, the cost of their manufacture and the price paid for them.[6] This can be employed to understand an aspect of the contemporary market where the object being sold disappears beneath a label 'Starbucks', 'Nike', 'Diesel'. The money paid for the object is divorced from what either the object is or how much it cost to produce; it is the 'label' that is being bought. Taken one step further, this can become part of a theological analysis, and apologetic, of current idolatries and how they are fashioned by the market.

The tools are a means for reading an object, a situation, an event; and they are only useful to the extent that they evoke a critical understanding not immediately evident in a surface description of the object, situation or event. They aid the production of new insights. I do not have to be committed to Foucault's plastic understanding of the subject – who can be bent in any direction given some hegemonic apparatus that enables the bending – or be a Marxist to use the tools. Reading is a practice; good reading is a highly sophisticated practice. The practice has to be learnt. I have heard from students who spent three years studying literature that the most valuable skill they acquired over that time was the ability to

---

6 See Karl Marx, *Capital* I, Book 1, tr. Ben Fowles (Harmondsworth: Penguin, 1976).

read well and pay attention to detail. The attention to detail is a mark of courtesy in the reader. If Christian apologetics is to 'speak' to the culture they are addressing, then without the in-depth reading of the culture they will not be effective; people won't listen because the apologetics is not helping them to understand something about that culture that they have not seen before; the apologetics is not helping them to understand the lives, values, activities that socially embed them in a specific cultural terrain. Apologetics, viewed in this way, assists the gospel in setting people free – from false desires, assumed needs, bewitching ideas, unreflected habits and substitutions for the real objects of their longing – to worship God and recognize the true orientation of the human heart towards such worship. As I said earlier, apologetics spearheads evangelism; and it begins with reading the 'signs of the times'.

9

Moments and Themes in the History of Apologetics

RICHARD CONRAD OP

A good way to learn Christian apologetics is by studying its history. Richard Conrad draws lessons for contemporary Christians from a survey of apologetics from the times of the apostles to the end of the twentieth century. He puts the emphasis on charity and a thorough knowledge of the faith. We encounter a succession of creative preachers and teachers who sought to find clear and imaginative language for their message, and often wrote theology of the first importance in the process. At the heart of their project was a desire to engage both the intellect and the desires of their hearers: the Christian faith makes sense of the world, and God answers the deepest needs of the human heart. **A.D.**

Rather than providing an analysis of apologetic techniques through the ages, I intend this chapter as a pointer to certain defining moments, and to certain figures worth watching, from which we can draw some lessons – and some warnings. I shall touch briefly on contemporary challenges and opportunities so as to show how the history of apologetics may teach us now; other chapters in this collection will explore current demands in greater depth.

I understand apologetics in a fairly wide sense, as the whole business of *explaining* the Christian faith *attractively*, in a way that engages *respectfully* with people's insights and instincts, that welcomes *home* all that is valid in them, but also *challenges* them as appropriate. It is not 'apologizing' for the Faith in the modern sense of apologizing; we should not be afraid to proclaim the beauty of God and the fullness of life God offers, the wisdom by which he meets our deepest needs. Apologetics is more proactive than merely *defending* the Faith. It should not be too rigidly distinguished from preaching, teaching, debating, broadcasting, writing and so on.

Pentecost

I see Pentecost as the great defining moment of apologetics. One of the readings for Pentecost in the Anglican Lectionary and for the Vigil of that Feast in the Roman Lectionary is the story of Babel from Genesis 11, telling of how human pride led to the break-up of the race into language groups that could not communicate with each other. We are encouraged to see Pentecost as Babel overcome. But the Holy Spirit does not 'put the clock back', abolishing human history as if it could not be redeemed. The Spirit does not suppress the different languages, with the richness of cultures and traditions they have served to express. Rather, the Spirit makes it possible to speak one truth in the many human languages. The Spirit incorporates the contributions of all humanity into a Catholic unity, while purifying what needs to be corrected and enlarging what is narrow.

Many depictions of Pentecost, both Eastern and Western, show Mary the Mother of Jesus at the heart of the infant Church (following Acts 1.14). Mary, who pondered the strange things that happened and cherished them in her heart (Luke 2.19, 51), stands for contemplative love. In the Roman Catholic Church, the Patron of the Missions is St Thérèse of Lisieux – an enclosed nun. She understood that without contemplative love at the heart of the Church, everything else would dry up. Her vocation was this: 'In the heart of the Church, I will be love.' If our apologetics is to express and to effect conviction, it must be nourished by the love of Christ, whose words, deeds and sufferings we ponder in liturgy, Scripture and personal prayer. This love, crafted by the Holy Spirit, must overflow into love and prayer for those to whom we preach.

One fresco of Pentecost, the one in the Spanish Chapel attached to Santa Maria Novella in Florence, shows Saint Peter standing over the infant Church, representing pastoral authority. But he is shown to one side, while Mary is central, for as Hans Urs von Balthasar was to point out six centuries later, the ministries of authority and preaching last throughout time, but contemplative love throughout eternity. In his first letter (3.15–16), Peter gives us a charter for our apologetics:

Always be ready to make your defence to anyone who demands from you an accounting for the hope that is in you; yet do it with gentleness and reverence. Keep your conscience clear, so that, when you are maligned, those who abuse you for your good conduct in Christ may be put to shame.

Our love for those to whom we speak must clothe itself in the flesh of gentleness and respect; our lives must not give scandal.

Our readiness to make a defence must not become neurotic and over-anxious; Jesus promises that the Holy Spirit will give us words to say when we are put on the spot (Matt. 10.19–20). Friendship with Christ in the Spirit will make our words more personally effective than a rhetorical skill or even a theological expertise that is without heart.

Likewise, the careful avoidance of 'notorious sins', the ones that cause scandal, cannot mean that we pretend to preach from a position of moral superiority. It is not given *us* to be free from all sin (see 1 John 1.8). We are more like the old-fashioned tramps who would leave a special mark on a gatepost to tell other tramps where a soft touch lived.[1] We preach to others the mercy we need for ourselves.

In his speeches on the day of Pentecost and subsequently (Acts 2.14–40; 3.12–26), Peter gave a lead in how to present Christian truth, and practised what he later advised. He deployed logical arguments; he appealed to details of what had happened, which he had witnessed or heard about, and whose meaning he had begun to recognize more deeply. He engaged with the hopes and speculations of his audience (all, or mostly, Jews, though in many cases pilgrims to Jerusalem from the Diaspora) by referring to their history, the prophecies they cherished, the promises they wanted fulfilled. He issued a challenge and a call to repentance: '. . . you crucified and killed by the hands of those outside the law . . .' Peter's words hit home: 'they were cut to the heart'. Yet – perhaps thinking of his own denial of Jesus – he could also say: 'I know that you acted in ignorance, as did also your rulers.'

It was not simply Peter's words that helped the gospel spread so rapidly, even though, as spoken in the Spirit, they had great force. The Lord confirmed the word by miracles he wrought. And he alone could penetrate the hearts of Peter's hearers. Hence the Pentecost event and its continuation is an answer to devoted prayer (Acts 1.14) – though it is the Spirit who draws us to pray in the first place, and our prayer is effective as a participation in the prayer Jesus made with uplifted hands on the Cross.

Notice, too, that in delivering the message he had to offer, Peter was enabled to 'do theology'. His speeches are a significant witness to the 'primitive'[2] Christology and soteriology of the early Church, and it was no doubt on the spur of the moment (better: under the guidance of the Holy Spirit in accordance with Jesus' promise) that Peter found himself

---

1 This is explored further by Simon Tugwell OP, in *The Way of the Preacher* (London: Darton, Longman and Todd, 1979), Chapter 7 and Appendices 5 and 6.
2 'Springboard' would be a better term.

creatively bringing together the Jewish hopes and thought-forms with which he was familiar, Jesus' strange words and gestures he had witnessed, and the recent world-shaking events.

Acts shows Pentecost perpetuated. When the Spirit brings Saint Philip and the Ethiopian eunuch together (8.26–39), the offer fits the moment. When Peter speaks to Cornelius (chapter 10) it is clear that the Spirit has got there first. At Antioch (13.14–43) Saint Paul engages with the hopes of his audience; at Athens (17.16–34) he engages with the religiosity of the people, but challenges its limitations and impurities. The fresco in the Spanish Chapel shows a Crimean Tartar knocking on the Church's door – Pentecost was continuing in the 1360s when the fresco was produced and the missionaries reached the Crimea.

Justin Martyr

Let us jump ahead a century or so to the best-known of 'the Apologists', Justin Martyr. He wrote two *Apologies,* and the *Dialogue with Trypho the Jew.* Justin seeks to meet his audience on common ground. To the pagans he recounts his search for a philosophy, a search they would have respected, and he speaks with gratitude of the Platonic tradition, which in his own century was beginning to 're-group', let us say, after the rather pick-and-mix approach that had led Saint Paul to be rude about 'philosophy'. Justin is happy to think of the Logos speaking in respected pagan thinkers of the past such as Heraclitus and Socrates. With his Jewish interlocutor, Justin shares a great respect for figures like Moses, and for the Old Testament text; he offers an account of the text's strange ways of speaking – a Christian account that explains what might otherwise seem inexplicable, such as Genesis 19.24, where 'the Lord rained . . . sulphur and fire from the Lord out of heaven'.

Justin takes trouble to *explain* Christian faith and liturgy to the pagans, who would only have known of the Church's beliefs and practices by garbled hearsay. In the course of his work he is able to do theology, to contribute to the development of the doctrine of the Holy Trinity by adapting a Platonic 'model' – for all that that model would have to be significantly reworked over the next couple of centuries.

Clement of Alexandria

In the next century Clement of Alexandria produced his *Protreptikos*, his 'appeal to the Greeks'. His very role as head of the Catechetical School in Alexandria was in itself an act of witness, since that school was very roughly equivalent to a modern Catholic university and as such was a declaration that the Christian faith is academically respectable and can hold its own in fruitful dialogue with the intellectual currents of the day. Clearly Clement shared a 'project' with many people of his day, a concern for truth. Indeed, his *Protreptikos* implicitly allies itself *with* contemporary currents of thought, for although it rubbishes the pagan myths, it stands with that tradition in Greek philosophy that was wary of attributing anything unworthy to the divine.

Clement, however, does not merely ally himself with the academics of his day, nor rely merely on an attractive style. He engages as tactfully as he knows how with the mentality and needs of his potential audience in its variety. While rubbishing the widely popular pagan myths, he borrows their motifs. Instead of a mythical Orpheus, Clement presents Christ as the truly existing divine Word, who sang the world into being, who has become flesh to be our Teacher, and who invites us to join in his New Song. In place of the stories of occasional heroes who became 'divine', Clement offers to everyone a real hope and sure means of truly becoming divine by journeying in Christ to communion with the authentic God. This hope, while more sure, is also more demanding, requiring as it does a 'moral apprenticeship'.

Athanasius

Moving forward another century, but remaining in Alexandria, we find Saint Athanasius writing two apologetic works before the Arian crisis occupied his energies: *Contra Gentes* and *de Incarnatione*. He, too, rubbishes the pagan myths – and by doing so stands *with* a pagan philosophical tradition that also set itself *against* nonsense. Athanasius engages with the current speculations on the origin of the cosmos, and offers a more coherent account of 'life, the universe and everything'. He takes care to explain Christian doctrine. He offers a hope of redemption: he shows people how the incarnate Logos restores us to being *logikoi* (rational beings), though this offer of being restored to our right minds is clearly also a challenge; likewise Athanasius shows those afraid of death how in making us truly divine the Logos offers immortality. And in doing so he does theology – for though the development of his Trinitarian thought was provoked by the Arian crisis, his *de Incarnatione* represents a quite agile and 'multi-valent' account of redemption.

Augustine of Hippo

One of Saint Augustine's most 'apologetic' works is his *City of God*. This is basically 'revisionist history'. After the Sack of Rome in 410, pagans had been saying, in effect, 'This wet and wimpish Eastern Christianity has sapped the classical moral fibre of the Roman Empire (not to mention introducing sacred writings that are in bad Latin and don't obey the conventions of proper Latin poetry). That is why we have begun to fall to the Barbarians.' Augustine refutes this by showing how the Empire was too much the city of this world, marred by pride and ruthless ambition; the classical 'gods' tended to promote depravity. But besides demanding a conversion, he engages with people's deepest longings, showing how even while waging war they long for peace (Book XIX); he ends with an attractive vision of celestial peace. On the way he also engages in a critical but respectful way with the widely valued (neo-) Platonism. The *City of God* at least raises the question of how the Christian people, on pilgrimage to a city built by God, should relate to civic life.

Although they might not be labelled 'apologetics', it is worth considering Augustine's polemical works against Manichees, Donatists and Pelagians: he offers a better answer to the problem of evil than the Manichees (and thereby does some original philosophy and theology); he insists on fraternal concern – and correction – for the Donatists, even when they will not regard Catholics as brethren. He certainly does theology in his anti-Pelagian writings, wrestling with intractable issues of grace and free will; according to R. H. Markus he also makes the Church more able to include sympathetically those who find it difficult to overcome their moral weaknesses.[3]

Augustine's *De Trinitate*, I think, continues his own 'personal research project', which he began with *The Confessions*. He was fascinated by how we can journey by love towards the knowledge of God, even though we cannot love something we do not already, somehow, know. It turns out that, in a way, we have an *inbuilt* sense of God even before we are consciously aware of it – to be precise, an inbuilt sense of the *Trinitarian* God in whose image we are made. Books I—VII of *De Trinitate* constitute an apology against Arians, one that takes logical, theological and scriptural problems seriously and builds important theological developments on the achievements of earlier theologians such as the Cappadocian

---

3 R. H. Markus, *The End of Ancient Christianity* (Cambridge: Cambridge University Press, 1990), Chapters 4 and 5.

Fathers.[4] The remainder of *De Trinitate* is an implicit apology against
the Neoplatonists by showing how, as one moves 'higher' in the human
psyche, one approaches an irreducible, yet coequal, *trinity* (the action
of our memory, intellect and will), not a mere monad; hence our mental
constitution points us to the Christian *Tri*-Unity and not the Neoplatonic
One. At the same time, by exploring the way in which the image of the
Holy Trinity has been corrupted by the sin of pride, Augustine invites
the Neoplatonists to abandon their attempt at a self-sufficient ascent to
the One, and to submit to a saving economy involving the Word's incarnation and passion, Scripture and sacraments. The apologetic implications of *De Trinitate* are wider, and perennial. Only in the light of Christ
can we really understand *ourselves* – how we are made in the image of the
Holy Trinity, and will be restless until we rest in the Holy Trinity.

Cyril and Methodius

If we now jump ahead to the ninth century, we can briefly consider
the work of Saints Cyril and Methodius, missionaries to the Slavs.
Earlier centuries were marked, on the whole, by a policy of 'inculturation', in which the Church and her liturgy crystallized in various Latin,
Greek, Aramaic, Armenian and other forms. Although on occasion it
was necessary to set herself against pagan institutions,[5] the Church
preferred, when it was safe to do so, to Christianize existing times and
places of worship.[6] In line with this policy, Cyril and Methodius sought
to provide the Slavs with not only a Slavonic Bible but also a Slavonic
liturgy. However, in this they were opposed (even persecuted) by German missionaries wishing to impose a Latin Liturgy on the Slavs –
despite the fact that Methodius had papal support for the Slavonic
mission.[7]

---

4 These developments include glimpsing the Holy Spirit as the Divine Love in Person,
and the recognition that not only the human power to know, but also the human power to
love, are part of our being in God's image.

5 For example, Saint Boniface cut down a sacred tree to show that the 'gods' could not
wreak vengeance on him.

6 The developed rite for consecrating a church was in effect a rite for 'Christening' a
pagan building – the building was itself 'baptized' and chrismated, and even taught to read
Scripture and tradition by having the Greek and Latin alphabets traced in ash on its floor.

7 He and Cyril went to Rome to obtain papal support (armed with the 'bribe' of Saint
Clement's relics), and Methodius returned to the mission after Cyril had died – being buried
with great pomp in San Clemente.

Dominic and Diego of Osma

Early in the thirteenth century, Saint Dominic and his bishop, Diego of Osma, saw the need for a preaching mission in the area of Toulouse. In those days most priests were not trained to preach, and there was a dearth of real Christian formation. As a result, many people had lapsed into what was effectively a form of Manichaean dualism. The problem was compounded by disillusionment with the Christian leadership: for some time there had been a widespread desire for 'evangelical poverty', but the Church had failed to harness it, and the Cistercian abbots, who were preaching in the Languedoc, went on horseback with retinues. With the support of the local Bishop Fulk, Diego and Dominic established a mission marked by poverty and mendicancy. Later, probably at the instigation of Pope Innocent III, Dominic made his band of friars a worldwide religious order. By approving the Franciscan and Dominican mendicant friars, Innocent captured the mood and the need of the moment. Dominic and his followers (notably Saint Thomas Aquinas, a 'third-generation' Dominican) validated the ongoing developments in civic, cultural and intellectual life even more explicitly than Saint Francis. They set themselves to oppose the Manichaean rejection of the goodness of creation, the body and marriage. Nevertheless, with his insistence on poverty, Dominic showed sympathy with the heretics' valid concerns. The reasons for the success of his mission[8] include his personal integrity and attractiveness, exemplified by his patience with the innkeeper with whom he and Diego lodged: he stayed up all night persuading the innkeeper into the Catholic Church.[9] Dominic was also renowned for his intense and prolonged personal prayer for the conversion of sinners.

Thomas Aquinas

Saint Thomas Aquinas, then, may serve as another example of respectful apologetics. His context includes the cultural and intellectual exchanges among Jews, Christians and Muslims; he quotes Jewish and Muslim authorities with respect, and *stands with* many of them in defending the value of Aristotelian natural philosophy and psychology against Christian 'fundamentalists', who did not want Aristotle studied or discussed.

---

8 The unattractive violent assault on heresy in the thirteenth century was of course a factor in the destruction of Catharism. But many people were genuinely converted by sincere preaching in those decades.

9 Hence I like to claim that my Order was founded in a pub.

In those days teaching methods included the *lectura* (reading and commenting on the great texts, notably Scripture), but also the 'disputed question' in which the class were required to offer arguments for both sides of an issue. Aquinas adopted the disputed-question format for his *Summa Theologiae*, indicating the intention to take both sides of each issue seriously, to see truth wherever it is to be found, and to respect the limitations and methods appropriate to each particular, precise question that may be asked. Obviously, Aquinas also wants us to take the right answers very seriously.[10] All the same, in the course of his *Summa Theologiae*, Aquinas was only rude twice.[11]

That *Summa* was in effect a first degree in theology. The earlier *Summa contra Gentiles* (which was not set up as a disputation) was more explicitly apologetic. Nevertheless, the first three of its four books covered issues discussed among Jews, Christians and Muslims (such as natural theology, creation, miracles, providence, the vision of God), where positions did not always divide along 'denominational lines'.[12] Having established a common area of discourse where 'denominational loyalties' did not predetermine people's conclusions, Thomas devoted the final book to specifically Christian teaching.

A lot of Aquinas' ethics is 'natural law morality', which draws on pagan as well as Christian sources. He defended the value, for Christians, of familial and societal relationships, and showed how the God-given virtues (not merely the Aristotelian, 'acquired' virtues) could 'take flesh' in the whole fabric of civic and academic life. He admits that Christians can be good citizens of non-Christian states, combining with people with whom they do not share a faith in projects to make life more human.

Aquinas' (largely neglected) teaching on the seven gifts of the Holy Spirit[13] sees them as ways in which the Holy Spirit makes us receptive to his guidance, attuned to his 'instincts'. The gift of knowledge, in particular,

---

10 His method tends to obscure the fact that the answer he gives is sometimes 'both . . . and . . .' The fact that he sometimes changed his mind is also not very obvious from his method – nor is it often recognized!

11 Towards David of Dinant who 'most foolishly thought that prime matter was God', and towards the Greeks who would not recognize the equivalence of 'from the Father and the Son' and 'from the Father through the Son'.

12 Such as the question whether God could delegate some work of creation to an angel (Aquinas says absolutely not), and whether in heaven we shall know the essence of God (against his own teacher, Saint Albert the Great, Thomas says yes). I am minded of how, by the end of the sixteenth century, similar positions on such issues as predestination, and how grace relates to freedom, could be found in different denominations.

13 Listed as seven in the Greek and Latin versions of Isaiah 11.2–3, and invoked in the Rite of Confirmation.

corresponds to Jesus' promise that the Holy Spirit will give us what to say when we have to make a defence of our Christian faith.

The Missionary Expansion of the Sixteenth and Seventeenth Centuries

The missionary expansion of the sixteenth and seventeenth centuries provides us with some lessons. The spread of Christianity into Eastern Asia was, sadly, probably hindered by the Dominicans opposing the Jesuit project of inculturation in China. Perhaps we acquitted ourselves better in the Americas by opposing mass baptisms of the barely instructed, let alone forced baptisms, and by preaching against the bad example set by the Conquistadores. Some good came out of the tragedies: reflection on the natural rights of the indigenous populations prompted people like Bartolomé de las Casas and Francisco de Vitoria to develop the modern theory of human rights in its embryonic form.

Henri de Lubac

I should like to mention three out of many twentieth-century figures who suggest ways of appropriating the apologetic lessons of the past. Henri de Lubac urged the development of a truly *Catholic* vision, an awareness of how the Church must embrace all humanity, bringing *home* all valid human aspirations. He reviewed the history of reflection on our natural, inbuilt thirst for God and concluded that Catholic theologians had for some centuries played down this theme, instead positing a gulf between the natural and the supernatural.[14] They had pictured human nature as a self-contained whole, with such well-defined civic and philosophical goals as Aristotle had explored; God's offer of a higher, a divine, life, would then break in 'out of the blue'. De Lubac saw this as weakening our apologetics: if human nature really is a self-contained whole, capable of a meaningful contentment within the dimensions of this world, then God's offer *will not feel relevant* to modern people – they experience no need for God. Let us recover Augustine's sense that God has made us for himself; let us help our contemporaries see that their hearts must

---

14 They did this for sound reasons. In the late sixteenth century Michel de Bay of Louvain had put forward a theory that God was *obliged* to grace Adam and Eve. In reaction Catholic theologians denied that human nature had a really positive thirst for God; they feared that such a thirst would constrain God to give himself to us, and grace would cease to be *grace*.

135

remain restless until they rest in God. Left to itself, human nature is ill-defined and open-ended; only in the light of Christ can we make sense of ourselves.[15] This conviction that 'Christ reveals man to himself' was confirmed by Vatican II in *Gaudium et Spes*.[16]

How are we to convince our contemporaries that their hearts must remain restless until they rest in God? De Lubac explores the history of humankind's spiritual aspirations, and seeks to show that they always aim too high or too low; fallen humanity cannot get it right until God be born at Bethlehem.[17]

Karl Rahner

Karl Rahner emphasized the 'transcendent dimension' of the human being, urging us to recognize how the human spirit reaches beyond the limitations of time and space. In part, this was an attempt to engage with the self-perception of the modern, post-Kantian West.[18] Rahner developed the concept of the 'supernatural existential'; that is, *everyone* exists in a context of vocation to communion with God, experienced implicitly, or known by revelation more-or-less explicitly. Hence *everyone* who has reached the age of moral responsibility says an implicit or explicit 'yes' or 'no' to God in every significant moral choice. This somehow-experienced

---

15 De Lubac's first essay on the subject was *Surnaturel: Etudes historiques* (Paris: Aubier-Montaigne, 1946). This provoked the fear that he *obliged* God to bestow grace, for if God makes a *nature* that *really needs* him, can he consistently withhold himself? De Lubac returned to the subject in *Augustinianism & Modern Theology* (Paris: Aubier-Montaigne, 1965; English translation, London: Geoffrey Chapman, 1969) and *The Mystery of the Supernatural* (Paris: F. Aubier-Montaigne, 1965; English translation, London: Geoffrey Chapman, 1967). He reasserted that we do naturally have a real thirst for God, which paradoxically *does not exact* grace from him. Note that in his later *A Brief Catechesis on Nature and Grace* (Paris: Fayaid, 1980; English translation, San Francisco: Ignatius Press, 1984), De Lubac reaffirmed a *distinction* (not a gulf) between nature and grace.

16 See paragraph 22, which closely echoes what De Lubac said in his first book: 'By revealing the Father and by being revealed by him, Christ completes [*achève*] the revelation of man to himself.' *Catholicisme* (Paris: Cerf, 1938), p. 264. [English translation: *Catholicism* (San Francisco, CA: Ignatius Press, 1988), p. 339.]

17 De Lubac, *The Mystery of the Supernatural*, chapter 7.

18 I see this as very roughly analogous to the way the Church Fathers engaged respectfully with the Platonic tradition. In due course many 'Platonic' perspectives had to be corrected by an 'Aristotelian' openness to the realities of the cosmos. At the beginning of the twenty-first century, I should prefer to *correct* the self-perception of the modern, post-Cartesian, post-Kantian, individualistic West that – by contrast with Aquinas' 'Aristotelian' perspective – has lost touch with the animal and social components of the complex-yet-single human psyche, and cannot make so much sense of up-to-date science, nor of modern discoveries (and re-discoveries) in animal and human psychology.

attraction to God is part of human nature *as historically experienced*;[19] hence we can help people to see that if they say 'no' to God, they contradict a constituent of their nature and doom themselves to frustration.

I consider that Rahner complements what we saw earlier of Augustine. Augustine showed that the 'core' of the human psyche is made in the image of the Holy Trinity for communion with the Trinity. Rahner suggested that the human race *in its historicity* is made receptive to the self-communication of the Trinitarian God. If this suggestion can be developed, it might help us present the Christian revelation to an age that is more sensitive to history than even Augustine was.[20]

John Paul II

Pope John Paul II is known for his own 'missionary' journeys; also for a combination of confidence in the Catholic Faith on the one hand, and openness to dialogue with other churches and religions on the other – a combination many people found perplexing. His first encyclical *Redemptor Hominis* reversed the usual picture of 'human beings journeying to God' and presented a picture of 'God journeying to humanity'. The Pope urged the Church to get more caught up in this divine journey to meet each human being – aware that when we bring the Good News to anyone, we will find that the Word and the Spirit have got there first, to awaken a thirst for truth and goodness. The Pope's second encyclical *Dives in Misericordia* continued this theme of being sensitive to the situation of 'everyone'. Concerned that the people of the day were not attracted by the image of the sinner crawling to God for mercy, John Paul expounded the Parable of the Prodigal Son to show that the father does not allow his son to crawl, but delights to reinstate him to his former dignity. The encyclical went further, and suggested that, in Christ, and in those who suffer in Christ, *God asks us* for mercy – thereby dignifying us.

---

19 See Karl Rahner, 'Concerning the Relationship between Nature and Grace', in *Theological Investigations* I (London: Darton, Longman and Todd, 1961), pp. 297–317; and 'Nature and Grace', in *Theological Investigations* IV (London: Darton, Longman and Todd, 1966), pp. 165–88. Written between De Lubac's *Surnaturel* and his *The Mystery of the Supernatural,* these papers sought to resolve the debate over the natural thirst for God. For Rahner, God *could* have made human beings without a real thirst for himself. But in fact he has freely given us a real thirst for himself, which is so universal it is experienced as natural (we 'find ourselves' within a 'supernatural existential'); yet it is already a *free gift.* We can say yes or no to it. And it comes through Christ – any allegations that Rahner allows salvation to bypass Christ incarnate are unjustified.

20 Rahner presents his suggestion – admittedly rather tentatively and obscurely – in *The Trinity* (London: Burns & Oates, 1970), part III, sections B–D.

In his concern to defend traditional Catholic sexual teaching, but also in his concern to point up human dignity, Pope John Paul significantly developed the theology of marriage, to show that husband and wife are called to image the Holy Trinity – a point about which earlier theology had been too reticent.

By employing the philosophy of 'personalism', the Pope engaged with the modern focus on human rights, and sought to present a helpful perspective on the issue of how the individual may be cherished in such a way that the common good is also upheld.

These three thinkers encourage us to a solidarity with others in their concerns for truth, for humanity, for human rights and for unity in a world where conflict remains. They speak of an empathy with the anxieties of people today, an openness to the insights of those who may not share our Faith and a willingness to engage with contemporary culture. We should be ready to work with others who believe in God, as far as possible. Nevertheless, without being arrogant or aggressive, we may be confident in what we have to offer, and should proclaim that God the Holy Trinity, revealed and *given* to us in the events that took place in the Holy Land 2,000 years ago, both clarifies and satisfies our deepest needs. We offer a deeper and wider vision, a hope of sharing the *divine* life and joy in a world God is going to re-create – yet this offer affirms and cherishes all that is truly human. At the same time, we expect to learn in the process of teaching; apologetic discourse enables us to *do theology* – we can balance our confidence in what we have to offer with a willingness to journey alongside those with whom we converse.

Present-day Considerations

Several further features of today's world demand special attention. One is the need to meet people where they are – both intellectually and in terms of the media they attend to. It has proved rather difficult in this country to provide much on TV or in the secular press that really explains or defends the Christian faith, even if competent Christians are called on to discuss or debate specific issues. This makes it all the more important for Christians to exploit the Internet. They must also take their part in every area of civic and academic life, with all the virtues Aquinas listed, so as to show our Faith is intellectually respectable, and that by promoting moral values and preaching Christian hope we are on the side of true humanity. Theology faculties provide an opportunity for ecumenical co-operation and concerted witness. Christians engaged in other academic areas, especially the sciences, in the arts, in politics, in sport and in economic life, should let it appear that their Faith supports them in practising their craft at least as well as those who do not share their Faith.[21]

So as to 'be prepared to make a defence to any one who calls [them] to account for the hope that is in [them]', it is essential for Christians 'in the world' to pray for the Spirit's guidance and to be supported by the prayers of the Christian community; it is essential, too, that they be well formed in the Christian faith. Sound Christian education is therefore vital. Writing as a Roman Catholic, I fear that our parishes and schools have not done as well as they should in this area, despite the obvious devotion and fidelity of parishes, and the fact that Catholic schools are known for their good ethical atmosphere. However, there are many signs of renewed concern for vigorous catechesis that is both authentic and intellectually aware.[22]

Apart from those who belong to, or are reached by, Christian communities in this country, it is clear that many people have a very minimal understanding of even basic Christian teaching and history, and know next to nothing of the Bible. We face the same problem as Justin Martyr. Addressing it will be an uphill struggle – maybe one way of getting information across is to connect it with our cultural history[23] and with the Christian artistic heritage, in the way exemplified by the *Seeing Salvation* exhibition at the National Gallery in 2000 and the accompanying TV programmes.

A further aspect of the need to 'get information out' has become urgent. Many Muslims fear that we water down the core doctrine of God's unity, and if we are to be in as much solidarity and converse as possible with Jews and Muslims, we need to make it clear that the doctrine of the Holy Trinity does not imply the slightest compromise over the divine unity.[24]

---

21 Of course, natural law and Christian virtues may well direct Christian artists, politicians and businessmen into different behaviour from their non-Christian colleagues. But this different behaviour should prove a *better* source of truth and beauty, justice and integrity, the common good and true well-being.

22 Examples include Maryvale Institute in Birmingham and the programme of publication undertaken by the Catholic Truth Society. The vigour of the Alpha Course deserves mention; it is also used in Catholic circles and has inspired the approach of the 'Catholic Faith Exploration' videos.

23 To some extent we need to engage in *revisionist* history, so as to show in how many ways Christianity has been an enriching force for the good, rather than a damper on progress, and to make it clear that (despite some hitches) Christianity has not *typically* been opposed to science – quite the opposite.

24 If we can recover the thirteenth-century element of respectful shared dialogue, we can mitigate the prejudice that Islam breeds extremism and the consequent suspicion that religion causes violence. The task (as urgent for us as for Justin and Athanasius) of explaining

At the same time, Christianity offers a dignity unknown to Judaism and Islam: being adopted as the Father's beloved children in his eternal Son, to whom we are conformed by the Spirit who enfolds us.

Early Christian theologians *stood with* those currents in Greek philosophy that were suspicious of unworthy myths. It is essential today that the Church appear as the 'critical friend' of science: critical but a friend nonetheless.[25] We are not on the side of anything and everything that calls itself 'faith' or 'spirituality'; we do not approve of magic, nor of the 'neo-pagan' worship of the natural forces that science investigates and technology can employ. In the face of the strange contemporary 'schizophrenia' that values the objectivity of science and technology, yet can also speak of 'my truth and your truth', we actually find ourselves *on the same side* as Richard Dawkins when it comes to opting for reason rather than superstition! Obviously, we have something richer to offer than he has. While we can appreciate that technology alone cannot satisfy the human heart (is that why there has been an upsurge of interest in the occult?), our Christian combination of Scripture, liturgy, sound doctrine and moral wisdom stands to nourish the whole human person. To use a cliché, we have something for both head and heart, a pattern of life for the present and the hope of future immortality.

As the 'critical friend' of science, the Church has a traditional, developing moral wisdom that can be brought to bear on ethical issues to do with technology and can judge what is and what is not truly humanizing; yet our sights are set on a coming kingdom neither nature nor technology can achieve. We even have *a more generous vision of science* than Richard Dawkins, for we can see more clearly how the human being, made in the image of God, has the power to grasp and – respectfully – employ the structures God has crafted into the cosmos.[26] The beauty of the cosmos,

---

the doctrine of the Holy Trinity is made more difficult by those Christian theologians who give the impression that the doctrine *does* qualify the assertion that 'the LORD is One'. The 'A Team' of theologians (Athanasius, Augustine, Anselm and Aquinas, with Barth and Rahner as honorary members) makes it clear that the divine unity is *not* to be compromised. This does not obscure the distinctions between Father, Son and Spirit; on the contrary, it makes them appear all the richer and more exciting.

25 Although Albert and Thomas had to oppose elements of 'fundamentalism' in the thirteenth century, it was typical of Christians (as of Jews) from the first century AD onwards to incorporate up-to-date cosmology into their thought. Thoroughgoing fundamentalism was an invention of the early twentieth century.

26 As a Thomist, I should claim that Aquinas' understanding of the cosmos is in some ways *closer to the reality* than is Dawkins's. On pages 182–3 of *The God Delusion* (London: Bantam, 2006), Dawkins suggests that, when faced with a tiger, to suppose it has a conscious intention to eat you is merely a short cut to predicting the behaviour determined by its physics and physiology. Whereas a follower of Aquinas can recognize that a tiger *is*

and the greater beauty of the human being, take on new lustre when they are recognized as reflecting the beauty of God.

The recent furore over child-abuse scandals (rightly so called) in the Catholic Church reminds us of the importance of following Saint Peter's rule, 'keep your conscience clear', and of heeding Jesus' warning not to cause a little one to stumble. Maybe one reason it is the Catholic, clerical instances of abuse that have excited most horror, is that human beings like to see hypocrisy punctured. Quite possibly, the popular perception of the Catholic Church is of a strict and unsympathetic moralist telling people, 'Don't do that', where 'that' is chiefly something to do with sex. We need to work harder at getting the full message of the gospel across – the offer of being incorporated into Christ by the Holy Spirit, so as to journey in Christ into the Father's embrace.[27] And we all (by which I mean the whole Christian people, not just the clergy) need to be renewed in our discipleship and in our prayer, so that we can be seen to love God, and each other, and all those whom we invite to share our journey into the Truth and Goodness that alone can satisfy humanity. This love must be fashioned by the Holy Spirit whom we invoke, and who alone can make the invitation attractive and effective. This love is to conform us to Christ, in whom the Father reaches out to his children.

---

conscious (some of the time, like us), and does (sometimes) really *want* to eat someone. I strongly suspect that Aristotle's recognition that an organism is not a machine and is more than the sum of its parts, is more in tune with quantum mechanics and other modern theories, than is the seventeenth-century 'mechanical' view of living bodies which still lurks in the Western subconscious. I should like to suggest that we abandon both materialism and dualism in favour of a recognition of the rich variety of creatures which God holds in being. But there is no space to develop this here.

27 Of course, it may be convenient for people to hear the bits of the Church's teaching they find it easiest to discount, and to ignore what demands conversion by being both more deeply attractive and more deeply uncomfortable.

The Natural Sciences and Apologetics

ALISTER E. MCGRATH

All apologetics has a context. The cultural context of the West is in an important sense one dominated by the claims made for science, not least for science over and against religion. Alister McGrath considers this supposed hostility of science to religious belief. It calls, in response, for a renewed historical imagination. A more accurate history of 'science and religion' might be told than is often given, one that is far less confrontational than is commonly supposed. More than that, it is important to see that science itself rests upon beliefs that cannot be proved scientifically. The scientific method also has limitations. When these are respected, and the sciences operate on their own sphere, they are a remarkably powerful mode of reason. When these limitations are ignored, the method fails. Sciences cannot answer questions beyond their remit, not least concerning questions of 'wisdom and meaning'. Nor can science guide us ethically as to how to make use of its own fruits. Here, McGrath is considering nothing less than the nature and scope of human reason (or modes of reason in the plural), a theme common to this book as a whole. In the second half of his chapter, he continues to discuss forms of rationality. Now, however, the question is how the apologist could usefully draw upon science's own methods. As one example, the practice of 'inference to the best explanation' serves as a good model for Christian theology. McGrath concludes the essay with the contention that it stands in Christianity's favour that it leads to health and balance in thinking. The sense and vigour of a typically Christian attitude towards science is a good illustration of this: it respects science without idolizing it. A Christian understanding of science therefore delivers us from the travesty visited upon the sciences, and upon the business of human life, when the scientific method is taken as the only admissible standard of rationality. **A.D.**

It is impossible to reflect on the challenges and opportunities facing Christian apologetics in the twenty-first century without engaging with the natural sciences. This, it must be emphasized, is not merely an intellectual issue; it is also a cultural matter, which links up to important debates about the location of authority and trust within culture as a whole.[1] Who do we trust? To whom do we turn when we seek guidance and wisdom? For an individual or institution to be perceived as untrustworthy is to undermine the plausibility of any statements that they may make.

There is little doubt that science was regarded as possessing immense cultural authority throughout much of the twentieth century. Sir Richard Gregory (1864–1952), who did much to establish the natural sciences as a benchmark of intellectual rigour and moral accountability, put it like this: 'My grandfather preached the Gospel of Christ; my father preached the Gospel of Socialism; and I preach the Gospel of Science.' It is no accident that the 'New Atheism', especially in the form associated with Richard Dawkins, appeals to the rationality of the natural sciences as part of its apologetic. The Chicago geneticist Jerry Coyne, for example, declared that 'the *real* war is between rationalism and superstition. Science is but one form of rationalism, while religion is the most common form of superstition.'[2] Given the cultural authority of science, it is essential that Christian apologetics demonstrates its ability to engage plausibly and comprehensively with its methods and ideas.

Apologetics 'seeks to show why it is reasonable, with the help of grace, to accept God's word as it comes to us through Scripture and the Church'.[3] There are two elements to the apologetic enterprise. Negatively, it seeks to identify intellectual emotional and imaginative suspicions and concerns about faith, and aims to offer culturally plausible responses to these. Positively, it seeks to commend the Christian faith in terms that relate to our culture, and have the capacity to captivate its rational, moral and aesthetic imagination.

So what issues are raised for Christian apologetics by the natural sciences?[4] In this chapter, we shall consider two representative concerns and possibilities for apologetics. Limitation on space means that only cursory

1 Onora O'Neill, *A Question of Trust* (Cambridge: Cambridge University Press, 2002), pp. 41–60.

2 As cited by Richard Dawkins, *The God Delusion* (London: Bantam, 2006), p. 67.

3 Avery Dulles, *A History of Apologetics*, 2nd edition (San Francisco, CA: Ignatius Press, 2005), p. 367.

4 There is a substantial body of literature dealing with these questions For example, John Polkinghorne, *One World: The Interaction of Science and Theology* (London: SPCK, 1986); Ian G. Barbour, *Religion in an Age of Science* (San Francisco, CA: HarperSanFrancisco, 1990); John Polkinghorne, *Belief in God in an Age of Science* (New Haven, CT: Yale University Press, 1998); Alister E. McGrath, *Dawkins' God: Genes, Memes and the Meaning of Life* (Oxford: Blackwell Publishing, 2004); Francis S. Collins, *The Language of God: A Scientist Presents Evidence for Belief* (New York: Free Press, 2006); Owen Gingerich, *God's Universe* (Cambridge, MA: Harvard University Press, 2006).

responses can be given, offering only an outline of what needs to be said; however, reference will be made to sources that will develop these points in greater detail.

Challenges from Science to Apologetics

The tensions between science and the Christian faith are complex, and are perhaps better understood in terms of competition for cultural authority rather than intellectual divergence. Nevertheless, there is no doubt that there are intellectual issues underlying these tensions, most notably concerning the manner in which reliable knowledge is derived and validated.

This conflict is often expressed more generally in terms of the phrase 'science and religion', which unhelpfully reifies both notions, attributing concrete identity to abstractions. Science and religion are not well-delimited entities, whose essence can be defined; they are shaped by the interaction of social, cultural and intellectual factors, so that both notions are shaped by factors that vary from one cultural location to another. Nevertheless, the phrase is so widely used that its use cannot be avoided, even if it is to be treated with caution.

In what follows, we shall consider two important concerns that arise for Christian apologetics: the idea that science is fundamentally opposed to the Christian faith, and the related notion that science will eventually be able to offer an explanation for everything – including religion itself.

Science is at war with religion

One of the oldest stereotypes which still dominates the agenda of the 'New Atheism' and much journalistic writing is that science and religion are at war with each other. They are locked in mortal combat, from which only one can emerge victorious. Religion, according to this stereotype, represents the dead, repressive hand of the past: science offers a bold and enlightened future. In the end, science will triumph and sweep religion from the field.

The origins of this 'warfare' model of the relation of science and religion date from the final quarter of the nineteenth century and reflect a complex sociological context in which science was trying to establish itself as an independent professional discipline, independent of the Church.[5] In the early nineteenth century, many clergymen were active,

5 Frank Miller Turner, 'The Victorian Conflict between Science and Religion: A Professional Dimension', Isis 69 (1978), pp. 356–76; Colin A. Russell, 'The Conflict Metaphor

if often amateur scientists. The continuing interest in natural theology led many to see the exploration of nature almost as a religious vocation, stimulating popular interest in natural history.[6] Yet as the century progressed, pressure grew for the emancipation of the natural sciences from any ecclesiastical association. It was, many argued, essential that science should be seen as independent of any political, religious or social influence or control.

Although the late nineteenth-century professionalization of science generally did not entail hostility between science and religion, a number of aggressive works poured petrol on this smouldering dispute, arguing – on the basis of a disturbing lack of historical evidence – that science was permanently at war with backward-looking religious communities, who resisted progress as a matter of principle. The general tone of the later nineteenth-century encounter between Christianity and the natural sciences was set by two works: John William Draper's *History of the Conflict between Religion and Science* (1874) and Andrew Dickson White's *The Warfare of Science with Theology in Christendom* (1896).

Although recent atheist writers have asserted that the publication of Charles Darwin's *Origin of Species* (1859) marks a point of transition, the historical evidence suggests that it was actually these two later works which crystallized a growing public perception of tension and hostility between science and religion.[7] Historical revisionism has since cast doubt on much of the historical evidence alleged to indicate continuous tension between science and religion.[8]

There have been, of course, tensions between science and religion – for example, those arising from Darwin's theory of natural selection. Yet neither Darwin nor his leading interpreters, such as T. H. Huxley (1825–95), saw this theory as necessarily challenging religious belief.[9] The construction of a metanarrative of conflict, ultimately leading to the scientific

and Its Social Origins', Science and Christian Faith 1 (1989), pp. 3–26; Peter J. Bowler, *Reconciling Science and Religion: The Debate in Early Twentieth-Century Britain* (Chicago: University of Chicago Press, 2001).

6 Jonathan Topham, 'Science and Popular Education in the 1830s: The Role of the Bridgewater Treatises', *British Journal for the History of Science* 25 (1992), pp. 397–430.

7 See especially the dominance of this paradigm in the writings of Bertrand Russell (1872–1970): Peter H. Denton, *The ABC of Armageddon: Bertrand Russell on Science, Religion, and the Next War, 1919–1938* (Albany, NY: State University of New York Press, 2001), pp. 83–109.

8 The best of these is Ronald L. Numbers (ed.), *Galileo Goes to Jail And Other Myths About Science and Religion* (Cambridge, MA: Harvard University Press, 2009).

9 See Alister E. McGrath, 'Religious and Scientific Faith: The Case of Charles Darwin's *The Origin of Species*', in Alister E. McGrath, *Mere Theology: Christian Faith and the Discipleship of the Mind* (London: SPCK, 2010), pp. 93–110.

elimination of religion, is arguably the outcome of atheist polemics, rather than historical analysis. Atheism is generally read into, rather than out of, the narrative of scientific development within its broader cultural context.

Huxley himself famously declared that science 'commits suicide when it adopts a creed'.[10] In making this point, Huxley was protesting against science becoming the servant of a doctrinaire atheism, or being seen as a weapon in a war against religious belief. Science, he argued, was *science*, not a tool in the hands of those with aggressive religious or manipulative anti-religious agendas.

Science, when at its best and most authentic, has no creed, whether religious or anti-religious. As Huxley himself pointed out, it nevertheless has one, and only one, article of faith:

> The one act of faith in the convert to science, is the confession of the universality of order and of the absolute validity in all times and under all circumstances, of the law of causation. This confession is an act of faith, because, by the nature of the case, the truth of such propositions is not susceptible of proof.[11]

While there are those who insist that science makes and requires no judgement of faith, this is clearly not the case, in Huxley's view. Science finds itself committed to working beliefs that are not 'susceptible of proof', which Huxley rightly terms 'acts of faith'.

Huxley's insight here contrasts sharply with the dogmatic insistence of Richard Dawkins that science is a faith-free zone. Dawkins is clearly wrong; science has to make some basic assumptions – the sort of thing that the psychologist William James helpfully termed 'working hypotheses'. The astonishing, almost pathological aversion of the New Atheism to faith-based judgements in science is ultimately a mark of its prejudice against religion, rather than a sign of an intimate familiarity with the scientific method.

Science will eventually explain everything

Richard Dawkins is one of a number of recent writers to assert the intellectual and cultural supremacy of the natural sciences.[12] Science is gobbling

---

10 Thomas H. Huxley, *Darwiniana* (London: Macmillan, 1893), p. 252.

11 *The Life and Letters of Charles Darwin*, ed. by Francis Darwin. 3 vols (London: John Murray, 1887), vol. 2, p. 200.

12 This approach is often referred to as 'scientism': see Frederick A. Olafson, *Naturalism and the Human Condition: Against Scientism* (London: Routledge, 2001).

up the conceptual space once occupied by superstition, magic and religion. It is just a matter of time before these are completely displaced by rational, scientific explanation. There will no longer be any good reason to believe in God, or any of the irrationalities to which religious belief is prone. Perhaps there are some areas in which science has yet to offer credible explanations of things. But it is just a matter of time before it does. What science cannot explain today, it will be able to explain tomorrow.

For Dawkins, science offers a persuasive explanation of the origin and maintenance of religious belief. Dawkins introduced the idea of the 'meme' in 1976 to designate a cultural replicator, analogous to the gene, which transmitted ideas within populations.[13] Memes, Dawkins declared, leap from one brain to another, spreading ideas in a manner analogous to a virus infecting a community. The supreme example of a meme, he argued, was a 'God-meme'. Its undoubtable efficacy did not lie in its veracity, but in its capacity to adapt and survive.

Atheist writers seized upon this as an integral element of their critique of religion. Indeed, the idea of the meme plays a critically important role in two of the leading works of the New Atheism: Richard Dawkins's *God Delusion* (2006), and Daniel Dennett's *Breaking the Spell* (2006). Yet the notion of the meme has failed to secure acceptance within the mainline scientific community, being seen as a curiosity or quirk, on the sidelines of scientific orthodoxy.[14]

Many scientists, however, resist the temptation to extend the scope of the scientific method beyond its legitimate remit. The very success of the natural sciences, they argue, is dependent upon limiting its purview to a restricted field of enquiry, where it can deliver results with conviction. Extending its scope runs the risk of discrediting it. In a 1992 critique of an anti-evolutionary work which posited that Darwinism was *necessarily* atheistic, the evolutionary biologist Stephen Jay Gould insisted that the whole question of God lay outside the scope of the scientific method:

> To say it for all my colleagues and for the umpteenth million time (from college bull sessions to learned treatises): science simply cannot (by its legitimate methods) adjudicate the issue of God's possible

---

13 Richard Dawkins, *The Selfish Gene*, 2nd edition (Oxford: Oxford University Press, 1989), pp. 192–3.

14 For a detailed analysis, see Alister E. McGrath, *Darwinism and the Divine: Evolutionary Thought and Natural Theology* (Oxford: Wiley-Blackwell, 2011).

superintendence of nature. We neither affirm nor deny it; we simply can't comment on it as scientists.[15]

Gould here reinforces the traditional argument that science is open to multiple interpretations, both atheistic and religious.

More significantly, other prominent scientists have argued that there are intrinsic limits to the scientific method, which mean that certain questions can never be answered on the basis of science. To demand that science answer questions that lie beyond its sphere of competence is potentially to bring it into disrepute. These questions are metaphysical, not empirical. Sir Peter Medawar (1915–87), who won the Nobel Prize in Medicine for his work on immunology, insisted that the limits of science must be identified and respected. Otherwise, he argued, science would fall into disrespect, having been abused and exploited by those with ideological agendas. There remain important transcendent questions 'that science cannot answer, and that no conceivable advance of science would empower it to answer'.[16] Medawar has in mind here 'ultimate questions' such as: What are we here for? What is the point of living? These are real and important questions. Yet they are not questions that science can legitimately answer, as they lie beyond the scope of the scientific method, as this is legitimately applied. Medawar was a rationalist who disliked religion; he was, nevertheless, quite clear about the limits of science in this respect.

In the end, science does not, and can not, provide us with the answers that most of us are seeking. For example, the quest for the good life has stood at the heart of human existence since the dawn of civilization. Even Richard Dawkins is willing to concede limits to scientific enquiry, when he agrees that 'science has no methods for deciding what is ethical'.[17] The inability of science to disclose moral values merely causes us to move on, to search for them elsewhere, rather than to declare the quest invalid and pointless. Science is amoral.

The point here is that science is morally impartial precisely because it is morally blind, placing itself at the service of both the dictator wishing to enforce his oppressive rule through weapons of mass destruction

---

15 Stephen Jay Gould, 'Impeaching a Self-Appointed Judge', *Scientific American* 267, no. 1 (1992), pp. 118–21. Available online at http://www.stephenjaygould.org/reviews/gould_darwin-on-trial.html.

16 Peter B. Medawar, *The Limits of Science* (Oxford: Oxford University Press, 1985), p. 66.

17 Richard Dawkins, *A Devil's Chaplain* (London: Weidenfeld & Nicolson, 2003), p. 34.

and of those wishing to heal a broken humanity through new drugs and medical procedures. We need transcendent narratives to provide us with moral guidance, social purpose and a sense of personal identity. While science may provide us with knowledge and information, it is powerless to confer wisdom and meaning.

This final point merits closer consideration. Can science ever satisfy the deeper human longing for meaning? The Spanish philosopher José Ortega y Gasset (1883–1955) celebrated science's capacity to explain our observations of the world, while nevertheless insisting on its failure to satisfy the deeper longings and questions of humanity. 'Scientific truth is characterized by its exactness and the certainty of its predictions. But these admirable qualities are contrived by science at the cost of remaining on a plane of secondary problems, leaving intact the ultimate and decisive questions.'[18] The fundamental virtue of science is that it knows when to stop. It only answers questions that it knows it can answer on the basis of the evidence. But human curiosity wants to go further than this. Human beings are unable 'to do without all-around knowledge of the world, without an integral idea of the universe'.

Ortega y Gasset declares that the twentieth century witnessed unparalleled efforts to restrain humanity within the realm of the exact and determinable. A whole series of questions were needlessly and improperly declared to be 'meaningless', because they went beyond the limits of the natural sciences. Ortega y Gasset declares that this premature dismissal extends to the great questions of life, such as: 'Where does the world come from, and whither is it going? Which is the supreme power of the cosmos, what the essential meaning of life?' However, we continue to wrestle with such ultimate questions of life, ignoring the demands of those who insist they are meaningless. We cannot evade these questions, because wrestling with them is an inalienable aspect of being human. 'We are given no escape from ultimate questions. In one way or another they are in us, whether we like it or not. Scientific truth is exact, but it is incomplete.'[19]

Both Medawar and Ortega y Gasset, though in different ways, raise fundamental questions about the intellectual and existential limits of science. Both delight in scientific success, and rejoice in the advancement in knowledge that it brings. Yet both demand a realistic approach to science, which recognizes its limitations – and possibly even its dangers.

---

18 José Ortega y Gasset, *History as a System and Other Essays Toward a Philosophy of History* (New York: W. W. Norton, 1962), pp. 13–15.

19 Ortega y Gasset, *History as a System*, pp. 13–15.

Even the atheist philosopher Bertrand Russell, perhaps one of the less critical advocates of science as the arbiter of meaning and value, was aware of its disturbing absence of moral direction. Science, if 'unwisely used', leads to tyranny and war.[20]

In this section, we have briefly considered two concerns that the natural sciences raise for Christian apologetics. But what of the opportunities?

Opportunities for Apologetics from Science

Science and the Christian faith can both be understood as attempts to make sense of things – to discover a deeper reality beneath the surface structure of things.[21] This is not to say that Christianity is purely about sense-making; nevertheless, part of the existential and relational transformation entailed by the Christian faith relates to how we see and understand reality. 'Do not be conformed to this world, but be transformed by the renewing of your minds' (Rom. 12.2). This allows some important apologetic openings, of which we shall consider two in the present section. We begin by considering the idea of the 'best explanation'.

Inference to the best explanation

Richard Dawkins regularly argues that science is to be contrasted with religious faith. Whereas science proves its theories, religious faith is 'blind trust, in the absence of evidence, even in the teeth of evidence'.[22] It is a 'process of non-thinking', which is 'evil precisely because it requires no justification, and brooks no argument'.[23] These core definitions of faith are hardwired into Dawkins's worldview, and are obsessively repeated throughout his writings. Science is evidence-based; religion runs away from the evidence.

Underlying Dawkins's approach is a form of scientific positivism, which probably reached its peak in the late nineteenth century. The simplistic mantra 'science proves its theories' unquestionably contains an element

---

20 Bertrand Russell, *The Impact of Science upon Society* (London: Routledge, 1998), p. 97.

21 On science, see Peter R. Dear, *The Intelligibility of Nature: How Science Makes Sense of the World* (Chicago: University of Chicago Press, 2006). On theology, see Alister E. McGrath, *The Open Secret: A New Vision for Natural Theology* (Oxford: Wiley-Blackwell, 2008), especially pp. 113–216.

22 Dawkins, *The Selfish Gene*, p. 198.

23 Dawkins, *The God Delusion*, p. 308.

of truth, even though it is more aspirational than actual. Yet Dawkins's positivist approach neglects the role of fiduciary commitments in science. The scientific evidence is often open to multiple interpretations, raising the question of which interpretation is the 'best', and what criteria might be used in making this judgement.

An example will help make this important point clearer. In his *Origin of Species* (1859), Darwin sets out his theory of natural selection. This theory, he argued, made more sense of the observational evidence than its alternatives – such as the doctrine of 'special creation' associated with William Paley (but which is not determinative of the Christian tradition as a whole),[24] or the evolutionary theory known as 'transformism', developed by a number of pre-Darwinian writers.[25] Yet Darwin was absolutely clear that he could not prove that his theory was right. He believed it was right, but was aware that it encountered difficulties. Towards the end of his account of natural selection in *The Origin of Species*, Darwin concedes that there is observational evidence that counts against his theory, and that it faced some significant challenges. Yet he believed it was right, and would ultimately be shown to be right:

> A crowd of difficulties will have occurred to the reader. Some of them are so grave that to this day I can never reflect on them without being staggered; but, to the best of my judgement, the greater number are only apparent, and those that are real are not, I think, fatal to my theory.[26]

We note here a characteristic feature of the scientific method – the willingness to hold a theory, while accepting that anomalies existed. These anomalies might be resolved through further investigation; on the other hand, they might ultimately force the theory to be abandoned.

I have engaged with Darwin in some detail, as the great English naturalist is often adopted as a mascot by the New Atheism. It is important to appreciate that Darwin himself was quite clear that science had to

---

24 For a detailed analysis, see McGrath, *Darwinism and the Divine*.

25 Pietro Corsi, 'Before Darwin: Transformist Concepts in European Natural History', *Journal of the History of Biology* 38 (2005), pp. 67–83.

26 Charles Darwin, *Origin of Species* (London: John Murray, 1859), p. 171. For examples of such 'difficulties', see Abigail J. Lustig, 'Darwin's Difficulties', in Michael Ruse and Robert J. Richards (eds), *The Cambridge Companion to the* Origin of Species (Cambridge: Cambridge University Press, 2009), pp. 109–28. For further comment, see McGrath, 'Religious and Scientific Faith'.

make judgements of faith. That was just the nature of things. Darwin believed that the ability of his theory of natural selection to accommodate observation was an indication of its truth:

> It can hardly be supposed that a false theory would explain, in so satisfactory a manner as does the theory of natural selection, the several large classes of facts above specified. It has recently been objected that this is an unsafe method of arguing; but it is a method used in judging the common events of life, and has often been used by the greatest natural philosophers.[27]

The theory, Darwin insisted, could not be proved. But it could be judged by its capacity to make sense of things. Darwin explicitly stated that 'the change of species cannot be directly proved', so that 'the doctrine must sink or swim according as it groups and explains phenomena'.[28]

Darwin's argument is now regarded as a textbook example of 'inference to the best explanation' – the approach to observational evidence, now widely recognized as characteristic of the natural sciences, which recognizes the role of fiduciary judgement in determining which of a number of theories offers the best explanation of the evidence.[29] A judgement has to be made about both the criteria by which this judgement is to be made (such as simplicity, elegance, coherence and fecundity) and the outcome of the application of these 'epistemic virtues' to the evidence.[30] Any adjudication concerning which of a number of possible theories offers the best explanation of the evidence is provisional and subject to revision; more importantly, it is also a matter of faith, based on the judgement of individuals and communities.

So what is the relevance of this to apologetics? Darwin's example allows us to suggest that, in certain respects, the Christian faith can be seen as a theory which is to be judged by its ability to accommodate reality. This is not a new idea; it is found, for example, in the writings of Ian T. Ramsey (1915–72), a noted philosopher of religion who ended his career as Bishop of Durham. Ramsey used the phrase 'empirical fit' to refer to

---

27 Charles Darwin, *Origin of Species*, 6th edition (London: John Murray, 1872), p. 444. This comment is not present in earlier editions of the work.

28 Francis Darwin (ed.), *The Life and Letters of Charles Darwin*, 3 vols (London: John Murray, 1887), vol. 2, p. 155.

29 Ernan McMullin, *The Inference That Makes Science* (Milwaukee, WI: Marquette University Press, 1992); Peter Lipton, *Inference to the Best Explanation*, 2nd edition (London: Routledge, 2004).

30 Paul Thagard, 'The Best Explanation: Criteria for Theory Choice', *Journal of Philosophy* 75 (1978), pp. 76–92.

the capacity of a theological doctrine to make sense of experience and observation.[31] Much the same idea is expressed by C. S. Lewis, one of Anglicanism's most significant apologists: 'I believe in Christianity as I believe that the Sun has risen, not only because I see it, but because by it, I see everything else.'[32] I have argued elsewhere that the rich Trinitarian ontology of classical Christian thought has a deep intellectual capaciousness, which proves able to accommodate our observations and experience of reality.[33]

At this point, an objection must be considered. Scientific theories do not simply aim to accommodate existing observations, they also predict novel observations. While Christianity may be able to offer a powerful and plausible explanatory framework for reflection on our experience of the world, it does not *predict* – and for that reason, must be judged inferior to the sciences, if not downright unscientific. As might be expected, things are far from being as simple as this objection presupposes. The philosopher of science Karl Popper (1902–94) found himself embarrassed when he challenged the scientific character of Darwin's theory of natural selection. Its failure to predict, he argued, negated its claims to be scientific.[34] Happily, Popper came to realize his error of judgement. He retracted this criticism, and conceded that the scientific character of Darwin's theory was not compromised by its incapacity to predict, nor to be open to the full range of verificatory mechanisms normally applied to scientific theorizing.

This issue is not new: it emerged as important in the mid nineteenth-century debate between William Whewell and John Stuart Mill over the role of induction within the scientific method.[35] Whewell emphasized the importance of predictive novelty as distinctive of the sciences; Mill argued that this amounted to nothing more than a psychological distinction between prediction of novel observations and theoretical accommodation of existing observations. More recent discussions of the issue suggest

---

31 Ian T. Ramsey, *Models and Mystery* (London: Oxford University Press, 1964), p. 17.

32 C. S. Lewis, 'Is Theology Poetry?', in Lesley Walmsley (ed.), *C. S. Lewis: Essay Collection* (London: Collins, 2000), pp. 1–21; quote at p. 21.

33 See especially Alister E. McGrath, *A Fine-Tuned Universe: The Quest for God in Science and Theology* (Louisville, KY: Westminster John Knox Press, 2009), pp. 61–82.

34 Karl R. Popper, *Unended Quest* (London: Routledge, 1992), pp. 194–210, especially p. 195: 'I have come to the conclusion that Darwinism is not a testable scientific theory, but a *metaphysical research programme*' (emphasis in original). See further Karl R. Popper, 'Natural Selection and the Emergence of Mind', *Dialectica* 32 (1978), pp. 339–55.

35 Laura J. Snyder, 'The Mill-Whewell Debate: Much Ado about Induction', *Perspectives on Science* 5 (1997), pp. 159–98.

that while prediction can occasionally be superior to accommodation, this is not always the case.[36] Reliable explanation does not necessarily entail prediction; as Darwin rightly noted, the capacity of a theory to explain may be taken as an indicator of its truth.[37]

The issue of fine-tuning in nature

In the previous section, we noted the importance of inference to the best explanation. This approach suggests that there are strong degrees of affinity – but most emphatically not *identity* – between the motivations and methods of both theological and scientific reflection on the world. Both engage the question: what theoretical framework makes the best sense of what is actually observed? The noted American philosopher Charles Sanders Peirce (1839–1914), himself a scientist, argued that the basic philosophical method characteristic of scientific investigation is what he termed 'abduction' – the generation of an explanatory framework that seems to offer the best fit with the empirical world.

Peirce sets out the process of thinking that leads to the development of new scientific theories or ways of thinking about reality as follows.[38]

1 The surprising fact, *C*, is observed;
2 But if *A* were true, *C* would be a matter of course.
3 Hence, there is reason to suspect that *A* is true.

Abduction is the process by which we observe certain things and work out what intellectual framework might make most sense of them. Sometimes, Peirce suggests, abduction 'comes to us like a flash, as an act of insight'. Sometimes, it comes about through slow, methodical reflection, as we try to generate every possibility that might make sense of what we observe. But the critical question does not concern how this framework is generated (the 'logic of discovery'); the real issue is how well it fits what is actually observed (the 'logic of justification').

---

36 Christopher Hitchcock and Elliott Sober, 'Prediction vs. Accommodation and the Risk of Overfitting', *British Journal for Philosophy of Science* 55 (2004), pp. 1–34.

37 For further discussion of what it means to 'explain' something scientifically and theologically, see McGrath, *A Fine-Tuned Universe*, pp. 51–60.

38 Charles S. Peirce, *Collected Papers*, ed. by Charles Hartshorne and Paul Weiss. 8 vols (Cambridge, MA: Harvard University Press, 1960), vol. 5, p. 189. For further reflection on the notion of 'abduction', see Sami Paavola, 'Abduction as a Logic of Discovery: The Importance of Strategies', *Foundations of Science* 9 (2005), pp. 267–83; Sami Paavola, 'Peircean abduction: instinct, or inference?', *Semiotica* 153 (2005), pp. 131–54.

So how does this relate to Christian apologetics? A case study will help us explore this point. In recent years, increasing attention has been paid to the phenomenon of 'fine-tuning' in nature.[39] The term 'fine-tuning' is often used to refer to the scientific realization that the values of certain fundamental cosmological constants and the character of certain initial conditions of the universe appear to have played a decisive role in bringing about the emergence of a particular kind of universe, within which intelligent life can develop. Many recent scientific studies have emphasized the significance of certain fundamental cosmological constants, the values of which, if varied even slightly, would have significant implications for the emergence of human existence.[40] In recent years, it has become clear that 'fine-tuning' can also be observed at the chemical and biological levels. The debate in the literature mainly concerns the *interpretation* of these phenomena, whose existence is generally conceded.

So what is the apologetic significance of this? The observation of fine-tuning is consonant with Christian belief in a creator God. It proves nothing; nevertheless, it resonates strongly with the Christian vision of reality, fitting easily and naturally into the map of reality which emerges from the Christian faith. The capacity of Christianity to map these phenomena is not conclusive proof of anything. It is, however, highly suggestive. It is one among many clues, accumulating to give an overall 'big picture' of reality. It is one among many threads, which can be woven together to yield a patterned tapestry. 'Fine-tuning' is a clue to the meaning of the universe, insignificant in isolation, but richly suggestive when set alongside other such clues.

In his study of the relationship of the natural sciences and Christian theology, the physicist-turned-theologian John Polkinghorne (born 1930) makes a point of no small relevance to our concerns in this chapter.

No form of human truth-seeking enquiry can attain absolute certainty about its conclusions. The realistic aspiration is that of attaining the best explanation of complex phenomena, a goal to be achieved by searching for an understanding sufficiently comprehensive and

---

39 For a thorough exploration of the scientific issues and their apologetic implications, see McGrath, *A Fine-Tuned Universe*, pp. 109–201.

40 Richard Swinburne, 'The Argument from the Fine-Tuning of the Universe', in John Leslie (ed.), *Physical Cosmology and Philosophy* (New York: Macmillan, 1990), pp. 154–73; Robin Collins, 'A Scientific Argument for the Existence of God: The Fine-Tuning Design Argument', in Michael J. Murray (ed.), *Reason for the Hope Within* (Grand Rapids, MI: Eerdmans, 1999), pp. 47–75.

well-motivated as to afford the basis for rational commitment. Neither science nor religion can entertain the hope of establishing logically coercive proof of the kind that only a fool could deny.[41]

Both, however, are committed to finding the best evidence-based explanation of what is actually observed and encountered in the world. For the Christian, apologetics is partly about affirming the conceptual resonance between the Christian theoretical framework and the deeper structures of the world, as uncovered by the natural sciences.

There is much more to apologetics than affirming the capacity of the Christian faith to make sense of things. Apologetics, we must recall, engages the mind, emotions and imagination. It appeals to beauty and morality, as much as to rationality.[42] Yet perhaps this allows us to make a point of some importance in closing this discussion. Most scientists would concede the rationality of the natural world, while puzzling about its origins and significance. The real question is whether the recognition of the accessibility of the world to human reason is in itself existentially significant. It is far from clear that this is the case. As the physicist Steven Weinberg once gloomily commented, 'the more the universe seems comprehensible, the more it seems pointless'.[43]

Apologetics must go beyond demonstrating the capacity of the Christian faith to make sense of things, and speak meaningfully of deeper issues of purpose, value and identity.[44] The New Atheism offers a superficial reading of nature, skimming its surface, superbly exemplified in Dawkins's famous statement that the universe has 'no design, no purpose, no evil and no good, nothing but blind pitiless indifference'.[45] As the wisdom literature of the Old Testament emphasized, we must go deeper – not resting with surface readings of the world, but probing and plumbing its depths.[46] The very fact that Christian ways of thinking can accommodate the sciences is both an affirmation of the penultimacy

---

41 John Polkinghorne, *Theology in the Context of Science* (London: SPCK, 2008), pp. 85–6.

42 See Thomas Dubay, *The Evidential Power of Beauty: Science and Theology Meet* (San Francisco, CA: Ignatius Press, 1999).

43 Steven Weinberg, *The First Three Minutes* (London: André Deutsch, 1977), pp. 148–9.

44 Roy Baumeister, *Meanings of Life* (New York: Guilford Press, 1991).

45 Richard Dawkins, *River out of Eden: A Darwinian View of Life* (London: Phoenix, 1995), p. 133.

46 Paul S. Fiddes, '"Where Shall Wisdom Be Found?" Job 28 as a Riddle for Ancient and Modern Readers', in John Barton and David Reimer (eds), *After the Exile: Essays in Honor of Rex Mason* (Macon, GA: Mercer University Press, 1996), pp. 171–90.

of science, and an invitation to discover a deeper and more satisfying understanding of the universe, and our place and purpose within it. In John Polkinghorne's words, 'My instinct as a scientist is to seek a comprehensive understanding and I believe that it is my religious faith that enables me to find it.'[47] Christianity does not displace scientific accounts of the world; rather, it lends them ontological depth and clarity, and in doing so, discloses a greater vision of reality – a vision that gives both intellectual resilience and existential motivation to the task of apologetics.

---

47 John Polkinghorne, *Beyond Science: The Wider Human Context* (Cambridge: Cambridge University Press, 1998), p. 101.

Bibliography

Books marked * are particularly recommended.

General Introductions to Apologetics

* Avery Dulles, *A History of Apologetics* (Philadelphia: Ignatius, 2005).
* Alister McGrath, *Bridge Building: Creative Christian Apologetics* (Leicester: IVP, 1992).

Evangelical Perspectives

W. C. Campbell-Jack and Gavin J. McGrath (eds), *New Dictionary of Christian Apologetics* (Leicester: IVP, 2006).
  A useful volume for those interested in the academic study of apologetics. The focus is firmly evangelical.
William Lane Craig, *Reasonable Faith: Christian Truth and Apologetics* (Wheaton, IL: Crossway Books, 1994).
Josh McDowell, *Evidence that Demands a Verdict: Historical Evidences for the Christian Scriptures* (San Bernardino, CA: Here's Life Publishers, 1981).
  Very much not what is being discussed in this volume: the classic example of apologetics based on history and biblical prophecy.
* John G. Stackhouse, *Humble Apologetics: Defending the Faith Today* (Oxford: Oxford University Press, 2006).
Cornelius Van Til, *Christian Apologetics*, edited by William Edgar (Phillipsburg, NJ: P & R Publishing, 2003).
  Although Van Til's approach is in some ways quite different from those found in this book, his 'presuppositional apologetics' saw that that the Christian faith holds out its own account of reason, and that this is part of what it has to offer.
Ravi Zacharias and Norman L. Geisler (eds), *Who Made God?: And Answers to Over 100 Other Tough Questions of Faith* (Grand Rapids, MI: Zondervan, 2003).

Catholic Perspectives

* Robert Barron, *Word on Fire: Proclaiming the Power of Christ* (Chestnut Ridge, NY: Crossroad, 2008).
Scott Hahn, *Reasons to Believe: How to Understand, Explain and Defend the Catholic Faith* (London: Darton, Longman and Todd, 2007).
  Hahn's book is one of the most accessible works of apologetics from a Roman Catholic perspective. It is something of a hybrid, partly aimed at converting non-Christians and partly at converting Protestants.

* Peter Kreeft and Ronald K. Tacelli, *Handbook of Catholic Apologetics: Reasoned Answers to Questions of Faith* (San Francisco, CA: Ignatius Press, 2009).

William Most, *Catholic Apologetics Today: Answers to Modern Critics* (Charlotte, NC: Tan, 1987).

* Timothy Radcliffe, *What Is the Point of Being a Christian?* (London: Continuum, 2005).
Radcliffe's book simply shows us what is attractive about the Christian faith and the Christian community, and for this it has already become a classic.

Liberal Perspectives

* Brian Hebblethwaite, *In Defence of Christianity* (Oxford: Oxford University Press, 2005).

Richard Holloway, *Doubts and Loves: What Is Left of Christianity* (Edinburgh, Canongate, 2001).
In this, as in his other works, Holloway chips away at Christianity until he obtains something he finds to be defensible: bleak reading.

Philosophical Approaches

Brian Davies op, *The Reality of God and the Problem of Evil* (London: Continuum, 2006).

Paul Helm, *Faith and Reason* (Oxford: Oxford University Press, 1999). *A reader covering a wide range of perspectives.*

* John Milbank, *Theology and Social Theory*, second edition (Oxford: Blackwell, 2006).
Perhaps the most significant book for theology of the last few decades.

Alvin Plantinga, *Warranted Christian Belief* (New York: Oxford University Press, 2000).
This is the third of three books in which he spells out his 'Reformed epistemology'. Plantinga argues that Christian faith can be 'warranted' without reference to evidence. It hovers between fideism and epistemological subtlety.

Kenneth Surin, *Theology and the Problem of Evil* (Eugene, OR: Wipf & Stock, 2005).

Richard Swinburne, *Is There a God?* (Oxford: Oxford University Press, 1996) and *Was Jesus God?* (Oxford: Oxford University Press, 2008). *These two more popular volumes complement Swinburne's academic output from the Clarendon Press. Both sets of books are largely dedicated to a starkly rational defence of Christian beliefs, which do not usually fare very well in the process.*

* Denys Turner, *Faith Seeking* (London: SCM Press, 2002).
Important for the chapter 'How to Be an Atheist'.

Historical Apologetics

L. R. Bush (ed.), *Classical Readings in Christian Apologetics AD 100–1800* (Grand Rapids, MI: Zondervan, 1983).

G. K. Chesterton, *Autobiography*. In *The Collected Works of G. K. Chesterton*, vol. 16 (San Francisco, CA: Ignatius Press, 2000).

* G. K. Chesterton, *The Everlasting Man*. Numerous reprints. In *The Collected Works of G. K. Chesterton*, vol. 2 (San Francisco, CA: Ignatius Press, 1986).

G. K. Chesterton, *Heretics*. Numerous reprints. In *The Collected Works of G. K. Chesterton*, vol. 1 (San Francisco, CA: Ignatius Press, 1986).

* G. K. Chesterton, *Orthodoxy*. Numerous reprints. In *The Collected Works of G. K. Chesterton*, vol. 1 (San Francisco, CA: Ignatius Press, 1986).

C. S. Lewis, *Essay Collection: Literature, Philosophy and Short Stories* (London: HarperCollins, 2002).

C. S. Lewis, *Mere Christianity* (London: Geoffrey Bles, 1952).

C. S. Lewis, *The Problem of Pain* (London: Geoffrey Bles, 1940).

* Josef Pieper, *The Human Wisdom of St Thomas: A Breviary of Philosophy* (San Francisco, CA: Ignatius, 2002). *This tiny anthology is the perfect introduction to Thomas Aquinas.*

* Dorothy L. Sayers, *Creed or Chaos* (London: Hodder and Stoughton, 1940). Reprinted as *Letters to a Diminished Church* (Nashville, TN: Thomas Nelson Publishing Group, 2004).

Thomas Aquinas, *Summa Contra Gentiles*, translated by A. C. Pegis, 5 volumes (Notre Dame, IN: University of Notre Dame Press, 1976).

Atheism

Julian Baggini, *Atheism: A Very Short Introduction* (Oxford: Oxford University Press, 2003).

Guy P. Harrison, *50 Reasons People Give for Believing in a God.* (Amherst, NY: Prometheus Books, 2008). *An analysis from a sceptical or atheist position.*

Michael Martin (ed.), *The Cambridge Companion to Atheism* (Cambridge: Cambridge University Press, 2006). *The forthcoming* Oxford Handbook to Atheism *will provide a more neutral discussion of atheism than that offered here.*

The 'New Atheists'

Richard Dawkins, *The God Delusion* (London: Bantam, 2006).

Daniel C. Dennett, *Breaking the Spell: Religion as a Natural Phenomenon* (London: Penguin, 2007).

A. C. Grayling, *Against All Gods: Six Polemics on Religion and an Essay on Kindness* (London: Oberon Books, 2007).

Sam Harris, *Letter to a Christian Nation* (London: Bantam Press, 2007).

Christopher Hitchens, *God Is Not Great: The Case Against Religion* (London: Atlantic Books, 2007).

Christopher Hitchens, *The Portable Atheist: Essential Readings for the Non-Believer* (Cambridge, MA: Da Capo Press, 2007). *An anthology.*

Discussions of and Replies to Recent Atheism

Tina Beattie, *The New Atheists: The Twilight of Reason and the War on Religion* (London: Darton, Longman and Todd, 2007).

John Cornwell, *Darwin's Angel: An Angelic Riposte to 'The God Delusion'* (London: Profile, 2007).

* Conor Cunningham, *Darwin's Pious Idea* (Grand Rapids, MI: Eerdmans, 2010).

* Terry Eagleton, review of *The God Delusion* in *The London Review of Books*. Vol. 28, No. 20 (19 October 2006), pp. 32–34. Available at http://www.lrb.co.uk/v28/n2o/terry-eagleton/lunging-flailing-mispunching. *The pithiest and most combative response to the New Atheists.*

* Terry Eagleton, *Reason, Faith and Revolution: Reflections on the God Debate* (New Haven, CT: Yale University Press, 2009).
Eagleton spares neither the New Atheists nor the Christian faith in his short and beautifully written book worked up from a set of lectures.

Stewart Goetz and Charles Taliaferro, *Naturalism* (Grand Rapids, MI: Eerdmans, 2008).
A penetrating examination of the worldview on offer by the New Atheists.

* David Bentley Hart, *Atheist Delusions: The Christian Revolution and Its Fashionable Enemies* (New Haven, CT: Yale University Press, 2009).
Bentley Hart is brilliant and withering in his philosophical discussion of the New Atheists, but is disheartened by what he takes to be the bleak prospect of a renewal of the Church and Christian thought in response.

Timothy Keller, *The Reason for God: Belief in an Age of Scepticism* (London: Hodder & Stoughton, 2008).

Alister E. McGrath, *Dawkins' God: Genes, Memes, and the Meaning of Life* (Oxford: Blackwell, 2004).

Alister E. McGrath, *The Twilight of Atheism: The Rise and Fall of Disbelief in the Modern World* (London: Rider and Co, 2005).

Alister McGrath, *The Dawkins Delusion?: Atheist Fundamentalism and the Denial of the Divine* (London: SPCK, 2007).

Keith Ward, *Why There Almost Certainly Is a God: Doubting Dawkins* (Oxford: Lion, 2008).

Introductions to Philosophy

* Diogenes Allen and Eric O. Springsted, *Philosophy for Understanding Theology.* (Louisville, KY: Westminster John Knox Press, 2007).

* Kelly James Clark, Richard Lints and James K. A. Smith, *101 Key Terms in Philosophy and Their Importance for Theology* (Louisville, KY: Westminster John Knox Press, 2004).

Frederick Copleston SJ, *A History of Philosophy.* Nine volumes (London: Continuum, 2003).

* Andrew Davison, *Love and Understanding: An Introduction to Western Philosophy for Theologians* (London: SCM Press, forthcoming).

Terry Eagleton, *After Theory* (London: Penguin, 2004).

* Fergus Kerr OP, *Theology after Wittgenstein* (London: SPCK, 1997).
* Leszek Kołakowski, *Why is there something rather than nothing?: 23 Questions from Great Philosophers* (London: Penguin, 2008).
John Lechte, *Fifty Key Contemporary Thinkers* (London: Routledge, 1994).
* Alasdair MacIntyre, *God, Philosophy, Universities: A Selective History of the Catholic Philosophical Tradition* (London: Continuum, 2009). *A particularly critical and illuminating study.*

Contemporary Religious Culture

* Michael Buckley, *At the Origins of Modern Atheism* (New Haven, CT: Yale University Press, 1990).
Jane Garnett, Matthew Grimley et al. (eds), *Redefining Christian Britain: Post 1945 Perspectives* (London: SCM Press, 2006).
See especially the essays by Grace Davie, 'A Papal Funeral and a Royal Wedding: Reconfiguring Religion in the Twenty-First Century' and Matthew Grimley, 'Public Intellectuals and the Media'.
Michael Hoelzl and Graham Ward (eds), *The New Visibility of Religion: Studies in Religion and Cultural Hermeneutics* (London: Continuum, 2008).
* Henri de Lubac SJ, *The Drama of Atheist Humanism* (San Francisco, CA: Ignatius, 1995).
* Charles Taylor, *A Secular Age* (Cambridge, MA: Harvard University Press, 2007).
Graham Ward, *Cultural Transformation and Religious Practice* (Cambridge: Cambridge University Press, 2004).
Rowan Williams, *Lost Icons* (London: Continuum, 2003).

Science and Theology

Francis Collins, *The Language of God: A Scientist Presents Evidence for Belief* (London: Pocket Books, 2007).
Thomas Dixon, *Science and Religion: A Very Short Introduction* (Oxford: Oxford University Press, 2008).
Alister McGrath, *Science and Religion: An Introduction* (Oxford: Blackwell, 1999).
Peter Medawar, *The Limits of Science* (Oxford: Oxford University Press, 1986).
Denis Noble, *The Music of Life: Biology Beyond Genes* (Oxford: Oxford University Press, 2008).

Literature, Architecture and the Visual Arts

Robert Barron, *Heaven in Stone and Glass: Experiencing the Spirituality of the Great Cathedrals* (Chestnut Ridge, NY: Crossroad, 2000).
Jeremy Begbie (ed.), *Sounding the Depths: Theology Through the Arts* (London: SCM Press, 2002).

Arthur Bradley and Andrew Tate, *The New Atheist Novel: Fiction, Philosophy and Polemic After 9/11* (London: Continuum, 2010).

David S. Cunningham, *Reading Is Believing: The Christian Faith Through Literature and Film* (Grand Rapids, MI: Brazos Press, 2002).

Paul Fiddes, *The Promised End: Eschatology in Theology and Literature* (Oxford: Blackwell, 2000)

Richard Kieckhefer, *Theology in Stone: Church Architecture from Byzantium to Berkeley* (Oxford: Oxford University Press, 2004).

James Leachman OSB (ed.), *The Liturgical Subject: Subject, Subjectivity and the Human Person in Contemporary Liturgical Discussion and Critique* (London, SCM Press, 2008).
Takes in theology, philosophy and literature.

Gerard Loughlin, *Telling God's Story: Bible, Church and Narrative Theology* (Cambridge: Cambridge University Press, 1996).

Richard Taylor, *How to Read a Church: A Guide to Images, Symbols and Meanings in Churches and Cathedrals* (London: Rider and Co., 2003).

Rowan Williams, *Grace and Necessity: Reflection on Art and Love* (London: Continuum, 2006).

Introductions to Christian Doctrine

Jeff Astley, *SCM Studyguide to Christian Doctrine* (London: SCM Press, 2010).
Particularly strong on the communal aspects of Christian belief.

Hans Urs von Balthasar, *Credo: Meditations on the Apostle's Creed* (San Francisco, CA: Ignatius Press, 2000.)

Richard Clutterbuck, *Handing on Christ: Rediscovering the Gift of Christian Doctrine* (London: Epworth Press, 2009).

Tony Lane, *A Concise History of Theology* (London: Continuum, 2006).

Fergus Kerr OP, *Twentieth-Century Catholic Theologians: From Neoscholasticism to Nuptial Mysticism* (London: SPCK, 2006).

Alister McGrath, *Christian Theology: An Introduction* (Oxford: Blackwell, 2006).

Alister McGrath, *The Christian Theology Reader* (Oxford: Blackwell, 2006).

Mark McIntosh, *Divine Teaching: An Introduction to Christian Theology* (Oxford: Blackwell, 2007).

Eric Mascall, *He Who Is: A Study in Traditional Theism* (London: Longmans, 1943).

* E. P. Sanders, *Paul: A Very Short Introduction* (Oxford: Oxford University Press, 2001).

* Rupert Shortt, *God's Advocates: Christian Thinkers in Conversation* (London: Darton, Longman and Todd, 2005). *No other book offers such a stimulating and relatively gentle way into the state of current theology at its most vigorous.*

Rowan William, *Tokens of Trust* (Norwich: Canterbury Press, 2007).

Anthologies of patristic writings are a particularly good way into theology. The following are strongly recommended:

* Henry Bettenson, *The Early Christian Fathers* (Oxford: Oxford University Press, 1969).

* Henry Bettenson, *The Later Christian Fathers* (Oxford: Oxford University Press, 1972).

* Erich Przywara, *An Augustine Synthesis* (London: Sheed and Ward, 1936 [and subsequent reprints]).

Doctrine for Apologetics

Diogenes Allen, *Christian Belief in a Postmodern World: The Full Wealth of Conviction* (Louisville, KY: Westminster John Knox Press. 1989).

Hans Frei, *The Eclipse of the Biblical Narrative: Study in Eighteenth and Nineteenth Century Hermeneutics* (New Haven, CT: Yale, 1980).

Fergus Kerr OP, *Immortal Longings: Versions of Transcending Humanity* (London: SPCK, 1997).

* Herbert McCabe OP, *God Matters* (London: Continuum, 1999).

* Herbert McCabe OP, *God Still Matters* (London: Continuum, 2005).

Herbert McCabe OP, *God, Christ and Us*, edited by Brian Davies OP (London: Continuum, 2005).

Herbert McCabe OP, *Faith Within Reason*, edited by Brian Davies OP (London: Continuum, 2007).

Herbert McCabe OP, *God and Evil: In the Theology of St Thomas Aquinas*, edited by Brian Davies OP (London: Continuum, 2010).

Alister McGrath, *The Open Secret: A New Vision for Natural Theology* (Oxford: Wiley-Blackwell, 2008).

Bruce Marshall, *Trinity and Truth* (Cambridge: Cambridge University Press, 2000).

Sandra Menssen and Thomas D. Sullivan, *The Agnostic Enquirer: Revelation from a Philosophical Point of View* (Grand Rapids, MI: Eerdmans, 2007).

John Sanders, *No Other Name: Can Only Christians be Saved?* (London: SPCK, 1994).

Kevin J. Vanhoozer (ed.), *The Cambridge Companion to Postmodern Theology* (Cambridge: Cambridge University Press, 2003).

Graham Ward (ed.), *The Blackwell Companion to Postmodern Theology* (Oxford: Blackwell, 2005).

Graham Ward, *Christ and Culture* (Oxford: Blackwell, 2005).

Theological Ethics for Apologetics

St Benedict, *The Rule of Benedict* (London: Penguin, 2008).

* David S. Cunningham, *Christian Ethics: The End of the Law* (London: Routledge, 2007).

Andrew Davison and Alison Milbank, *For the Parish: A Critique of Fresh Expressions* (London: SCM Press, 2010).

Stanley Hauerwas, *The Hauerwas Reader* (Durham, NC: Duke University Press, 2001).

* Josef Pieper, *The Four Cardinal Virtues* (Notre Dame, IN: University of Notre Dame Press, 1967).

Josef Pieper, *Faith, Hope, Love* (San Francisco, CA: Ignatius Press, 1997).

Graham Ward, *The Politics of Discipleship: Becoming Postmaterial Citizens* (London: SCM Press, 2009).

Index

abduction 14, 154–7

accommodation 24, 117, 152–4, 156

Acts of the Apostles 47, 67–8, 127–9

Adorno, Theodor 117, 119

advertising 116, 120, 122

Alpha Course 139

Amis, Martin 49, 53–5, 56

analytic philosophy 16, 111

angels 32, 58, 122, 134

Anglicanism 5, 57, 127, 153

animals 13, 39, 118, 136

Anselm of Canterbury 10, 102, 140

apocalyptic 120, 122

Aquinas, Thomas 4, 10, 38, 102–103, 133–6, 138, 140

argument 3–11, 14–16, 19, 42, 69–70, 72–3, 75, 78, 90, 93, 99, 110–11, 128, 134, 148, 150–2, 154

Aristotle 102–3, 133–4, 135, 136, 141

arts 31–45, 46–58, 67, 70, 117, 127, 139

Athanasius of Alexandria 130, 139, 140

atheism 3–4, 6, 16, 25, 48–56, 53, 69, 81–97, 99, 143, 146–7, 150–1, 156

Augustine of Hippo 41, 131–2, 137, 140

Balthasar, Hans Urs von 89, 92, 127

baptism 34, 42, 92, 116, 135

Barth, Karl 6, 140

belief 3, 5–10, 12, 15–16, 19, 22, 25, 31–3, 40, 47–9, 51–4, 57, 59, 67–8, 70–1, 74, 77–8, 81, 84–6, 88–9, 94–6, 98–100, 118, 121, 129, 138, 142–3, 145–7, 151–3, 155, 157

Benedict XVI 82, 89

Berger, Paul 122

biology 49, 147, 151, 155

bishop 24, 83, 133, 152

body 16, 38, 42, 58, 101, 103, 116, 119–20, 133, 141

Booth, William 58

Bradley, Arthur 48–9, 56

Buckley, Michael 6, 90

Cappadocians 131–2

Casas, Bartolomé de las 135

Cassirer, Ernest 32

Cézanne, Paul 38

character 50, 100–3, 106, 120

Chesterton G. K. 36–8, 42

Christ, *see* Jesus

Church 5, 12–3, 24–6, 28, 35, 39, 42, 46–7, 56–8, 72, 81–4, 86–8, 91, 93–9, 103, 107, 110–11, 116, 122–4, 127–9, 131–3,

sacrament 42, 63, 77, 132, *see also* Baptism, Eucharist
sciences 7–8, 17, 19, 34, 49, 53, 67, 84, 121, 136, 139–40, 142–57
scientism 146
Scotus, John Duns 7
scripture 5, 43, 48, 50, 54, 67, 70, 77, 106, 116, 127, 132, 134, 140, 143, *see also* individual books
secularity 7, 8, 10, 13, 17, 46, 49, 51–2, 55–6, 86, 88, 95, 116–7, 122–3
semiotics 32, 34, 38, 43, 46, 118–25
Sensus Communis 13
sex 55, 111, 119, 141
Socrates 129
Stewart, Robert B. 95
Stott, John 71
suffering 51, 93, 110, 120, 127, 137
Swedenborg, Emmanuel, 32
Swinburne, Richard 4, 155

Tate, Andrew 48–9, 56
Taylor, Charles 23
technology 118, 140
teleology 4–5, 100–4, 106–8
terrorism 49, 51–2, 139–40
Tertullian 123
theology 3–8, 10–1, 13, 18, 21, 35, 42, 51, 54, 65, 71, 77, 89, 103, 117, 120–1, 123–4, 128–31, 134, 136, 138, 145, 155, *see also* doctrine
Theresa, Mother 93–4
Thérèse of Lisieux 127
Tillich, Paul 117
Tolkien, J. J. R. 39–44, 64, 66
Tractarians 43
Tran, Jonathan 111
Tutu, Desmond 104
Twilight novels and films 48, 55–8, 119

univocity 7, 69–70
utilarianism 105

vampire 55–8, 118–20, 122
virtue 9, 36, 73, 76, 100–7, 134, 138–9, 149, 152
Vitoria, Francisco de 135
voluntarism 6

Walsh, Chad 71
Ward, Graham 7, 115, 122, 123
Ward, Keith 96
Whewell, William 153
Williams, Rowan 70–1
Wittgenstein, Ludwig 20, 26–8
worldview 7–8, 46, 54–5
Wright, N. T. 71

Žižek, Slavoj 33